MORAL DEVELOPMENT

Advances in
Research and Theory

James R. Rest

**In collaboration with Robert Barnett,
Muriel Bebeau, Deborah Deemer, Irene Getz,
Yong Lin Moon, James Spickelmier,
Stephen J. Thoma, and Joseph Volker**

PRAEGER

New York
Westport, Connecticut
London

Library of Congress Cataloging-in-Publication Data

Rest, James R.
  Moral development.

  Bibliography: p.
  Includes index.
  1. Moral development — Research.   I. Title.
BF723.M54R48   1986   155.2′5   86-21708
ISBN 0-275-92254-5 (alk. paper)

Library of Congress Catalog Card Number: 86-21708
ISBN: 0-275-92254-5

First published in 1986

Praeger Publishers, 521 Fifth Avenue, New York, NY 10175
A division of Greenwood Press, Inc.

Printed in the United States of America

∞

The paper used in this book complies with the Permanent
Paper Standard issued by the National Information Standards
Organization (Z39.48-1984).

10 9 8 7 6 5 4 3 2 1

This book is dedicated to the participants
at the Center for the Study of Ethical Development
at the University of Minnesota —
an embodiment of a community of scholars.

Contents

List of Tables and Figures

TABLES

FIGURES

Preface

In the 1960s and 1970s the cause of social justice prompted people to action in the civil rights movement, the Vietnam protests, the black movement, and the women's movement. In the 1980s the rise of the religious and political right challenges many of the assumptions that seemed commonplace and hardly worth debating a decade ago. Moral judgment research gained popularity in the 1970s at the same time that social justice was the dominant public concern. Nowadays, social justice is less of a public concern, and support for moral judgment research seems to have likewise waned. Nevertheless the central question of moral judgment research is more relevant today than ever: How do people arrive at their notions of what is morally right and wrong? Current political and social debates are not merely over choice of methods and matters of timing. They are also over fundamental differences in what is right and what is just in our society. Therefore, more than ever, it is important to understand where people's sense of morality comes from, and to understand how their moral intuition works.

This book is primarily focused on research conducted with the Defining Issues Test (DIT). (See the Appendices for a copy of the test and a summary discussion of its characteristics.) Over 500 studies with the DIT have been reported, produced by researchers from virtually every state in the United States and from over 20 foreign countries. This data base constitutes the largest and most diverse body of information on moral judgment that exists, and the studies lend themselves to comparison and summarization because they use the same method of assessing moral judgment. But it is difficult to conduct such literature reviews because the individual reports of studies are widely scattered and much is as yet unpublished. This book integrates this literature, summarizes the cumulative findings from similar studies, and puts this knowledge in theoretical perspective.

THE FIRST PHASE OF RESEARCH

This book draws on the work of hundreds of researchers. It represents a new phase of research since my book in 1979, *Development in Judging Moral Issues*. The 1979 book focused on measurement issues.

That discussion dealt with questions such as how to collect information from subjects that can be used to infer something about their moral judgment, questions about the reliability of assessment procedures, threats to internal validity, and the rationale for building a case for the validity of a measure of moral judgment. In this earlier phase of research the case for the validity of the DIT rested on four major kinds of evidence:

1. Demonstration that subjects were fairly consistent and stable (over short periods of time) in their moral judgments.

2. Demonstration of upward change over time in accord with the theoretical characterization of what was "upward." We looked at cross-sectional data, longitudinal data, and sequential analyses of longitudinal data. We also contrasted groups expected to be "expert" (moral philosophy and political science Ph.D. students) with "novice" groups.

3. Demonstration of a convergent-divergent pattern of correlations with other psychological measures. That is, we looked to see if DIT scores correlated more highly with other psychological measures that were theoretically similar to moral judgment, but correlated less with other psychological measures that were theoretically less similar. Furthermore, we looked to see if DIT scores were distinct from other constructs, such as general cognitive development, or IQ, or SES (socioeconomic status), or political liberalism/conservatism. We found that although DIT scores are correlated with these constructs, the DIT represents unique and useful information above and beyond that accountable by its shared covariation with these other constructs.

4. Demonstration that DIT scores can be changed experimentally by treatments theoretically designed to shift it upward (appropriate moral education programs), but that DIT scores are resilient to experimental manipulations that ought not to change it (e.g., instructing subjects to "fake" good—note that some very recent research confirms these interpretations; see Chapter 5).

In sum, many studies were performed, and the convergence of findings from many different kinds of studies and the replications by various researchers lead to the conclusion that moral judgment (as defined by our psychological constructs) is a robust phenomenon for which the DIT provides a useful assessment.

THE SECOND PHASE OF RESEARCH

Since 1979 research interests have shifted from primarily measurement and validity issues to other questions. Since 1979 researchers have assumed that the DIT has adequate reliability and validity, and have gone on to new questions (Berndt 1985). The new studies seek to determine what life experiences seem to affect moral judgment, whether diverse kinds of people all follow the same course of development, what role (if any) moral judgment plays in actual decision making and real life behavior, what kinds of moral education programs can facilitate development, and so on. The chapters in this book attempt to portray our answers to these questions.

Chapter 1 presents an overview of the psychological processes involved in morality. It starts off with the question, "What processes or functions must have occurred in order for an individual to perform a moral act?" Chapter 1 suggests that there at least four major processes. One of these is the person's judgment as to what is the morally right thing to do in a particular situation. This is the special function of the construct of moral judgment. Chapter 1 places moral judgment in a larger context and theoretically links this process with the other processes. Chapter 1 also suggests how the Four Component Model guides programmatic research and educational program development.

Chapter 2 reviews studies of the natural development of moral judgment—that is, how over time moral judgment changes in the direction postulated by theory. The discussion deals with the theoretical issue of how to conceptualize the natural conditions that facilitate development, and the methodology of how to collect and categorize information on life experiences that relate to moral judgment development. A longitudinal study provides some vivid images of how people on a course of high development differ in life styles and activity pattern from people on a course of less development.

Chapter 3 deals with deliberate educational interventions designed to promote moral judgment development. It summarizes our current picture of what kinds of educational programs seem to work with what kinds of people, and discusses some of the problems in conducting studies in this area.

Chapter 4 discusses the effects of cultural/national differences as well as sex differences and religion. A central theoretical question here is whether the usual stage model of development really applies to all people who live in diverse life situations, or only to some people with special life situations. This leads us to consider whether some form of universalism is theoretically required in the basic assumptions of our structural-developmental approach, or whether the approach could accommodate some form of relativism.

Chapter 5 deals with the relation of moral judgment to behavior. First we review several studies that show that there is some empirical link. Next we outline a strategy for tracing both theoretically and empirically what the linkages are between moral judgment and behavior, and report on recent progress in verifying these linkages.

Chapter 6 summarizes our advances in terms of three lists: the major empirical findings that are now reasonably well established; conceptual refinements and new theoretical perspectives; and new directions for research. Some readers may want to take a look at this chapter first in order to gain an idea of the end of the story before starting with the other chapters.

While DIT research is closely related to the Kohlberg system (and the research of his colleagues using the new scoring system; see, for example, Colby, Kohlberg, Gibbs, and Lieberman 1983), there are still several reasons for having a book that focuses only on DIT studies. First, there is the obvious practical limitation that we here in Minnesota have access to and knowledge of studies using the DIT but not the same "inside track" on the literature using the Kohlberg scoring system. Then too, the DIT has been in use since the early 1970s, whereas the Kohlberg system has been standardized only relatively recently. There are over 500 studies using the DIT but not nearly that number yet using the Kohlberg system. So there is a more substantial data base on the DIT ready to be summarized than on the recent Kohlberg measure. But more profoundly, there are important methodological and conceptual differences between the DIT and the Kohlberg system (see Appendix). The tests correlate generally in the 0.3 to 0.7 range, depending on which version of the Kohlberg scoring system is being used, and on sample homogeneity. Therefore the tests cannot be regarded as equivalent. Given these differences, much clearer statements about moral judgment can be made by summarizing studies that are comparable in measurement of the chief variable. For readers not familiar with the DIT (and for those who wish a brief overview), the Appendix provides a copy of the questionnaire, discussion of its major characteristics, and comparisons with Kohlberg's test.

This book is written with the hope of encouraging other researchers—particularly students new to the field—to contribute to the field. Accordingly, we try to help others gain access to the tools and research strategies, and to the pertinent literature. Most importantly, we try to make clear what trends have solid and replicated empirical support; these are the conclusions that new research can build on and that new researchers can be confident are reliable phenomena, not just some half-baked ideas.

Acknowledgments

I wish to acknowledge the important contributions of many researchers. both those at the University of Minnesota and elsewhere. First of all, thanks to the many researchers who have been sending in reports of their studies using the DIT. Their studies make up the bulk of the 500 studies completed with the instrument and upon which the reviews were conducted. Many of their names are cited as authors of the studies that are reviewed in this book. Second, thanks to the group of students and faculty colleagues here at the University of Minnesota who have been meeting for several years together as the "Center for the Study of Ethical Development." This group is an embodiment of the ideal, a "community of scholars," who meet to share and mutually advance our understanding and interest in a topic worth our investment of time and energy. It is to this group that the book is dedicated. Third, the particular group of people who have had special roles and responsibilities in the compilation of this book are listed as co-authors of the various chapters. Their original studies, reviews of the literature, and discussions form the backbone of this work.

1
An Overview of the Psychology of Morality

James Rest
With Muriel Bebeau and Joseph Volker

THE DOMAIN OF MORALITY

Morality is rooted in the social condition and the human psyche. It arises from the social condition because people live in groups, and what one person does can affect another. If someone likes to shoot a rifle in a crowded city, other people are likely to be hurt. If someone dumps poisonous chemicals in his or her backyard, other people are likely to be poisoned. If one house catches fire, it is likely to spread if other people do not help to put the fire out. If one person invents a cure for disease, the most effective protection for everyone is to share the cure and eradicate the disease. Humans live together and interact with one another, and if they are to avoid a situation in which all are at war against all, then some basis for social cooperation and coordination of activity must be found.

The function of morality is to provide basic guidelines for determining how conflicts in human interests are to be settled and for optimizing mutual benefit of people living together in groups. It provides the first principles of social organization; it remains for politics, economics, and sociology to provide the second-level ideas about the specifics for creating institutions, role-structure, and practices. As Turiel, Nucci, and others have stated (Turiel 1978; Nucci 1981), morality is distinguishable from other domains of social functioning such as etiquette, social convention, and economics. It is morality's special province to provide guidelines for who owes whom what, to provide guidelines for determining how the benefits and burdens of cooperative living are to be distributed (to use the terminology from Rawls 1971). A moral system is functioning well when all the participants in a society know the principles that govern their interactions, when they appreciate that their interests are taken into account, when they see that there are no arbitrary imbalances in the distribution of burdens and benefits, and when they want to support the system because the system is optimizing the mutual benefits of living together.

Morality is also rooted in the individual human psyche as well as in the rudimentary requirements of cooperative social organization. First, the emerging field of "prosocial behavior" suggests that empathy is a very early human acquisition, if not genetically wired into human nature (see, for instance, Eisenberg 1982; Hoffman 1981; Radke-Yarrow, Zahn-Waxler, and Chapman 1983). That is, people feel bad when they witness distress in others. Second, a caring and mutually supportive relationship with another person is one of the primary goods that humans value. And so, when some individuals are assessing how their interests are being treated by a particular set of social arrangements, one of their major interests is in how the set of social arrangements encourages close relationships, bonds of affection, and loyalty. That is, good relationships with other people (the social relationships themselves) are one of the most important welfare outcomes of a social system. Third, there is emerging evidence that as the individual personality system develops, involving the development of self-concept, people generally want to think of themselves as basically decent, fair, and moral, and that the development of individual identity as a moral person carries at least part of the motivation to be moral (Damon 1984; Blasi 1984). Fourth, humans reflect upon their social experience and develop an increasingly richer, more penetrating picture of the social world. They develop the ability to use social information in drawing ever more complicated inferences and making more encompassing plans, and some people develop even to the point of constructing ideal visions of society. To a certain extent, the development of social cognition is the emergence from egocentrism into viewing one's own place as part of larger social networks.

There are other strands in human development that are also relevant to the psychology of morality in addition to these four, but these instances are sufficient to illustrate the point that there are natural tendencies in individual human development in which moral development is rooted. Of course this is not to say that people inexorably become better and better in every way every day. The developmental tendencies that support moral development can also be channeled in other directions, become distorted, or be preempted by other tendencies. Empathy can become prejudice, intimate relationships can become constrictive, the evolving self-concept system can organize itself around nonmoral values, and sophistication in social cognition can be used for exploitation as well as for moral purposes. I mean to assert, however, that our conception of moral development concerns all these ingredients, and when the term "morality" is used throughout this book, we intend to refer to a particular type of social value, that having to do with how humans cooperate and coordinate their activities in the service of furthering human welfare, and how they adjudicate conflicts among individual interests. (See Frankena 1970 for further discussion on defining morality.)

THE FOUR-COMPONENT MODEL

The story of moral development has strands that interweave and interact. We have found it useful to approach the complexity of morality by posing this question: When a person is behaving morally, what must we suppose has happened psychologically to produce that behavior? Our answer to that question (still somewhat tentative) is to postulate that four major kinds of psychological processes must have occurred in order for moral behavior to occur. As a shorthand, we refer to these ideas as the "Four-Component Model."

Assume that someone has just acted in a particular situation in a way that we would say was "behaving morally." Logically we would claim that the person must have performed at least four basic psychological processes:

1. The person must have been able to make some sort of interpretation of the particular situation in terms of what actions were possible, who (including oneself) would be affected by each course of action, and how the interested parties would regard such effects on their welfare.

2. The person must have been able to make a judgment about which course of action was morally right (or fair or just or morally good), thus labeling one possible line of action as what a person ought (morally ought) to do in that situation.

3. The person must give priority to moral values above other personal values such that a decision is made to intend to do what is morally right.

4. The person must have sufficient perseverance, ego strength, and implementation skills to be able to follow through on his/her intention

to behave morally, to withstand fatigue and flagging will, and to overcome obstacles.

The Four-Component Model has been useful in organizing existing research on the psychology of morality, as an analytical tool in approaching theoretical problems (such as the relations between cognition, affect, and behavior), as a framework for programmatic research, and as a basis for formulating objectives for moral education programs. Before describing the model in more detail, there are several things to note about the model.

First, note that a four-component model denies that moral development or moral behavior is the result of a single, unitary process. Although one process might interact and influence others, the four processes have distinctive functions. A person who demonstrates great facility at one process is not necessarily adequate in another. We all know people who can render very sophisticated judgments but who never follow through on any course of action; we know people who have tremendous follow-through and tenacity but whose judgment is simple-minded. In short, the psychology of morality cannot be represented as a single variable or process.

Second, note that I do not portray the basic elements of morality in terms of cognition, affect, and behavior. It is commonplace for reviewers of morality to state that cognitive developmentalists study thinking, psychoanalytic psychologists study affect, and social learning psychologists study behavior—and to assume that cognition, affect, and behavior are the basic processes and distinct elements, each having a separate track of development. In contrast, I take the view that there are no moral cognitions completely devoid of affect, no moral affects completely devoid of cognitions, and no moral behavior separable from the cognitions and affects that prompt the behavior. Although for some theoretical and research purposes it is possible to highlight cognition or affect or behavior, in the reality of moral phenomena, cognitions are always interconnected with affect, and vice versa, and both are always involved in the production of moral behavior. I submit that when we consider each of the four basic processes of morality carefully, we find many cognitive-affective interconnections, never cognition or affect in isolation. Each of the four component processes involves different kinds of cognitive-affective interconnections—there is not just one connection. In the discussion below, I will try to illustrate this point.

Third, note that the four components represent the *processes* involved in the production of a moral act, not general traits of people. The four components are not presented as four virtues that make up the ideally moral person, but rather they are the major units of analysis in tracing out how a particular course of action was produced in the context of a particular situation. The four components depict the ensemble of processes that go into the production of moral behavior in a specific situation.

Last, note that I do not intend to create the impression that the four components depict a linear sequence in real time—that is, that a microanalysis would show that first a person executes Component 1, followed in turn by Components 2, 3, and 4, in that order. In fact, there is research that suggests complicated interactions among the components. For instance, a person's way of defining what is morally right (Component 2) may affect the person's interpretation of the situation (Component 1). The four processes are presented in a *logical* sequence, as an analytical framework for depicting what must go on for moral behavior to occur.

Now some further description of each of the components will be given. Examples of research will be cited under each component to illustrate the meaning of the component and to show how various research traditions make contributions to our understanding of each component. I will also try to provide examples of cognitive-affective interconnections in each component.

Component 1

Interpreting the situation involves imagining what courses of action are possible and tracing the consequences of action in terms of how each action would affect the welfare of each party involved. A person may say to her/himself, "This is a *moral* problem" or may think about some specific moral norm or principle that applies to the case. But this is neither necessary nor inevitable. Minimally in Component 1, a person realizes that she/he could do something that would affect the interests, welfare, or expectations of other people. (Note that realizing that one's actions might be violating some moral norm or principle is one of the ways that a person's action can affect others. In this case, society in general has a stake or interest in the action because a general law, norm, or moral principle is involved.)

Several findings from psychological research are especially pertinent to Component 1. The first is that many people have difficulty in interpreting even relatively simple situations. Research on bystander reactions to emergencies shows this. For instance, Staub (1978) showed that helping behavior was related to the ambiguity of cues in the situation—if subjects were not clear about what was happening, they didn't help as much. We must not underestimate the difficulty in interpreting social situations nor must we assume that all misinterpretation is defensive in nature, even though people sometimes may not "see" things because they are defensively blocking them from conscious recognition. We are just beginning to understand how complicated it is to interpret social situations. The vast new emerging field of social cognition (e.g., Collins, Wellman, Keniston, and Westby 1978; Shantz 1983) is clarifying the complications in cue detection, information integration, and inference-making that are involved in developing the ability to interpret social situations.

Second, research shows striking individual differences among people in their sensitivity to the needs and welfare of others. Before it occurs to some people that a moral issue may be involved, they have to see the blood flowing. Other people are so supersensitive that every act, work, or grimace takes on momentous moral implications. Research by Schwartz (1977) documents individual differences in this regard on a variable he calls "Awareness of Consequences."

A third research finding is that a social situation can arouse strong feelings before extensive cognitive encoding. Almost instantaneously we may feel a strong dislike for someone, or we may feel instant empathy; this may occur even before we reflect on and ponder a social situation (Zajonc 1980). This is not to say that feelings are independent of cognition, but rather that more primitive cognitions (which may be tacit and automatic) and their accompanying feelings can proceed without waiting for a considered, reflective judgment and careful weighing of the facts. These first impressions and "gut feelings" therefore become part of what we need to interpret in Component 1 when we are faced with a social problem. Sometimes these feelings signal important aspects of the situation and provide motivation for our "better selves"—for instance, when we empathize with a victim and go to his aid. But sometimes the affects aroused in a situation can hamper our better judgment—for instance, when we instantly dislike the way someone looks and are tempted to deny the person her full rights. In any event we must attend to and clearly recognize our initial impression, and yet must also realize that first impressions are often poor guides for actions. Nevertheless, affective arousal happens to us whether we invite it or not, and these feelings are part of the situation that needs interpreting (that is, our own immediate feelings are part of what needs to be interpreted in Component 1). In sum, Component 1 involves identifying what we can do in a particular situation, figuring out what the consequences to all parties would be for each line of action, and identifying and trying to understand our own gut feelings on the matter.

The interconnection of cognition and affect in Component 1 is illustrated in work by Hoffman on empathy (1976, 1981). Hoffman proposes that the rudiments of empathy (distress felt by the self which is triggered by the perception of distress in another person) is a primary affective response that can be aroused in very young infants and requires very little cognitive development for its activation. For instance, newborn babies cry upon hearing other babies cry. Hoffman's account is particularly interesting in suggesting how this primary affective response already present in very young children comes to interact with cognitive development to produce more complex forms of empathy:

1. During the first year the child may be discomforted and become alarmed upon seeing distress cues from others. At this point, however, the child does not clearly distinguish him/herself from others and is unclear about what is happening to whom.

2. Then, gradually, the child comes to realize a clear distinction between the self and others; thus when another person is hurt, the child knows it is not the self, but still feels sympathy for the other. Nevertheless, the child may respond to the other person in ways that would comfort the self but are not appropriate for the other (e.g., to offer one's own doll to one's mother when seeing her sad).

3. At 2 or 3 years, the child is aware that other people's feelings and needs can differ from her own and begins to use information about the world and others to infer what is required in the situation to give effective help to the other.

4. By late childhood, the child has developed a conception of other people as each having his/her own particular life history and identity. The child's empathy at this point may be aroused by the awareness of some deprivation in the other person's general life situation rather than by specific signs of distress. For instance, one may feel sad for a retarded child even while observing him/her playing joyfully in a playground. Hoffman's account, therefore, depicts how affective responses (the arousal of empathic distress) interact with the development of conceptions of the other. Affect (empathy) is never

completely separate from cognition, and the development of cognition transforms the quality of the affect.

Component 2

Recall that the outcome of Component 1 is that one is aware of various possible courses of action and what the consequences are for people's welfare. Now how does one decide which one of these courses of action is morally right? This is the business of Component 2.

Making moral judgments seems to come naturally to people. Even young children seem to display fits of moral outrage when they sense something unfair or wrong was done to them. As adults in our society, we face immensely difficult moral problems in allocation of health care, the arms race, social justice for minorities, use of military force, and so on. And yet, despite the enormity and complexity of these issues, most people seem to have at least intuitions about what's morally right or wrong regarding such issues as abortion, the military draft, affirmative action, and other issues. It almost seems as if humans are either genetically built to make moral judgments or are quickly conditioned by social experience to make them. Equally striking is the fact that people's moral intuitions are so drastically different. And furthermore, people can hold their moral opinions about very complex matters with great fervor and certitude. One person can be completely convinced in the rightness of one solution to a problem while another person can be completely convinced that the opposite solution is right. In short, people readily make moral judgments (or at least have intuitions about right and wrong), this activity seems to come in early in development, their intuitions differ dramatically as to what's right and what's wrong, and they can have great certainty about their moral convictions. The psychologist's job is to figure out how people make these judgments (how moral intuition works), to account for the differences in judgment, and to account for the certitude of people in these judgments, even about immensely complicated matters.

Cognitive developmental psychologists (including Piaget, Kohlberg, and DIT researchers) have made contributions in this area. While I would not consider Piaget's or Kohlberg's work (or DIT research) to constitute a total theory of moral development (understood as all four components), this work has given us much in explaining Component 2. Cognitive developmental research has gone about studying the phenomena of moral judgment in a very straightforward way—find out about people's strategies for defining right and wrong by presenting them with some moral problems, then ask them what's right and wrong. The explanations and justifications that people give then constitute the data base upon which to characterize different systems for making moral judgments. Note that this kind of data base zeros in on Component 2 processes and is ill-suited for providing information about the other components. Component 1 cannot be studied in this way because the very presentation of the moral dilemmas (as written paragraphs or as short vignettes verbally presented by an interviewer) has already precoded and interpreted the situation (already identifying what courses of action are possible, identifying who has a stake in the situation, suggesting what the consequences are of each course of action). Since this information is already given in the stimulus material, we cannot then discover how the subject carries out Component 1 processes. Also, information about Components 3 and 4 is not elicited by the usual moral judgment procedure either. The moral judgment task requires that subjects talk about what ought to be done, what is morally right or wrong. It is not well suited for determining how the subject would actually prioritize his/her values if really in the situation (Component 3) or whether the subject has the stamina, resolution, and implementing skills to actually reach an intended goal (Component 4). Nevertheless, despite these limitations, cognitive developmental research in moral judgment has suggested some very interesting things about Component 2 processes (to which this book hopes to contribute).

This is not the place to attempt a review of cognitive developmental research on moral judgment (see Rest 1983 for one such attempt). However, some short characterization of the general yield of this research can be given here in order to flesh out the discussion of the Four-Component Model. The key to understanding the cognitive developmental contribution to the question, "How do people decide what's right or wrong?" lies in a few assumptions. The first of these is that as people have social experience they develop more elaborate conceptions of the social world, in particular, how it is possible to organize cooperation among people. This is to say that people are automatically reflecting upon social experience and making meaning structures that organize that social experience. One of the important conceptions that develops is how people can arrange cooperation and positive social relationships. (One could easily speculate on the evolutionary and ontogenetic pressure in the social environment to attend to such an issue. Consider, for instance, the life prospects of an individual who is oblivious to the issue of getting along with others.) According to the cognitive developmental view, young children at first form very simple conceptions: a person can get along with significant others by giving in to them or obeying their commands; a person can get along with others by arranging to exchange favors, making deals with others. Later on, more complex conceptions evolve: establishing positive long-term relationships with others based on mutual understanding, loyalty, and affection, Still later, conceptions emerge involving society-wide networks of cooperation based on formal institutions, role-systems, and publicly enacted laws. And for some, their thinking about organizing cooperation develops to the point of having schemes for organizing ideal societies according to principles that optimize human welfare. (See Rest 1979a, chapter 2, for a more extended discussion.) The basic point here is that with social experience people develop more elaborate conceptions of how to organize cooperation. The cumulative impact of social experience therefore is not just learning a longer list of rights and wrongs, but developing conceptions of how cooperation is organized in the social world.

The second critical assumption in the cognitive developmentalists' account is that along with each conception of social organization, there is a distinctive sense of fairness, a notion of what I owe to others and what others owe to me. For instance, in the notion of simple, direct exchange of favor for favor (Stage 2 in the theory), the sense of fairness is that while I am giving something of value to another, I am also getting something in return; therefore, the reciprocity of value for value is what makes the arrangement fair. In the notion of maintaining positive, long-term relationships (Stage 3), the sense of fairness comes from realizing that I know that I can count on you and you know that you can count on me, and hinges on being able to count on our mutual loyalty and mutual dedication to each other's welfare. In the notion of society-wide networks of cooperation (Stage 4), the sense of fairness comes in realizing that I will do my job and stay within the law, expecting that others in society will do likewise. Similarly, for the other conceptions of organizing social cooperation (the other stages), there is a distinctive sense of fairness and an appreciation of the reciprocity of cooperation.

The third critical assumption of the cognitive developmental account is that when a person is faced with deciding what is morally right in a social situation, the sense of fairness that derives from a particular concept of organizing cooperation drives the moral judgment. Let us depict the task before a subject in this way: I am aware of various lines of action that I could take in a particular situation; I am aware that various people are involved and have a stake in what I do; my task is to decide which course of action is morally right. The cognitive developmental view is that the various concepts of social co-operation and their accompanying notions of fairness provide heuristics for solving this problem. Subjects must have a way of identifying what considerations are relevant, and must have a way of balancing or prioritizing the various claims of people. If a subject can assimilate a particular social problem to one or another concept of cooperation and its accompanying sense of fairness, then the subject will have a basis for judging what is morally right. Indeed, the degree of fit of the situation to a general scheme is what gives the subject a sense of conviction and certainty. For instance, if I can completely assimilate a social problem to a Stage 4 scheme of justice, then I will have firm certainty in my moral judgment.

An example of how this is supposed to work may help clarify things. Let us suppose that a subject is presented with Kohlberg's classic dilemma of Heinz and the drug. (If by some chance the reader has escaped hearing about Heinz and the drug, here is the scenario: Heinz's wife is dying of cancer and a drug invented by a druggist in town might save her. The druggist, however, is charging an exorbitant price for the drug, which Heinz can't raise. Should Heinz steal the drug from the druggist in order to save his dying wife?) Let us suppose that our subject has available from long-term memory a Stage 4 scheme (dubbed the "law and order" stage). This general structure then alerts the subject to considerations involving the maintenance of society and upholding the law. Of critical importance then is the consideration that if Heinz stole the drug, he would be breaking the law. The subject might search the story for information about whether the druggist was acting within the law by refusing the drug. But the story leads the reader to infer that the druggist is within the law. Of course, the person is aware of the need that Heinz's wife has for the drug. But if one puts the wife's claim alongside the concern for the countless people whose welfare depends on law maintenance, then a problem-solving heuristic derived from a Stage 4 scheme ends up with the priority going to the law. It would be wrong for Heinz to steal the drug (although one can sympathize with him or understand why Heinz's morality might weaken enough to transgress in this instance).

In general, the cognitive developmental view is that through social experience, people develop concepts of how to organize cooperation. Accompanying these different concepts are different senses of fairness (usually referred to in terms of "stages" of moral judgment). The stage schemes reside in long-term memory and are invoked to help make sense of problematic social situations in arriving at a judgment of what is morally right. The general stage scheme directs the subject to attend to certain considerations and to prioritize people's claims so as to advocate one or another line of action. The stage schemes serve as heuristics in solving moral problems. When situations lend themselves to easy or complete assimilation under a general scheme, the subject has a feeling of certainty and conviction in his/her moral judgments. Since different schemes are available to different people and since it is possible for different people to apply a general scheme in different ways to the same situation, differences among people arise in their judgments about what line of action is morally right, although each is convinced of the certainty of his/her position.

In Component 2, the interconnectedness of cognition and affect is presupposed in the association of a person's conceptions of organizing social cooperation and the distinctive sense of fairness that accompanies them. Cognitively understanding a particular form of social organization carries with it a feeling that the participants have moral responsibilities to reciprocate and to do their respective shares, or else they are trying to take unfair advantage of the cooperativeness of others.

Having sketched out the cognitive developmental view, let me hasten to add that other theorists and researchers have proposed other psychological processes by which people arrive at judgments of what is morally right. Some convincing evidence for an alternate process comes from a study by Lawrence (1979), who studied radically fundamentalist seminarians. Her study presents some clear indication that these people deliberately and self-consciously set aside their own sense of fairness about a situation. They told her that their own personal views about what seemed fair or just should not intrude in deciding what was morally right inasmuch as all questions of value have been decided by a higher authority (truth as revealed by God). Therefore, the way they decide what is right is to attempt to assimilate a situation to some church teaching or scriptural reference and let that determine their moral judgment.

The general implication of Lawrence's study is that there seem to be different kinds of problem-solving strategies in making moral judgments besides stage schemes of justice as described by cognitive developmentalists. Lawrence's study indicates that allegiance to belief systems and ideologies can override the influence of a person's own sense of fairness in making decisions of moral rightness. We need not limit this mechanism to ideologies of the right—ideologies of the left could also preempt one's sense of fairness in deciding what is morally right.

In addition, there is the possibility that other concepts besides that of justice and fairness could be the key in determining how people judge what is morally right. Philosophers and theologians have proposed other concepts on which to base morality; for instance, the Christian concept of *agape* goes beyond justice in defining what is morally right. Gilligan (1982) has contended that women use "a different voice" from the subjects in Kohlbergian research. Researchers of non-Western populations have contended that people in different cultures develop their moral sense in ways radically different from those of people in Western culture. In Chapter 4 we will review the evidence and take up this important point again.

Component 3

Component 2 has labeled one possible course of action as the morally right one. But moral values are not the only values that people have. People value advancement in their careers, art, projects that they have worked long and hard on—many things besides fairness or morality. These other values can come into conflict with moral values. Doing the moral thing sometimes prevents one from realizing other values. It is not unusual for non-moral values to be so strong and attractive that a person will choose a course of action that preempts or compromises the moral ideal. For instance, John Dean (1976) writes in his book, *Blind Ambition*, that his activities as special counsel to President Nixon were motivated by his ambition to succeed in the Nixon administration, and that questions of morality and justice were preempted by wanting to convince everyone that he could play "hard ball." As a research example, Damon (1977) asked young children to theorize how ten candy bars *ought* to be distributed as rewards for making bracelets. In interviews, the children described various schemes for a fair distribution of rewards, explaining why they thought a particular distribution *ought* to be followed. However, when these same children *actually* were given the ten candy bars to distribute, they deviated from their espoused schemes of justice, and instead gave themselves a disproportionate number of candy bars. Thus the children's espoused moral ideals were compromised by other motives—in this case, by a desire for those tasty candy bars.

Given that a person is aware of various possible courses of action in a situation, each leading to a different kind of outcome or goal, why then would one ever chose the moral alternative, especially if it involves sacrificing some personal value or suffering some hardship? What motivates the selection of moral values over other values? The more one ponders these questions, the more one can appreciate the challenge to psychological theories.

Nevertheless, there have been many answers from psychological theorists to account for the motivation to prioritize moral values over other values. I will briefly list here some of the major theories and their proponents (see Rest 1983 for a fuller discussion):

1. People behave morally because evolution has bred altruism into our genetic inheritance (Wilson 1975).
2. "Conscience makes cowards of us all." That is, shame, guilt, and fear motivates morality (Aronfreed 1968; Eysenck 1976).
3. There really isn't any special motivation to be moral. People just respond to reinforcement and/or modeling opportunities and "learn" social behavior that nonscientists may wish to call "morality" (Bandura 1977; Goldiamond 1968).
4. Social understanding of how cooperation functions and how one's own stake in building a desirable social world motivates morality (Dewey 1959; Piaget 1965). The tradition of liberal enlightenment subscribes to the view that education is a broadening experience that can overcome prejudice and pettiness and foster social responsibility.
5. Moral motivation is derived from a sense of awe and self-subjugation to something greater than the self. One can identify with a crusade, one's country, the sacred (Durkheim 1961; Erikson 1958).
6. Empathy is the basis for altruistic motivation (Hoffman 1976).
7. The experience of living in just and caring relationships and communities leads to moral commitment (Rawls 1971; Kohlberg 1985).
8. Concern for self-integrity and one's identity as a moral agent is what motivates moral action (Blasi 1984; Damon 1984).

These eight theories about moral motivation indicate the diversity of views on the issue. At present, research has not proceeded very far along on any one of these lines. Part of the complexity of doing research on moral motivation is that more than one determinant may be operating in a person at any given point in time, and therefore the researcher's task is not to prove one theory right and all the others wrong, but to figure out how to assess the motive strength of a particular source (or sources) in a given situation.

There are many interconnections between cognition and affect in Component 3. One obvious one is that imagining a desired goal or outcome implies having some sort of cognitive representation of it, and *desiring* it implies having positive affect toward it. Another less obvious interconnection is discussed in work by Isen and her colleagues (1970). She found that subjects who were induced to feel happy by being provided a success experience (being told they did extremely well on a perceptual-motor task) tended to donate more money for charity than subjects with a failure experience (being told they did extremely poorly) or than controls. Similar results have been found in studies of children donating more to charity after success in a bowling game, or college students volunteering to participate in a study after being given a cookie, of people who helped pick up spilled papers after finding a dime in a pay phone, and of children giving more to charity who had reminisced about happy experiences (see review in Staub 1978). The general finding is that people who are in a good mood (from pleasant memories, a recent success experience, being given something, etc.) usually are more positive, generous, and cooperative. These researchers talk about the "positive effects of looking on the bright side." They speculate that mood plays a role in the retrievability of cognitions, and influences the availability of cognitions that emphasize the advantages of helping and cooperating, and that a bad mood heightens the availability of the cognitions that emphasize the disadvantages of helping. This would be another instance of the interconnectedness of affect and cognition (in this case, in a Component 3 process).

Component 4

Component 4 involves executing and implementing a play of action. As popular wisdom tell us, good intentions are often a long way from good deeds. Component 4 involves figuring out the sequence of concrete actions, working around impediments and unexpected difficulties, overcoming fatigue and frustration, resisting distractions and allurements, and keeping sight of the eventual goal. Perseverance, resoluteness, competence, and character are attributes that lead to success in Component 4. Psychologists sometimes refer to these processes as involving "ego strength" or "self-regulation." A biblical term for failures in Component 4 is "weakness of the flesh." Firm resolve, perseverance, iron will, strong character, and ego strength can be used for ill or for good. Ego strength comes in handy to rob a bank, prepare for a marathon, rehearse for a piano concert, or carry out genocide.

In one study of Stage 4 "law and order" subjects, those subjects with high ego strength cheated less than the Stage 4 subjects with low ego strength. Presumably the former had "the strength of their convictions," whereas the latter had convictions but didn't act on them (Krebs 1967). Other lines of research also suggest that a certain inner strength, an ability to mobilize oneself to action, is a factor in moral behavior. Barrett and Yarrow (1977) found that social assertiveness was an important component in children's "prosocial" behavior. London (1970) interviewed people who were involved in saving persecuted Jews in Nazi Germany, and was struck by the adventurousness of the helpers as well as their caring.

Some recent research on self-regulation processes has described techniques for improving or altering self-regulation. One technique involves the "cognitive transformation" of the goal object. For instance, Mischel (1974) studied the ability of young subjects to wait for reward objects (marshmallows). Some subjects were instructed to think about the marshmallows as cotton balls while other subjects were instructed to think about the chewy, sweet, soft taste of marshmallows. Subjects who focused on the consummatory qualities (chewy, sweet, soft taste) were unable to wait as long as subjects who concentrated on something else. Mischel and Mischel (1976, 94) state:

> By knowing the relevant rules of cognitive transformation and utilizing them during self-control effects, individuals may be able to attain considerable self-mastery in pursuit of their goals, even in the face of strong countervailing situational pressures.

Staub (1979, 134) adds, "What a person thinks about in the course of helping another person may well determine the persistence of his helpfulness." Note that this research illustrates an interconnection of cognition with affect in Component 4 and suggests an approach for educational intervention.

Masters and Santrock (1976) illustrate the technique. Self-regulatory processes can be manipulated by instructing subjects to consider a task as fun, easy, or satisfying. While performing some tasks, some children were instructed to say to themselves, "This is fun, really fun." These children tended to work longer than children instructed to say, "Ugh! This is no fun." Thus a positive affective state induced by certain cognitions was related to persistence of effort. Individuals who can act as cheerleaders to themselves seem to be able to increase their staying power. Bandura states that expectations of efficacy (e.g., "I can do it," "This is fun!") determine "whether coping behavior will be initiated, how much effort will be expended, and how long it will be sustained in the face of obstacles and adversive experience" (1977).

With older subjects, Rational Emotive Therapy (Ellis 1977) employs basically the same technique as that of Masters and Santrock, and attempts to change behavior by engendering expectations of efficacy.

Interaction among the Components

We have seen that perseverance in a task and self-mobilization to work for a goal require the subject's attention and sustained effort. Sometimes the attention and effort needed to carry out a task are so great that the subject can attend to little else. Darley and Batson (1973) found this to be the case in a study of seminarians at Princeton Theological Seminary. Seminarians were asked to prepare and deliver a short talk on the parable of the Good Samaritan and then to deliver their talks in another building, requiring a short walk between campus buildings. Darley and Batson used the walk as an analogue of the road between Jerusalem and Jericho, and to complete the scenario, positioned a student confederate along the way who was slumped over, shabbily dressed, coughing and groaning. Darley and Batson wanted to see how much the subjects would help the "victim." The factor that made a large difference in helping behavior was the time pressure put on the subjects. Those seminarians who were put under great pressure tended to help less than the seminarians who were given a more leisurely pace to compose their short talks. The seminarians under pressure seemed not to have processed the new situation (the "victim"), since they were so absorbed with fulfilling their first duty, preparing the talk. "Indeed, on several occasions, a seminary student going to give his talk on the parable of the Good Samaritan literally stepped over the victim as he hurried on his way!" (Darley and Batson 1973, 107). My interpretation of this is that the time-pressured subjects were so engaged in completing their first duty (allocating most resources to Component 4 in response to the first situation), that they were insensitive to the new situation (Component 1 processing of the new situation). This study suggests that the overlap in time of situations can determine one's reaction (being dutiful with regard to one moral concern can cause insensitivity to another that begins before the first is completed). Concentrated effort in one component can diminish attention to another component (steadfastness can interfere with sensitivity, and perhaps vice versa).

Another sort of interaction among the components is illustrated by Schwartz (1977). Subjects sometimes engage in defensive evaluations to deny or minimize feelings of moral obligation. As the costs of moral action come to be recognized, a person may distort the feelings of obligation by denying the need to act, denying personal responsibility, or reappraising the situation so as to make alternative actions more appropriate. In other words, as subjects recognize the implications of Component 2 and Component 3 processes and the personal costs of moral action become clear, they may defensively reappraise and alter their interpretation of the situation (Component 1) so that they can feel honorable, but at less cost to themselves. Other researchers have also studied such defensive operations and the devaluation of victims (Bandura, Underwood, and Fromson, 1975; Walster and Walster 1975).

Further examples could be given of the interactive nature of the four components; however, the major point here is that moral behavior is an exceedingly complex phenomenon and no single variable (empathy, prosocial orientation, stages of moral reasoning, etc.) is sufficiently comprehensive to represent the psychology of morality.

The Four-Component Model as a Guide to Research

The Four-Component Model has been useful in helping us place our research on moral judgment in the larger historical perspective of the psychology of morality and in providing a perspective for designing future research. Researchers working in the cognitive developmental tradition have not always appreciated their particular place in a larger enterprise, and at times have represented research in moral judgment as the whole of the psychology of morality, using the term "moral judgment development" interchangeably with "moral development." Accordingly, the work of other researchers on other aspects was regarded as irrelevant to the psychology of morality or simply wrong. This attitude of some cognitive developmentalists was provoked in part by challenges from other research traditions that asserted that research on moral thinking itself was irrelevant or wrong (Bandura and McDonald 1963). Countless studies over the ensuing twenty years have tried to provide the "critical experiment" to disprove the entire cognitive developmental approach or the entire social learning approach. All these studies, pitting one approach against the other, assumed that if one perspective had something useful to say about one aspect of the phenomenon of morality, then the other approaches must all be wrong.

A review of the psychology of morality by Pittel and Mendelsohn in 1966 looked at research efforts from the turn of the century to the early 1960s. In their view, the attempt to predict behavior from a subject's verbalizations had repeatedly been a failure, and they suggested that an improvement in the field would be for researchers to investigate moral values as subjective phenomena in their own right. Pittel and Mendelsohn were particularly impressed with Piaget's pioneering work in moral judgment. In effect, Pittel and Mendelsohn's suggestion became the dominant view of cognitive developmentalists for almost 20 years—namely, that moral judgment was worth studying in its own right regardless of its relation to behavior. By limiting research in this way to a subject's justification of a decision about a hypothetical moral dilemma, cognitive developmentalists made progress in studying the subjective phenomenon in its own right, while ignoring other aspects. Sometimes the criticisms of other researchers outside the cognitive developmental tradition were bothersome (e.g., that morality is more than cognitive decision making, that how people actually behave is more important than how they talk about behaving), but such criticism did not deflect the focus on moral judgment processes.

Looking backward, we can see that much progress came from the sustained focus on moral judgment. Now we do have a greater understanding of how people arrive at judgments of right and wrong conduct. At the same time, cognitive developmentalists must also admit that this research has not been integrated with other moral processes. The Four-Component Model helps place progress on the moral judgment component alongside what else needs attention.

Into the 1970s, cognitive developmentalists were primarily occupied with developing measurement instruments. The scathing review by Kurtines and Grief (1974) of Kohlberg's research pointed mostly to reliability and validity issues of the methods of measuring moral judgment. The verdict in that review was that cognitive developmentalists had failed to make a case that development in moral judgment could be measured. It took almost a decade for Kohlberg and his associates to publish their massive and elegant counterargument (Colby, Kohlberg, Gibbs, and Lieberman, "A Longitudinal Study of Moral Judgment," 1983). Research on the DIT was initiated in the early 1970s, and *Development in Judging Moral Issues* (Rest 1979a) was largely devoted to measurement issues. The major question in the 1970s was whether a stage approach to moral judgment could produce acceptable assessment instruments.

The focus of research has changed, however. At a recent convention symposium (1985), Thomas Berndt suggested that moral judgment researchers are beyond a concentration on measurement issues:

During the 1970s, one critical question for moral development research was whether a person's characteristic pattern of moral judgment or reasoning could be measured reliably and validly.... I believe most psychologists are now convinced that individual patterns of moral reasoning can be assessed reliably and validly.... In short, the controversies over the measurement of moral reasoning have subsided, ending this old phase in research on moral development.

What then defines the new phase in moral-development research? ... Basic questions about the experiences that contribute to progress in moral reasoning, and individual characteristics that increase or reduce people's openness to moral experiences ... [Berndt 1985, 1-3]

The new phase in moral judgment research that Berndt talks about is the central thrust of this book. I would locate the bulk of the research discussed here as moving away from issues of instrumentation to the more substantive theoretical questions of the life conditions that influence moral judgment and considerations of how moral judgment influences life directions. The studies discussed here virtually assume the validity of the DIT, and go on to investigate the nature of moral judgment and its interconnections with other events. We are now beyond studying subjective moral values in their own right.

Unlike some of the earlier treatments of moral judgment research, we do not assume that moral judgment is the only process in the psychology of morality. My colleagues and I at the University of Minnesota have been using the Four-Component Model as a guide for further programmatic research. The ultimate aim is to understand and predict actual moral behavior and decision making. The study of verbalizations to hypothetical moral dilemmas has provided many insights into the psychology of morality, but one must not stop there. Eventually we wish to have a theory and a methodology for studying morality in the flow of real life events. Research on moral judgment on other components of the morality process has provided many leads for conceptualizing various facets of this complex phenomenon. Moving from the study of verbalizations to hypothetical dilemmas, however, into the realm of real life moral behavior, entails a quantum leap in complexity and juggling many variables and processes simultaneously. We hope to build on the findings of research over the past decades (as summarized in the Four-Component Model) to guide our venture.

One of our first decisions has been to study real life morality in the context of moral decision making by health care professionals. There seems to be a number of advantages to starting with professional decision making. One advantage is that decision making of professionals about issues that arise in their work will often involve reflective, deliberate reasoning that the person can articulate and explain. In fact, many of these decisions are arrived at in terms of how well the person can defend the decision and produce justification. The decision maker anticipates that he/she may be called upon to give a justification, hence the justifiability of a decision enters into the original choice of action. The researcher asks the subject of study to give a justification for a decision, and this is something the subject will have already given much thought to, not something produced anew only for research purposes. Note that I am not claiming that all moral decision making is of this deliberate, reflective, articulative kind; rather, I am stating that we have chosen to start with deliberate, reflective, articulative moral decision making for reasons of research strategy. While I do not assume that any of us fully knows his or her own mind, nevertheless it would seem to make sense to start the study in the most public, rational, reflective parts of human behavior rather than attempting to study first its more secret, irrational, least accessible areas.

A second advantage of studying professional decision making is that incidents and instances can be selected in which there is not so strong a conflict between self-interest and doing the right thing. That is, there are many instances in which the self-interest of the professional is to figure out what is the right thing, to choose that line of action which is most defensible. For instance, a doctor facing the decision about whether to pull the plug of an artificial respirator on a terminally ill patient is most interested in doing the right thing; the doctor himself or herself does not have a personal vested interest one way or the other in the decision. Similarly, there are many professional decisions in which the self-interest of the decision maker is to figure out what is right (or at least most defensible or least likely to come back to haunt you). Studying such dilemmas has the advantage of starting off with decisions that are loaded on Component 2 rather than also being complicated by heavy involvement of Component 3 processes (which we know least how to study).

There has been a third advantage in studying the moral decision making of health professionals (doctors, dentists, nurses, etc.). This group of people has been willing to cooperate with us in trying to understand how moral decisions are made. Even a casual reader of the newspapers will be aware of the difficult moral dilemmas now facing health professionals: for instance, the Karen Quinlan case, Baby Doe cases, the prospect of health care rationing as medical costs have risen so precipitously, abortion, and so on. Health professionals are sensitive and concerned with these problems, and we have found that many of them are willing to give time for psychological research that might lead to better decision making and educational programs that better prepare them to deal with the moral problems that are an inevitable part of the job.

And so the first step in our research program has been to identify a site for conducting research on real life moral decision making. The next step is to attempt to devise measures for each of the four components. Work on Component 1 has been under way for several years, principally by Dr. Muriel Bebeau at the School of Dentristy, University of Minnesota. That research is briefly described below.

Research on Component 1 in the Real Life Context

Bebeau began by identifying what the recurrent and important dilemmas in the practice of dentistry are. She interviewed practitioners, then conducted a statewide survey of 700 dentists to determine what kinds of situations and issues come up in this health care profession. She found, for instance, that there are dilemmas concerning what to do when one dentist finds substandard work being performed by another dentist; there are dilemmas arising from a patient who asks for treatment (e.g., pulling all the teeth) that is against the patient's long-term health interest; there are dilemmas arising when patients appear in the office who have serious health problems (beyond just dental problems) but are resistant to attending to the more serious problem; there are dilemmas that arise from having costly options that are optimal treatments and less costly options that are less optimal but adequate treatments; and so on (Bebeau, Reifel, and Speidel 1981).

Having identified the important kinds of moral dilemmas in the profession, Bebeau then wrote dramatizations of them. The dramatizations consist of dialogue between a dentist and a client such as one might find in a typical dental office. Scripts were developed, read by actors, and tape-recorded. These scripts serve as the stimulus material that subjects hear and are then tested on to determine how they perceive what is going on, what the issues are in the dramatization, and how the subjects (usually students in dental school) would role-play their treatment of such a situation. For instance, one of the dramas depicts a person new in town, Mrs. Harrington, who goes to a new dentist for the first time. The student hears a lot of the usual polite chatter that typically goes on in a dentist's office as an examination begins. Then the dentist in the drama begins to comment on the extensive (and no doubt expensive) work that has been done, and with further examination begins to comment that some of the crowns have defects that cannot be repaired without remaking the crowns. The dentist in the drama also notes that there is evidence of advanced periodontal disease (which, obvious to a dental student, has not been attended to by the previous dentist). As these difficulties are mentioned by the drama dentist, Mrs. Harrington begins to ask some pointed questions, like, "What do you mean I am going to have to replace some of the crowns when I've just recently paid to have that job done?" At this point in the dramatization, the student listening to the tape is asked to assume the role of the dentist in the drama and to deal with the situation. Then the student is interviewed to determine how he or she interprets the situation, how he or she understands what is going on in the situation.

Note that this kind of stimulus material differs from the usual Kohlberg interview or DIT questionnaire in several important ways: (1) the situation is not pre-interpreted for the subject, nor are alternative courses suggested. The stimulus material consists of dialogue between two people, not a condensed synopsis of a dilemma. (2) The situation is one selected and developed for its realism and frequency of occurrence. The dramas were developed with the assistance of practitioners in the field to depict lifelike situations and conversation. (3) The main goal of the procedure is not to elicit from the subject a solution for the problem and a justification; rather, the goal is to determine how the subject interprets or encodes the situation. (4) In order to deal with the situation the subject must simultaneously track technical information and problem solving (i.e., the symptoms of periodontal disease and inadequate crown application) along with the moral/value issues. We believe that professional dilemmas usually are a mix of technical and moral issues. Also, it is usual for a person's professional education to highlight the *technical* aspects of the profession, so that the student is conditioned not to recognize and deal with the *moral* aspects of the job. Without intending to do so, present professional schooling tends to overemphasize the technical so as to blind the professional to the moral.

Bebeau found that dental students produced varied responses to the Harrington dilemma. Some students did not imagine possible courses of action that were open to them. For instance, it did not occur to some that the new dentist might contact the previous dentist to ask about the circumstances leading to substandard crown work. It did not occur to some students that the new dentist might approach the previous dentist about some sort of financial support to Mrs. Harrington to alleviate the costs that result from paying twice for a job that should have been done right the first time. It did not occur to some students that this case might be reported to a peer review board. Bebeau found that some students were not clear about who had a stake in this situation and just what that stake was. For instance, some students did not recognize that the dental profession as a whole has a stake in quality assurance for health services, and that the public has a right to expect minimal standards of work.

Bebeau devised a scoring scheme that yields a score for Component 1. Subjects who were clear about the possible lines of action open to the actor got higher scores than subjects who were not so clear. Some subjects were clear about who had a stake in the situation and how the special characteristics of the participants have to be taken into account. They were scored higher than subjects who were not so clear. The mechanics of scoring involves analyzing interview material of a subject for each dilemma into a half-dozen or so criterion points, and assigning a number from 1 to 3 to each point. In the first round of studies, four dramatic situations were used. Aggregating over the set of cases yielded scores ranging from 34 to 102 points. Another set of four situations has also been developed (Bebeau, Oberle, and Rest 1984). On either set of cases, high scores are interpreted as indicating greater facility in Component 1 processes, or higher "moral sensitivity." It is noteworthy that the scoring criteria were developed in collaboration with practicing dentists as well as with the help of moral philosophers.

The reliability of Bebeau's measure is reported in several studies (Bebeau, Oberle, and Rest 1984; Bebeau, Rest, and Yamoor 1985). Interjudge agreement in terms of correlations averaged 0.87 for the four cases. Agreement averaged 86.5 percent in one study and 89.8 percent in another. In several analyses internal consistency produced an average Cronbach alpha ranging from 0.70 to 0.78; test-retest correlations over several weeks averaged 0.68 at the individual story level, and by the Spearman-Brown formula were estimated at 0.90 for the test as a whole. In short, the measure shows adequate psychometric properties.

Research exploring the properties of this measure of moral sensitivity in professional situations is still under way. Some of the findings indicate the following:

1. Moral sensitivity (Bebeau's measure of Component 1 processes in the dental situations) correlates only moderately with DIT scores

(in the 0.2 to 0.5 range). This is further evidence in support of the view that Component 1 processes are separable from Component 2 processes, and that morality is not a single, unitary process. It is possible for a person to be very high on moral sensitivity but not very sophisticated in working out a balanced view of a just solution, and vice versa.

2. At the same time, there is evidence for both convergent and divergent validity. Practicing dentists from the American College of Dentists and the University of Minnesota School of Dentistry reviewed tapes of subjects responding to the dramatized dental situations. Without using the scoring scheme devised by Bebeau, the practitioners intuitively ranked the protocols for moral sensitivity. Bebeau's moral sensitivity measure had a correlation of 0.69 with the practitioner's intuitive rankings of moral sensitivity and correlated with a frequency of only 0.20 to 0.40 with measures of verbal fluency, technical knowledge, and word count of the subjects' responses (Tsuchiya, Bebeau, Waithe, and Rest 1985). Practitioners agreed more with Bebeau's measure than among themselves. In short, the DEST (Dental Ethical Sensitivity Test) is correlated with variables that are theoretically similar and is different from variables that are theoretically dissimilar.

3. There is evidence that each type of situation contributes specific variability in moral sensitivity. We do not regard evidence of situational specificity as an indication that there is no underlying construct of moral sensitivity (since the Cronbach alphas are adequately high), but rather view it as indication that moral sensitivity cannot be viewed as a strong, pervasive personality trait. Component 1 processes seem to be affected by different situations, and a next goal of research is to devise ways of identifying the situational features and personal history factors that affect Component 1 processes. If we want to be able to eventually understand moral behavior in real life situations, then we will have to be able to understand what affects people's initial encoding and interpretation of the situations they face.

Stemming from Bebeau's pioneering work, Dr. Joseph Volker devised a procedure for assessing moral sensitivity in counselors, a profession that is also a helping profession but concerned with a very different aspect of health. Volker capitalized on the fact that counselor training often involves the use of tapes of therapy sessions (discussions between counselor and client) and having counselors analyze the sessions of other counselors. Volker developed two tapes. In both tapes the client discloses information about potential danger to a third party. In one tape the client disclosed information suggesting sexual abuse of a third party. In the second tape the client is a medical intern and discloses that she had been endangering her patients in the hospital due to the distraction of extreme stressors in her own life. The disclosures about danger to third parties, however, is presented in a subtle manner and for only a small portion of the counseling session. After listening to the tapes, subjects responded to a series of probe questions, including asking about the next steps that the counselor in the tape ought to take. Subjects were blind to the purpose of the study and were not specifically cued to respond to the ethical issues of the case. The critical response of interest was whether the subject listening to the tape limited his/her concerns only to the relationship between the counselor and client, or whether some concern was mentioned about the welfare of the third party in danger and included in recommendations for the counselor's next steps that something be done to safeguard the third party.

Volker's procedure differs from Bebeau's in several ways:

1. Of course, there is the obvious difference in professional field (counseling versus dentistry).

2. In Volker's tapes, the ethical issues are subtle, inconspicuous, and embedded within the larger business of the tape; a high score depends on noticing the ethical issue and in breaking the usual orientation to stay focused on the counseling dyad and to go outside of the counseling relationship to intervene in the outside world. In Bebeau's tapes, the ethical dilemma is the main focus of the tape and all subjects recognize that there is some sort of value/moral problem; a high score depends on drawing inferences from information about the various people and their special characteristics, and having full awareness of the possibilities of action.

3. The success of Volker's procedure depends on subjects being blind to the real purpose of data collection. This is not true of Bebeau's procedure.

4. Volker's scoring system is a global rating (1 to 5) on each dilemma and is essentially keyed to the degree of awareness, concern, and willingness to act on behalf of the third party. Bebeau's scoring system breaks aspects into many more points (roughly 7 to 12 aspects per dilemma) and is keyed more to particular features of the dilemma rather than a characterization of the global response.

As with Bebeau's measure, Volker obtained good interjudge reliability in scoring moral sensitivity (the correlation averaged 0.86). Also, as with Bebeau, Volker found that moral sensitivity is not equivalent to DIT scores, and found a fair degree of situational specificity in moral sensitivity. Also, Volker asked experienced clinicians to rate the transcripts of subject responses on moral sensitivity (without knowledge of Volker's scoring system). This he compared to the scores produced by his scoring system (the correlation was 0.95), thus demonstrating considerable agreement between his formalized measure of moral sensitivity and the more intuitive judgments of experienced clinicians and demonstrating convergent validation to his measure. On the other hand, he demonstrated that moral sensitivity scores are not due simply to verbosity inasmuch as the correlation there was -0.52. Also, comparisons between experienced and novice counselors were made; however unexpectedly, no significant differences were found on moral sensitivity (although there were significant differences between the novice and expert groups on the DIT). Volker discusses these findings, and as well, suggests explanations for some of the situational differences on moral sensitivity between his two dilemmas.

The work by Bebeau and Volker, although different in some aspects, illustrates our general strategy to researching moral decision making by professionals in the work setting. Of course, as yet only a start has been made on Component 1, and the other three remain virtually untouched in investigating these processes in specific work settings. Also, we have not begun to study the interactions of the components or how to combine information from them in order to better predict behavior. But hopefully our overall plan is apparent. Chapter 5 describes another aspect of relating moral judgment research to other processes and events.

The purpose of this chapter has been to present our general view of what the study of morality consists of, and to present some perspective on where our research has come from and where it is going. The purpose of the chapters that follow is to provide a much closer view of more specific issues and to review and summarize data from hundreds of studies using the DIT.

2

Life Experiences and
Developmental Pathways

James Rest and Deborah Deemer
With Robert Barnett, James Spickelmier,
and Joseph Volker

AGE TRENDS IN MORAL JUDGMENT

Virtually all research in the cognitive developmental tradition starts out by looking for age trends—that is, to see if older, presumably more advanced subjects show "higher" stage responses (as defined by a particular theory). Without this kind of empirical support, a developmental theory does not get off the ground. Piaget's preliminary work in moral judgment produced this kind of empirical support (1965), and Kohlberg's brilliant 1958 dissertation contained age trend data. Twenty-five years later, Kohlberg and his colleagues at Harvard (Colby, Kohlberg, Gibbs, and Lieberman 1983) have published a more precise and elaborated report of longitudinal trends in the same sample of subjects. The major empirical findings of this report deal with age trends. The age trends of Kohlberg's original sample have been replicated many times on many other samples using his new scoring procedure, including longitudinal studies in foreign countries (e.g., Nisan and Kohlberg 1982; Snarey, Reimer, and Kohlberg 1985; see also Gibbs and Widaman 1982). Nothing is more crucial to a developmental theory than to demonstrate that people do change over time in the direction postulated by the theory. The first question of validity of a measure of moral judgment is whether or not the measure shows age trends.

So also in research using the DIT, evidence of age trends was sought in the first phase, which focused on reliability and validity of the instrument. In my 1979 book, age trend data for the DIT was reported, involving cross-sectional data, longitudinal data, and sequential analyses. The cross-sectional data was summarized in a secondary analysis of about 3,000 subjects, and the age/education factor accounted for 38 to 49 percent of the variance in DIT scores. The longitudinal studies showed upward movement (about ten times more upward than downward movement). Sequential analyses (suggested by Baltes 1968 and Schaie 1970) indicated that the upward trends could not be explained away as being due to cohort or cultural change. Analyses also indicated that upward trends could not be attributed to testing effects.

Recent evidence on age trends in the DIT is in line with the earlier data. A meta-analysis of over 6,000 subjects in cross-sectional data by Thoma (1984; see Chapter 4) shows that age/education accounts for 52 percent of the variance of DIT scores. Cross-cultural studies on the DIT also show age trends (see Chapter 4). Indeed, the list of citations of studies that report age trends in cross sectional samples would fill several pages, and are adequately represented by the two large-scale meta-analyses.

Moreover, about a dozen new longitudinal studies of the DIT also show upward trends. (See Table 2.1 for descriptions.) As Table 2.1 shows, all the longitudinal studies show upward trends over time, and the trends are significant when the intervals between testings is more than two years. Also, recently we have completed a ten-year follow-up study on over 100 subjects who originally took the DIT in the early 1970s. As before, the general trends are upward for the sample as a whole and for males and females separately: correlated t-test (95 d.f.) $= -9.7, p < .0001$; for males, $t = -3.2$; for females, $t = -5.6$.

Taking all this together (including the Kohlberg and the DIT studies, the cross-sectional and longitudinal studies, and the cross-cultural studies) one must come to the conclusion that the evidence for a general developmental trend in moral judgment (as measured in the Kohlbergian tradition) is overwhelming. Of course, arguments still remain over the extent or existence of reversions and regressions, and disputes remain over how much error (and what kinds) are part of each measurement device. Nevertheless, the overall trend of change in the direction defined by the theory as upward is quite clear. While there are a few people who deny that moral judgment develops at all (e.g., Beck 1985; Emler, Renwick, and Malone 1983), their claims are not based on examining the age trend data (nor do they produce new age trend data that contradicts the existing findings); rather, they base their claims on personal conviction. If a person remains skeptical on

Table 2.1 Review of longitudinal studies

Author, date (length of study)	Sample characteristics	n	T1	T2	T3	T4	Test statistic	Probability
			Mean at time of testing					
Kitchner et al. (1984) (2 years)	Junior high school	16	43.34	46.93	—	—	$F(1,106) = 4.92$ Time	$p = 0.05$
	Junior college	26	44.61	49.51	—	—	$F(2,106) = 20.85$ Group	$p = 0.001$
	Graduate school	14	60.54	69.98	—	—		
Bridges and Priest (1983) (5 years)	West Point Cadets							
	Sample 1	24	—	38.3	39.8	41.5	$F = 0.6$	
	Sample 2	37	33.0	—	37.8	41.8	$F = 5.8$	$p < .05$
	Sample 3	17	32.6	—	—	41.4	$F = 2.5$	
	Sample 4	113	36.7	38.5	41.3	—	$F = 9.2$	$p < 0.05$
	Sample 5	27	34.9	35.3	40.8	45.9	$F = 5.8$	$p < 0.05$
Mentkowski and Strait (1983) (4 years)	College students	140	39.24	46.61	48.94	—	$t = 40.79$ T1-T2	$p = 0.001$
							$t = 4.48$ T2-T3	$p = 0.05$

Study	Sample	N					Statistic	Significance
McGeorge (1976) (2 years)	College students	93	42.7	44.2	—	—	NA	NS
Rest et al. (1978) (8 years)	Mixed education Age 13-23	41	36.5	47.5	49.8	51.3	$F = 17.6$	$p = 0.0001$
Kraack (1985) (2 years)		117	22.5	28.4	—	—	$t = 6.19$	$p = 0.00$
Spickelmier (1983) (6 years)	College students	24	42.46	48.09	46.80	—	$t = 1.048$	$p = $ NS
Thoma (1983) (1 year)	College freshmen	44	45.34	50.35	—	—	$t = 5.92$	$p = 0.02$
Whiteley (1982)	College students	187	38.12	42.20	—	—	$t = 15.88$	$p = 0.001$
Sheehan, Husted, and Candee (1981) (3 years)	Medical students	52	53.7	58.0	—	—	$t = 6.4$	$p = 0.02$
Biggs and Barnett (1981) (4 years)	College students	82	38.60	48.03	—	—	NA	$p = 0.001$
Broadhurst (1980)	Social workers	52	43.54	47.36	50.56	—	$t = 2.82$	$p = 0.01$

NA, not available; NS, not significant.
Source: Compiled by the authors.

the point that there are age trends in moral judgment, it is doubtful that any finding in all of social science will be acceptable.

In sum, one of the findings that has come from the first phase of research in moral judgment is that it is related to age, and this finding is replicated again and again.

What Causes Development: Formal Education

Age trend data indicates that people do develop over time, but it does not indicate *why* or *how*—that is, the causes, conditions, and mechanisms of development. As researchers move beyond the question of the validity of instruments, this question of the nature of development becomes more important.

According to Piaget (e.g., 1970), cognitive development takes place because humans are active interpreters of their experiences. Humans construct meanings to make sense of their experience, they form general categories of meaning by which experiences are assimilated, and they form expectations about what is likely to happen. When new experiences cannot be assimilated into existing categories of experience or when expectations are violated, humans attempt to revise their categories and expectations so that experience will once again make sense and be predictable. Change in one's cognitions then comes from experiences that do not fit one's earlier (and simpler) conceptions. Cognitive disequilibrium is the condition for development.

According to Kohlberg, the special kinds of *social* experiences that are particularly conducive to development in moral thinking come from "role-taking" experiences (1969). Role-taking experiences are those social experiences in which a person takes the point of view of another. And so the sharing of confidences among friends in childhood is a role-taking experience. Discussion between parents and children about the reasons for moral rules provides another occasion for role-taking experiences. Moral debates are another source for learning about another's point of view. Assuming a job in which one must think about the concerns of one's colleagues or subordinates is another occasion for a role-taking experience. Presumably, greater role-taking opportunities lead to devising more and more elaborate ways of coordinating human interests, and thus to more developed conceptions of justice.

It turns out, however, that morality researchers have not been able to measure directly cognitive disequilibrium or role-taking opportunities. Berkowitz (1980), for instance, describes his attempts to measure cognitive disequilibrium in the context of moral education programs and that he and a research assistant were unable to agree when disequilibrium was occurring.[1] Similarly, researchers have not been successful in developing measures of how much role-taking experience a particular subject is receiving. Both of these formulations seem to be too general and elusive for direct assessment, and seem to function more on a purely theoretical level than as operational constructs. Researchers have had to be more concrete in operationalizing what particular experiences promote development (and perhaps, intermediately, cognitive conflict and role taking).

One of the strongest and most consistent correlates of development in moral judgment has been years of formal education, even more so than chronological age per se. The power of formal education has been somewhat surprising. In the study of Colby, Kohlberg, Gibbs, and Lieberman (1983), the correlation of moral judgment development with formal education was 0.53 and 0.60. In the secondary analysis of demographic correlates of the DIT (1979a), format education was the strongest correlate. Our recent 10-year longitudinal study of DIT scores shows the effects of formal education more dramatically. In Figure 2.1, DIT scores are shown over four testings (roughly 1972 to 1983). Subjects are divided into three education groups. The high line represents the course of development for subjects with a high degree of education since high school, the middle line represents the course of development

Figure 2.1 Longitudinal mean DIT by education

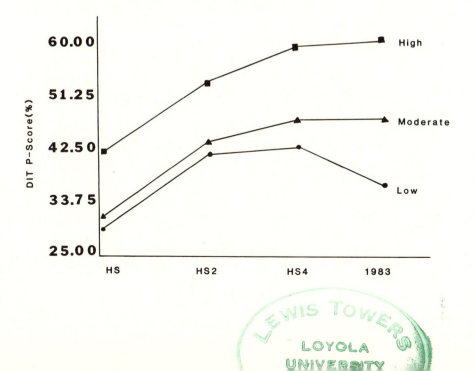

for subjects with a moderate amount of education, and the bottom line the course of development for subjects with a low amount of education. The high group continues to increase over time, the mediate group increases some and then levels off, and the low group actually increases only for the two years immediately following high school, then falls off. The initial differences between the three groups at the first testing (in high school) are dramatically increased according to their educational level. In other words, whether a person continues schooling seems to determine his general course of development after high school.

Therefore, the empirical link between years of formal education and increases in moral judgment scores definitely seems to exist. But the theoretical interpretation of this finding is not clear. It is not clear what years of formal education actually represent in terms of experiences, subject activity, or processes and mechanisms (see Rest and Thoma 1985 for a more extended discussion):

1. It may be that the college environment "socializes" certain attitudes and forms of verbalization. More time in college may represent more reinforcement and modeling opportunities to become "collegiate" (assuming that the DIT in some way measures how "collegiate" someone is becoming).

2. Alternatively, it may be that some particular skill or piece of knowledge is taught in college (like learning the names of the U.S. presidents, or extracting square roots), and the upward trends reflect more students learning these skills over time. (This assumes that the DIT reflects this particular skill or piece of special knowledge.)

3. It may be that college activities slowly imbue students with a general perspective. This alternative would not view college as directly teaching a particular set of values or beliefs, but rather as indirectly influencing a more general world view. (This assumes that the DIT reflects adherence to some general world view.)

4. It may be that college provides a generally stimulating environment in which individuals work out their own ideas about morality. This alternative does not presume that the college environment is promoting any ideology in particular (as assumed in nos. 1-3 above), but rather promotes reflection and self-discovery. (This alternative assumes that self-constructed development in moral judgment inevitably leads to more principled thinking.)

5. It may be that years of education represent nothing about the environment itself but rather indicate something about the people who

seek extended schooling. Perhaps people who chose to go to college are those who are predisposed to be more reflective, who seek intellectual stimulation, who are self-motivated to develop cognitively. It so happens that college is a place that attracts a disproportionately large number of such individuals, but the gains that are made during the college years are not attributable to college per se, but to the individuals who self-select to attend college.

Logically, any one of these explanations (or combinations of these explanations) could account for the empirical findings that moral judgment development is related to years in formal schooling. The critical experience that fosters growth could be in the extracurricular activities or atmosphere of college, in conversations over coffee, in the formal curriculum and course readings, in the life style of college students, in the movies that are shown at near-campus theaters, or in the individual disposition to be reflective and curious (apart from anything in the college situation).

Several waves of studies have been undertaken to better understand the relation between formal education and moral judgment development, and more generally to understand what life experiences foster moral judgment development. The consistent and strong empirical findings that relate moral judgment to formal education make this an opportune place to start investigation. Barnett and Volker (1985) recently reviewed ten studies, and their summary of findings is given in Tables 2.2 and 2.3.

One type of study was designed to link certain activities, interests, and life styles with moral judgment. The basic question here was, Do subjects with high moral judgment scores have interests and activities different from those of subjects with low moral judgment scores? Subjects were asked to fill out checklists of activities and interests. For instance, the "academic-conceptual" dimension of Biggs, Schomberg, and Brown (1977) involved responding to an item asking whether the subject had read about (a) Marxism, (b) mathematical induction, (c) psychoanalytic therapy, (d) the Victorian age, or (e) the Periodic Table. The more items that the subject checked having read about, the higher the "academic-conceptual" score. Similarly, subjects were asked if they had ever heard of (a) U Thant, (b) Earl Warren, (c) Mao-Tse Tung, (d) Melina Mercouri, or (e) James Shannon. The more people that subjects had heard of, the higher the score on "social/political figures." The first three studies in Table 2.2 used this way of characterizing life experience, indicated by the term "checklist" in the column under

Table 2.2 Relationship of life experiences to level of moral judgment

Study	Methodological problems	n	Sample	Experience measure	Experience related to high moral judgment	Experience related to low moral judgment
Biggs, Schomberg, and Brown (1977)	A, C	767	College freshmen	Checklist	Academic-conceptual[a] Social/political figures[a] Literary[a] Artistic[a]	
Schomberg (1978)	A	407	College freshmen	Checklist	Academic-conceptual[a] Study[b] Artistic[a] Literary[a] Intercultural[a] Social Issues[a] Cultural Affairs[a]	
Barnett (1982)	A, C	128	College seniors	Checklist	Social issues[a] Political activities[a] Literary[a] Social/political figures[a] Cultural experiences	Campus activities[a] Religious experiences[b]
Spickelmier (1983)	C, D	24	Young adults	Ratings based on interviews	Strong educational orientation[b] Academic success[b] Tolerant of diversity[b] Academic post-college environment[b]	Weak educational orientation[a] Academically unsuccessful[b] Apathetic/intolerant[b] Nonacademic post-college environment[a]

Study		N	Population	Measure		
Volker (1979)	A, E	42	College students	Checklist (MREC)	Formal instruction[b] Exposure to mature thinking[b] Political activities Adjusting to roommates	Assuming responsibility for others[b] Tragedy, facilitative relationships, career decisions Conservative religious beliefs/practices
Cady (1982)	A, E	57	Clergy	Checklist (MREC)	Education[b] Choosing a major[b] Learning about controversial issues[b] Exposure to different perspectives[b] Trusting and open relationships[a] Exposure to mature thinking via work[b] Experiencing suffering[b] Liberal religious theology[a]	Conservative religious theology[a] Religious experiences

[a] $p < .01$.
[b] $p < .05$.

Methodological problems key: A, Nonrandom or nonrepresentative sampling; B, significant (greater than 40 percent) subject mortality; C, no statistical control for regression to the mean; D, insufficient number of subjects to warrant statistical tests or no statistical tests conducted; E, multiple statistical tests, potential problem with type I error.

Source: Compiled by the authors.

Table 2.3 Relationship of life experiences to change in moral judgment

Study	Methodological problems	Sample	n	Experience measure	Experience related to growth in moral judgment	Experience not related to growth in moral judgment
Rest (1975)	A, B	Young adults	88	Experiences nominated by subjects	Formal instruction, reading, study[a] New real world responsibilities[a]	Maturation Expanding social world Religious experience Involvement in community affairs
Rest (1979)	A, B, C, D	Young adults	59	Experiences nominated by subjects	Current issues/events Contemplating issues New real world responsibilities Making decisions for the future Religious experiences Involvement in community affairs Personal stress Change in life style Travel	Reading Formal instruction Maturation New social contacts Specific influential people Making decisions Living away from home Experiencing tragedy

Kraack (in preparation)	B	177	College under-classmen	Checklist	Work/noncampus activities
					Campus involvement
					Amount of participation
					Type of involvement (e.g., political, religious, athletic, cocurricular, social, publications)
					Leadership (self-reported)
					Leadership (judged)

$^a p < .05.$
$^b p < .01.$

Methodological problems key: A, Nonrandom or nonrepresentative sampling; B, significant (greater than 40 percent) subject mortality; C, no statistical control for regression to the mean; D, insufficient number of subjects to warrant statistical tests or no statistical tests conducted; E, multiple statistical tests, potential problem with type I error.

Source: Compiled by the authors.

"Experience Measure." In general, these studies indicate that subjects with higher moral judgment scores tend to be better read, more knowledgeable and involved in academic experiences, and more socially active through their freshman year. As seniors, people with higher moral judgment scores remain more involved socially, politically, academically, and culturally. Nevertheless, the power of the trends using these "experience" measures was not much greater than the correlations with the more simple variable, years of formal education.

A second wave of studies used the "Moral Reasoning Experience Checklist" (MREC) designed by Joseph Volker. Volker's instrument asks subjects whether they have had certain experiences (e.g., "attending a course which presented material from different perspectives," "work experience which exposed the individual to persons of more mature thinking," "experiencing brutality or suffering," "experiencing a significant decision involving a family member"; see Table 2.2 for lists of "experience" categories). It also asks subjects to estimate how important this experience was to them. Volker derived items for the MREC from intensive interviews with college students and from suggestions throughout the moral judgment literature. One innovation was to provide separate analyses for whether or not subjects had experienced a certain event and for whether or not subjects thought the experience was especially important for their own development. (Presumably, some subjects may have experienced certain events, but the events might have had little impact on them.) Despite the care and inventiveness with which the MREC was devised, studies using the MREC checklist were also disappointing in that they yielded inconsistent results or low levels of significance.

A third type of study approached the characterization of life experiences by simply asking subjects what, in their own view, had influenced their development in moral thinking. In response to this open-ended question, subjects supplied their theories of what was influential in their own lives by giving a phrase or a few sentences. A categorization system was inductively devised to classify this material. Instances of categories were "new real world responsibilities," "formal instruction, reading and study," "involvement in community affairs," and so on (see entries in Table 2.3 for "experience" categories). In the Rest studies (1975, 1979a) this life experience data was related to the amount of gain in moral judgment scores over a several year period. And so the study design was not based on concomitant correlations but on longitudinal gains related to life experience. As with the MREC studies, however, results were disappointing in producing inconsistent or weak findings.

These disappointments caused us to reexamine our assumptions. On one hand, there had been the consistent and strong correlations between moral judgment and years of formal education. The variable, "years of formal education," must stand indirectly for some kind of enhancing experience or psychological process that fosters development. On the other hand, when we had attempted to specify more exactly what experiences were responsible for this correeation, we could not find any characterization of life experiences that produced more consistent and more powerful correlations. What was wrong?

Several possibilities came to mind. One difficulty may be in seeking a single life experience that is characterized at too concrete and too specific a level of description. As an analogy, suppose we were interested in what causes weight gains. We might ask subjects if they ate hamburgers, or fish, or nuts and berries, and so on. Some subjects would say yes to each of these. Were we to correlate each of these specific food categories with weight gain, we might find inconsistent or low correlations (because people who eat lots of hamburgers may not eat lots of nuts and berries; because some people may eat a wide mixture of foods, but small amounts of any specific food, yet show large weight gains). High correlations with a specific food show up only if the group of people with high weight gains eat a lot of that specific food and the group of people with low weight gains eat little of that specific food. Upon finding that none of these single food categories had high correlations with weight gains, we would be wrong to conclude that none of these food categories is associated with weight gains (e.g., that eating hamburgers has nothing to do with weight gains). The fact of the matter is that some people may gain weight from eating lots of hamburgers, others from nuts and berries, and others from eating moderate amounts of lots of different foods. The flaw in our logic is in attempting to correlate the amount of one specific food with weight gains of the group in general. The proper level of description is in a more encompassing term, calories. If we convert hamburgers, fish, nuts and berries to calorie equivalents, then we would find a correlation. (Of course, other factors influence weight gain in addition to calories, such as metabolism, energy expenditure, etc.) Drawing the comparison to morality research, it may be that trying to link moral judgment development to experiences such as travel, group discussions, and real life responsibilities is like asking whether hamburgers, fish, or nuts and berries separately is related to weight gain. Therefore, we should search for a level of description that is comparable to the calorie term in our example. It may be that some people profit from travel, some from group discussions, and some from real life responsibilities, yet each of these categories would not show up as a single strong correlate of moral judgment gain because strong correlations would only show up if the group of subjects in general gained by virtue of amounts of one experience. In short, our strategy for discovery was ill-suited to the task.

Another question is how objectively or subjectively to characterize the experience. The problem in being too objective is that the same event may affect different people differently. For instance, two people may travel, and one of them might be profoundly affected by the experience, yet the other person may be hardly affected at all. And so it matters not only that the subject was exposed to some event, but it also matters how the particular person reacted or subjectively experienced the event. On the other hand, our attempts to assess subjective impact have largely relied on the subject's own retrospective theory about how the event affected him/her. In other words, we ask the subject to theorize how significant the event was for the subject's development. But there is no basis to believe that people in general are accurate in knowing what affects their moral judgment development. In fact, people are not usually aware that the basic structures of their moral judgment change over time, and even less aware of what is affecting the basic structure. Therefore our assessment of the subjective impact of an experience was also faulty.

A New Approach

These considerations have led us to attempt another approach to characterizing life experiences, one that is not too concrete and includes information about the subjective reaction to the experience (but does not depend on the subject's own theory about development). An exploratory case study was completed by James Spickelmier (1983), and a follow-up study is now in progress (Deemer, in press). Spickelmier began by devising a structured interview that included questions on a wide range of experiences that are hypothesized to influence development. Questions were formulated not only to cover aspects of experience that had been tapped in previous moral judgment research, but also aspects of experience from the larger student development literature (e.g., Astin 1978; Bowen 1978; Chickering 1969). The topics of the interview included the following: living situation, peer relations, relationships with faculty, academic involvement, learning preferences, non-classroom involvements, exercising responsibility, relationships with the opposite sex, relationships with family, occupational goals, personal goals and values, experiences of crisis or trauma, and post-college experiences. Some sample questions are the following: (1) Describe a typical evening in each of your college living situations. What did you or your roommates tend to be doing? What did you talk about? (2) Give me the first names of some of your best friends in college. Describe them to me. Compare your friends with the other students at your school. (3) Can you tell me about a book, a lecture, a particular intellectual problem that impressed you during college? (4) How dependent were you on your parents for financial support and how did that change over the college years?

Information from this kind of interview seemed to give a fairly detailed picture of what was happening in the lives of the subjects and which experiences had major impacts, yet the information did not depend too much on the subject's theory about his/her own development. Spickelmier attempted to collect concrete descriptive material from which the coder could draw inferences and interpretations. The subjects for Spickelmier's study were all college students at the same institution, and so the questions all refer to the college setting. The subjects had been tested on the DIT as freshmen, in their junior year, and two years after college graduation.

Spickelmier went through several cycles of formulating ways to code the interview material. Since Spickelmier's study was exploratory and contained a non-random small sample, we do not want to make too much of the statistical findings. Its special value lay in suggesting ways to construct characterizations of experience that relate to moral judgment development. After much analysis and experimentation, Spickelmier developed coding guides for a dozen dimensions. Of these, three "academic" codes seemed to be most predictive of moral judgment development. One code (named "socializing environment") characterized how fully the student was immersed and involved in the college milieu versus simply attending college and being influenced by strong non-college socializing forces. For instance, one subject (who was scored low on socializing environment) commuted from her rural home throughout college, made few college friends, and continued to be oriented more to home than to college. In contrast, other subjects seemed to enjoy the break from high school and home, excitedly embraced their new environment, and became very immersed in their new collegiate worlds—they were scored high on this code.

A second academic code (named "academic success") attempted to differentiate students on one hand who formulated a clear academic goal, did well in academic work, and made normal progress toward their academic goals, in contrast to those students, on the other hand, who did not have clear goals and were frustrated in achieving them. Clearly this code represents more than simply the number of years in school.

A third academic code (named "educational orientation") represents the degree to which the students worked hard at their studies, enjoyed academic life and the world of ideas and the activities of reading and discussing, and chose friends who were similarly serious students.

In Spickelmier's study, subjects who started off as freshmen with higher DIT scores tended to be higher on these academic variables (in other words, moral judgment scores predicted life styles). And students who scored higher on these life experience variables showed greater gains in moral judgment scores from freshman year to two years after college (in other words, certain life experiences predicted moral judgment gains). In a multiple regression analysis, predicting DIT scores at two years beyond college, the freshman DIT score was entered first (so as to control statistically for initial differences) and then the academic codes were entered. The academic codes added 16 percent to the predictability of the later DIT scores, above and beyond the variance accounted for by the freshman DIT scores.

Deemer's study takes off from Spickelmier's, but is a much larger-scale study, involving over 100 subjects tested over 10 years, from a diversity of backgrounds. The subjects were those first tested as high school seniors in the early 1970s and reported in several intermediate longitudinal studies (Rest 1975, 1979a; Rest and Thoma 1985). Thirty-seven subjects had no college experience, 25 had some college experience but did not graduate, 40 graduated, and 13 have gone on to graduate school. Sex is evenly divided: 52 males and 50 females. Fifty are currently married. Approximately half of the sample have moved from the location of their high school; 38 continue to live in an urban area, 12 in a rural area, and the others have lived in a mix of environments. The scope, size, and diversity of Deemer's sample permit a more extensive exploration of the relation of life experience to moral judgment development.

Deemer adapted the interview questionnaire from Spickelmier, primarily adding questions appropriate for the non-college subjects, and extending the time period covered by the interview. This is a massive study, involving as much as five testings per subject, hundreds of variables, and often 50 pages and more of interview transcript. Deemer incorporated much of Spickelmier's codes in her life-experience categories, but was not constrained by the previous codes.

Since the Deemer study is so vast and complex, I will attempt to convey a sense of the findings by first giving some general impressions instead of proceeding directly to details of procedure, specific codes, and statistical analyses. There are so many parts to this study that it will be easier to understand by telling the ending to the story before going into the steps that lead there. Imagine two caricatures: one is of the ten-year course of development leading to high scores in moral judgment; the other is of the course of development leading to low scores in moral judgment. We begin looking at subjects as seniors in high school and follow them into their late twenties, as young adults. (For convenience, we will refer to their early testing in the 1970s when they were 17 and 18 years old as "high school," and to the most recent testing in the 1980s when they are in their late twenties as "young adulthood.") Already in high school there are discernible differences between the subjects who follow the path of high development and those who follow the path of low development; these differences, however, become more dramatic over time as the two groups diverge. In high school, the "high group" (in contrast to the "low group") gets better grades, is more interested in reading and studying and in ideas, plans to go to college, associates with friends who are also more academically inclined, and already has somewhat higher DIT scores. After high school, the high group is more adventuresome in seeking new growth experiences—it is more likely to go to college, and more interested in meeting new people, broadening their experiences, trying new work possibilities, and trying to learn new things. The high group is more reflective, more engaged in making sense of their own lives and the social structures in which they live. The high group makes and remakes plans and goals; they are busy imagining various future possibilities and trying out those plans; they assume more responsibility for what happens to them and are more active in maneuvering and working toward goals. The high group seems to have more energy than the low group, is more willing to take moderate risks, seems to be less devastated by disappointments and failures. By the time our subjects are in their late twenties, the high group continues to live in a highly stimulating social and work milieu (i.e., work that involves a high level of decision making and responsibility and has higher social status) and has more contacts with other people who are interested in ideas and intellectual topics. The people in the high group are more successful in attaining career objectives and more identified personally with their careers. Also, the high group is more politically aware and active, and participates more in civic and community organizations in leadership positions.

Note that our caricatures do not draw distinctions between the high group and low group in terms of leisure activities, socializing, or marriage patterns. Although the high group is more academically oriented and more intellectual, it is not characterizable as "grinds," or social isolates, or as always working and never having fun. In fact, the high group seems to spend a moderate amount of time in leisure activities such as sports, TV watching, and reading novels. The two groups are not discernibly different in terms of marital status. Furthermore, the high group has a moderate amount of hardships, emotional setbacks, disappointments, and hindrances. Moreover, the high group draws from both men and women, urban and rural settings, high SES and low SES.

Also note that these caricatures do not mention "political activists," "student radicals," "conscientious objectors," "religious evangelicals," or followers of Jesse Jackson, Jerry Falwell, Gloria Steinem, or members of Hari Krishna. As national surveys indicate (Levine 1980), young people in the 1970s in general did not have heros, and the subjects in this study did not mention being influenced by any well-known political, social, religious, or folk personage. Neither were our subjects much into causes or crusades. Consistent with national trends, young people in our sample were not "radicals," "revolutionaries," or "activists" in the images of the mass media of the 1960s.

Third, note that these caricatures do not mention grappling with existential crises, personal moral dilemmas, or specific moral problems (such as deliberating whether or not to register for the draft, or over deciding an abortion, or over whistle-blowing on some organization). This is not to say that our subjects had no personal moral dilemmas, but rather that they did not attribute special importance to a particular moral dilemma as an influence in their development. It was rare to hear of anything comparable to the "conversion" experience of St. Paul on the road to Damascus. Moral issues seem not to be the central concerns of most of these subjects, and moral crises were not pivotal life experiences.

From these interviews with over 100 subjects, we get the impression that development in moral judgment is a by-product of general social development, not a special result of particular moral courses, particular moral crises, or particular moral leaders. Those elements that differentiate the high group from the low group are not specifically "moral" experiences, but events that are likely to foster social development in general. Accordingly, development in moral judgment seems to be a flag for social development in general.

Our two caricatures, like all others, are oversimplifications. They depict general trends, but do not represent the range of diversity. The reader is advised to begin with these caricatures, and then to attend to the qualifications that will be mentioned in the further description of the Deemer study that follows.

In order to illustrate Deemer's study more concretely, several of her "experience" codes will be discussed. Table 2.4 presents the selection of the codes discussed in this chapter (see Deemer, in press, for further discussion). All of these experience codes have acceptable interjudge reliability (perfect agreement averaged 77 percent; Cohen's kappa averaged 0.68). The descriptions that follow are short excerpts from the interviews that are intended to convey the general sense of what subjects said and how it was coded. In order to preserve the anonymity of the subjects, the excerpts are edited of any identifying details. For economy of presentation, the full range of codes is not given, and the excerpts are abbreviated in some places to read more smoothly. Features essential to the codes are preserved.

Table 2.4   Experience codes and moral judgment in the Deemer study

Experience codes		
High school	Interim period	Young adults
Academic orientation	Educational/career orientation	Career fulfillment
Further education	Continued intellectual	Political awareness
encouraged	stimulation	Civic responsibility
	Other variables	
DIT	Number of years of education	DIT
		Duncan scale

Source: Compiled by the authors.

Life Experience Codes for High School

In the interviews, subjects were asked to describe their high school experience. One life experience code was "high school academic orientation." Subjects who studied hard, made good grades, enjoyed reading, and took challenging courses were scored "high" on this code, and subjects who didn't do well academically, didn't work hard, and took easy courses were scored "low." For example, the following excerpt illustrates a high score:

> I just felt like the whole world was opening up because my teacher was so wonderful. She had us read all sorts of things and had us do lots of writing. I love to write. I wrote a whole book in my senior year.

Examples of low codes on this dimension:

> I had fun. I kind of regret some things I missed in high school. I skipped out a lot the last year of high school. And the other two years weren't all that important to me. I got average grades, maybe a couple of D's. It wasn't that important. I missed out of trying to get better grades. But I graduated. That was my big goal . . . to get out.

> I didn't take what you'd call really heavy classes. I took slough-off classes, easy classes. I had to take some required math and I didn't do well in that class at all. I just didn't give it enough chance.

> I had a lot of truancy problems in high school and stuff like that. I wasn't into school like I should have been.

Another code for high schools was "further education encouraged." A high code represents encouragement by the parents and/or school personnel to go on to college. A low score represents lack of encouragement or pressure to do something else (earn money, succeed in athletics) rather than education. Example of a high code:

> My father was a person who was always helping me along in school and suggesting classes I should take. When it came to choosing my major, that was up to me, but I think he had a big influence on me. At one point I might be thinking about going into something, and he'd say, "Look, there's not that many jobs in that, maybe you should decide to do something else." I guess I was always encouraged to keep pushing along in my studies, but I was not told exactly what to do.

Example of a low code:

> My parents never really sat down with me and set any goals or said anything to me about it. It was left pretty much up to me. I would have had to pay for it, and I never would have had the money. They never really

seemed to push on it at all. I don't know if it wasn't important to them, or what.

Deemer's analysis indicates that both of these codes are significantly related to the subject's DIT score in high school—that is, the more academically oriented subjects and the subjects with greater family support for academics tended to have higher DIT scores in high school; and interestingly, these high school experiences were significantly predictive ten years later of DIT scores in their young adulthood ($rs = 0.42$ and 0.36), even after adjusting for initial differences in high school DIT scores.[2] In multiple regression analyses, the unique variance contributed by high school academic orientation to the adult DIT score (over and above that accounted for by the high school DIT score) was $R^2 = 6.0$ percent, $F = 5.81$, $p = .018$. For further education anticipated, the unique $R^2 = 6.9$ percent, $F = 6.40$, $p = .014$. And, not surprisingly, these experience codes also predicted the number of years of formal education acquired by the subjects after high school.

Life Experiences in the Interim Period

After high school, over half the subjects in our sample continued in some form of formal education. From previous studies, we know that simply the number of years of formal education is highly related to eventual DIT scores. Spickelmier's study and Deemer's study go beyond this and indicate that people differ in taking advantage of their years in schooling, and that how people use these experiences is more related to later development than to merely whether they were matriculated in some college. An important difference is represented by the code, "educational orientation," that Deemer adapted from Spickelmier. A high score on this code is given to those students whose interviews indicate that they worked hard at their studies, enjoyed learning and engaging ideas, worked toward academic goals, and chose friends who were serious students. A low code represents little studying, confusion over academic goals, choosing friends who are not academically oriented, and not investing in the academic side of college life. Examples of high codes:

I really enjoyed the academic support groups, and the professors. I liked many of my classes. I liked to be in the academic atmosphere. You would go and you would talk to interesting people about interesting things. Life just seems higher pitched. I like that atmosphere.

I was in the honors program. That was really good training. I had good grades, about a 3.7 approximately. I studied real hard especially right before a test. I enjoyed living on campus because there were always people around to do something with, something to talk about.

With my roommate, we got extremely close. We'd talk about all sorts of things, like should we be organ donors? What happens when you die? Does God exist? We had fantastic talks, it was terrific.

Examples of low codes:

I was always undecided. I never had a major. Somebody would tell me, "Hey, this is an easy course," and I'd take it. I took a little of everything, mostly entry level classes. I never applied towards anything. [Interviewer: How did you spend your time?] I didn't do much. I worked a little. I was living at home and probably worked half the week. I was doing a lot of drugs at the time. And I did a lot of partying. Hence the effect on my GPA. They weren't particularly happy or productive years. There isn't anything that sticks out in my mind that was really enjoyable.

I went to college right after high school. I was sort of forced to by my folks. I didn't particularly want to but parental pressure dictated. I went to a college close by my home. I figured that's as good a place as any. I never had a major. I eventually dropped out. I'd go for a quarter or two, then take a quarter off, and then go back the next quarter. All the time I was going to college I didn't really have any interest in it, and I was just more or less buying time, and I didn't study.

[Interviewer: what did you like most about school?] I don't know what I enjoyed most. Dating. Partying. Summers.

With these codes, Deemer found the same thing that Spickelmier found: among students in college, academic orientation accounted for later DIT scores in young adulthood ($r = .50$), even after adjusting for initial high school DIT scores. In multiple regression analyses, academic orientation uniquely accounted for 12.6 percent of the variance in DIT scores in young adulthood after controlling for high school DIT scores. Furthermore, high school DIT scores significantly predicted ($r = .47$) academic orientation in college.

Deemer's analysis of interview material points to one major crosscurrent in the two caricatures presented earlier: namely, that all those who go to college are not academically oriented, and hence formal education is not invariably linked with moral judgment development. A second cross-current is that among those who do not go to college, some subjects find engaging and challenging work, and find opportunities for growth and development. In a code called "career orientation," Deemer represents for non-college subjects the degree to which these subjects worked hard, had clear goals, desired to advance, and chose friends who were likewise career oriented. An example of a high code on career orientation:

My first responsibility was just to make sure the electrical jobs got installed. Then I got into computer programming. I really blossomed there. I got a good understanding of electricity. I guess I learned a lot about computers and about electronics, and it got to a point where I was actually doing like engineering training. I started putting in a lot of hours again. . . . I'm fairly intelligent and can use my brain and I wanted to do something that I could use my brain and physically do something for people.

An example of a low code on career orientation:

At first when I got out of high school I worked in an office and thought that being in an office would be all right, but it was just a bore anyway. Then I went into factory work because I knew there was money in that. You get paid nothing unless you really had a good education which I didn't have. Where I am working now is a real drag, but it is good money. That is what I'm after. I just want my paycheck and the rest of my life is my time and I'll do with it what I want. I enjoy what is *after* work. Work is not my highlight in life. I don't want to stay where I am. I'll let my husband do the work. That's the way I see it.

Since the "educational orientation" and "career orientation" codes are parallel (one for the college setting, the other for the non-college setting), it is possible to pool both college and non-college subjects. The combined "educational/career orientation" code is highly predictive of later DIT scores in young adulthood (simple $r = .53$). The amount of variance in DIT scores in young adulthood uniquely attributable to this code (after controlling for initial DIT scores in high school) is 18 percent.

It is important to note a general architectural feature in Deemer's design of life experience codes. Some of the codes emphasize person characteristics and other codes emphasize environmental characteristics, although all codes presuppose a complex, reciprocal interaction of person and environment. For instance, in the high school codes, the "academic orientation" code is primarily a characterization of a person variable, and the code, "further education encouraged," is primarily an environmental variable. It is not supposed that all people would profit from college if all were encouraged to go, nor is it supposed that all academically oriented high school students will ensure their own development regardless of environmental opportunities. Rather, it is supposed that people, to a greater or lesser degree, help make their own environments and often self-select themselves into situations of challenge and opportunity, while at the same time in order to develop, people need certain environmental supports and advantages. Development proceeds most when the person seeks to develop and when the situation fosters and supports development. Personal characteristics and environmental characteristics mutually influence each other. The main point here is that no simple, unidirectional, causal relationships are presupposed: that is, events causing development, or personal characteristics causing certain situations. Rather, accounting for development is a story of the mutual influences of individual characteristics interacting with situational opportunities and difficulties, and the serendipity of how these factors happen to be timed.

The next code, "continued intellectual stimulation," characterizes the extent of intellectual stimulation provided by one's environment over the ten-year period and continuing into the present. For instance, a person who goes to college and secures a professional job involving many challenges would be coded high; a person who went to college but then worked in a stifling job would be coded lower; a person who worked in a routine job in a factory or was unemployed over the ten years would receive very low codes. Examples of high codes are not difficult to imagine: some of the previous excerpts convey the excitement of college and later work. Also included are some non-college subjects whose work has been challenging. In the intermediate codes are included people whose work may not be particularly stimulating, but whose community involvements are rich, or whose circle of friends and spouse are enlivening, or who have made family life particularly stimulating. Examples of low codes:

> I get bored easy. Most of the jobs that I had were for a couple of months here, a couple of months there. I get bored real easy with what I'm doing. I don't like to get stuck in a rut. All those places I worked until I couldn't go no higher.

> All I do is stay home with the baby. With a small baby you don't get a chance to meet people. I don't go out except to the grocery store.

Continued intellectual stimulation is correlated with DIT scores in young adulthood ($r = .58$). After controlling for initial DIT scores in high school, this code uniquely accounts for 22 percent of the variance of later DIT scores. It does not simply reflect years of formal education. In fact, in multiple regression analysis, when high school DIT is first entered, then years of education, and continued intellectual stimulation is entered third, this experience code accounts for 14 percent of the variance of DIT scores in young adulthood, above and beyond the variance accounted for by the first two variables.

Life experiences in young adulthood

For the end point of this longitudinal study, we will consider only the experience codes that characterize how the subjects are "turning out" as young adults. We will describe "career fulfillment," "political awareness," and "civic responsibility." The theoretical interest here is to determine how pervasively moral judgment development is linked to social development in general, to responsible citizenship, and other qualities of young adults that are usually regarded as desirable.

"Career fulfillment" can best be described in terms of the criteria for scoring this five-point code (rather large parts of interviews are used to make these inferences, and therefore short excerpts do not convey the sense of this code; see Table 2.5). Deemer found that career fulfillment was significantly associated with the subjects' DIT

Table 2.5 Career fulfillment

Score	Description
5	Have identified a career that subjects find challenging and meaningful. Includes individuals who have pursued work in the community that they find meaningful and provides a sense of identity but for which they don't receive a salary. Their career means something to them that is part of their identity.
4	Individuals who have made a commitment to a career field but are currently in transition between school and work or are still in school. Individuals who have found a means of survival while they pursue their career.
3	Never planned to have a career or were unable to succeed in their chosen field. Got a job and work to survive, but are not personally invested or identified in what they do. (Includes individuals who found a job in their field but now realize it was not a good choice for them. Also includes housewives who are not merely a satellite of their husbands. People not invested or identified with their work.)
2	Individuals who suffer from job insecurity or prolonged unemployment or individuals constantly under the threat of lay-offs, and who have realistic concern about meeting their basic survival needs.
1	No meaningful work; no earned income; prolonged dependence; satellite housewives.

Source: Compiled by the authors.

scores as young adults (r = .43), and this relationship is significant even when initial DIT scores in high school and years of education are partialed out (F to enter = 11.64, p < .001). Just as this code is not simply the amount of education, it is also not simply the amount of money being made. Note that the scoring guide gives more importance to the subject's own sense of identity and doing personally meaningful work than to financial security. Also, Deemer's code does not simply reflect the social status of the subject's occupation. The subject's occupations were scored by the Duncan scale, a scale based on perceived prestige and social status of the occupation. The correlation of the DIT with the Duncan scale was significant (r = .39) but not quite as high as the code, career fulfillment. In any event, moral judgment development in young adulthood is associated with career success.

"Civic responsibility" codes the extent to which the subject is concerned about the community and actively contributing to the welfare of the community. High codes reflect taking leadership roles in community welfare projects, intermediate codes reflect helping out when called upon to do so or maintaining membership in a community group, and low codes reflect no participation and active opposition to civic participation. Example of a high code:

> Toward the end of school I had become active in politics. I developed a relationship with a State Representative and I believed that he was the best candidate, and so I started working on his campaign. It has been like an annual type of thing where I get some job and end up working for this candidate. This is part of my social conscience, the human rights type of an issue. I believe that it is just a basic type of issue that covers the way races treat each other, the way sexes treat each others, whether it is in the work place or whether it is a national basis involving a war or something like that. . . . The human rights issues and the human equality issues is the big issue that encompasses a lot of sub-issues. I think it is very important and that was probably the primary reason why I felt that I should be active in politics.

Example of a medium code:

> If they were going to go out and plant trees, or something like this, I'd be willing to help, and that kind of stuff. If I can help somebody else. Its important to feel good by helping somebody else. I don't mind if I don't get anything for it. Even just a "Thank you" is fine with me. I'm willing to pitch in. If somebody came around from town and asked me to pitch in to help with this or that, if I had the time and I could do it, I'd do it.

Example of a low code:

> I don't like to get involved where people use my time.

Deemer found that civic responsibility is significantly associated with DIT scores (F [4,96] = 4.94; $p < .001$).

"Political awareness" reflects the extent to which the person is interested, informed, and articulate about the larger "macro" issues of society. High codes are given to subjects reading several sources of information and participating frequently in political discussions. Medium codes are given to subjects who watch the news on TV, do some newspaper reading, and have occasional political discussions. Low codes are given to people who seldom read about political issues, and take little interest in them. Political awareness was significantly related to DIT scores, F (3,93) = 11.13, $p < .0001$.

In short, DIT scores in young adulthood are related to certain life styles and patterns of activities. High scores in moral judgment tend to be more successful in their career aspirations, are more involved in their communities, and are more informed about the wider issues of society.

Note that so far in describing Deemer's results, only one experience code at a time has been reported. We can group several of these codes together to represent experience more generally. This is done by simply adding the ratings for several codes together into one variable. We add the five codes together that represent life experience since high school: "educational/career orientation," "continued intellectual stimulation," "career fulfillment," "civic responsibility," and "political awareness." What does the sum of these ratings represent? Recall the two caricatures introduced at the beginning of this section, of the "high road of development" and the "low road of development." The composite variable can be interpreted as the extent to which a subject is following the "high road of development." Thus, it stands for personal characteristics, educational and career opportunities, support, stimulation, and challenge by one's social environment, and civic and career activities that go along with the development of high moral judgment scores (which we have reported separately, above). In many ways this score is similar to Spickelmier's "academic" code composite. This "high road" score is highly correlated with DIT scores in young adulthood ($r = .69$). In multiple regression analyses, if we first control for the high school DIT score, the "high road" score accounts for an additional 26 percent of the variance of DIT scores in young adulthood (above and beyond that accounted for by initial DIT score). If we also add a second control variable (years of education), then the "high road" score accounts for an additional 18 percent of the variance (above and beyond that accounted for by high school DIT and years of education). The multiple *r* with all these three variables predicting to DIT scores of young adults is .70. Thus the Spickelmier/ Deemer approach has proved to be very fruitful in accounting for adult development in terms of life experiences. The experience codes from the interviews clearly give useful information beyond the simple variable of years of education. Because the experience codes can account for so much of the variance in adult DIT scores, it is reasonable to assume that the way that these codes characterize experience is representing important elements in what fosters natural development in moral judgment. We have succeeded in going beyond the proxy variable, "years of education."

Conclusions

We return now to the initial question of this chapter, What causes development in moral judgment? As we follow young people from the common gathering ground of high school, as over the years they do so many different things and go so many different ways, what do we observe distinguishes those who continue to develop in moral judgment from those who do not?

Starting with the persistent finding that development is related to years of formal education, we want to understand what is behind this proxy variable. Years in school must indirectly represent some psychological process, some conditions of experience that are directly responsible for development. We began our investigations by listing likely candidates of specific experiences: moral discussions with peers, provocative books, travel, suicide of a friend, caring for a child or spouse, taking on a new job, moving to a new locale, and so on, and we ask subjects to indicate which of these events they have experienced. Then our analysis indicates that none of these specific experiences carries much power in predicting development. Something is wrong in our research strategy.

With hindsight, we realize that any or all of these specific experiences might foster development if they happen to receptive, reflective individuals, and if the specific experience is accompanied by other experiences in a cumulative pattern. By switching our examination of life experiences from a myopic count of specific events to a broader characterization of the overall level of social stimulation and social support for development, we achieve a quantum leap in the power of predictability. From being able to account for hardly any variance in the DIT scores of the young adults (after controlling for initial DIT differences in high school), we are now able to account for 26 percent over initial DIT scores. This increase in predictability makes us believe that our theoretical formulations are on to something.

The picture we get from these analyses is that development in moral judgment occurs in concert with general social development. It is not specific *moral* experiences (i.e., moral education programs, moral leaders, moral crises, thinking about moral issues) as much as a growing awareness of the social world and one's place in it that seems to foster development in moral judgment. The people who develop in moral judgment are those who love to learn, who seek new challenges, who enjoy intellectually stimulating environments, who are reflective, who make plans and set goals, who take risks, who see themselves in the larger social contexts of history and institutions and broad cultural trends, who take responsibility for themselves and their environs. On the environmental side of the equation, those who develop in moral judgment have an advantage in receiving encouragement to continue their education and their development. They profit from stimulating and challenging environments, and from social milieus that support their work, interest them, and reward their accomplishments. As young adults, the people who develop in moral judgment are more fulfilled in their career aspirations, have set a life direction of continued intellectual stimulation and challenge, are more involved in their communities, and take more interest in the larger societal issues. This pattern is one of general social/cognitive development.

The good news in this is that DIT scores may serve as indirect indicators of general social development (at least for populations like ours). As discussed in Chapter 1, strictly speaking, moral judgment is theoretically and operationally distinct from other moral processes, and is certainly not conceived as a characterization of personality organization in general. However, the present research seems to indicate that at least in populations like ours, social development seems to proceed on a broad front with many elements of personality tending to cluster together. To some extent then, the DIT may serve as a proxy variable for social development in general and for stimulating and supportive social environments.

The bad news in this is that clues are not provided in this research for planning deliberate and focused attempts to foster development in moral judgment through education. If development in moral judgment naturally develops as one aspect of a very broad front of social development, the specific targets of opportunity for intervention are not suggested. The next chapter reviews work on deliberate educational interventions.

NOTES

1. Turiel, in his classic 1966 study, introduced an experimental manipulation designed to operationalize cognitive disequilibrium. Exposing subjects to statements one stage above their own spontaneous stage was assumed to produce more cognitive disequilibrium than exposing subjects to statements at the stage below their own spontaneous stage. This assumption has never been checked, however. There are no manipulation checks or independent measures of cognitive disequilibrium. Other interpretations of this manipulation are possible.

2. Since the Deemer study is still in progress, the numbers in the statistical analyses may change if her final study redefines some of the codes, producing some inconsistencies between this report and her final report.

3

Educational Programs and Interventions

James Rest and Stephen J. Thoma

Over the past decade, considerable interest and investment have been devoted to devising moral education programs in the expectation that development in moral judgment would be facilitated. Educators influenced by cognitive developmental theories have attempted to facilitate the natural progression of moral judgment development by providing various types of enriched and stimulating educational experiences. Previous reviews of moral education programs (Enright, Lapsley, and Levy 1983; Leming 1981; Lockwood 1978; Lawrence 1980; Rest 1979a) have suggested that some moral educational programs (roughly half of those reviewed) are effective in promoting moral judgment development, particularly if the program lasts longer than a few weeks and if the intervention involves the participants in discussion of controversial moral dilemmas. This active practice in moral problem-solving, buttressed by interactive exchanges with peers, seems to speed up the natural development of moral judgment. In the few studies with delayed follow-up testing, the gains seem to be maintained.

The gains on the average are not great, however, and are not equivalent, say, to changing the moral reasoning of junior high students into

This chapter is adapted from an article by Schlaefli, Rest, and Thoma. "Does Moral Education Improve Moral Judgment? A Meta-Analysis of Intervention Studies Using the Defining Issues Test." *Review of Educational Research* 55, 3 (1985): 319-52. Reprinted with permission. Our thanks to the researchers who sent us reports of their studies.

the reasoning comparable to moral philosophers. Rather, the magnitude of change in these moral education programs tends to be the equivalent of four to five years' natural growth (if we use the rate of development in longitudinal studies as the basis for comparison).[1] The lack of huge changes in moral judgment is not too surprising considering that the tests that are most frequently used (Kohlberg's or the DIT) were designed to depict rather broadly gauged changes in thinking over the life span, and are intended to represent fundamental, underlying structures of social thought rather than fine descriptions of specific concepts and ideas. That is, the kinds of contrasts that researchers in the Kohlberg tradition attend to are analogous to contrasting general cultural development in terms of the Stone Age, the Bronze Age, the Middle Ages, and so on—the contrasts are not like contrasting cultural changes in terms of the 1960s with the 1970s. Hence, using these tests to assess the impact of a half-year course is not like using, say, a standardized achievement test that is constructed to be sensitive to yearly changes. Nevertheless, even small gains on these measures of moral judgment are of theoretical and practical interest if it is true that the gains are maintained and cumulative, and that differences in moral judgment scores are related to real-life decision making (see Chapter 5).

Since these earlier reviews, the number of intervention studies has more than tripled. Not only do the additional studies provide a test of the generality of the earlier conclusions, but this data base also permits us to use some meta-analytic methods to give us a more precise and differentiated picture of the impact of moral education programs on moral judgment. The 55 studies reviewed here all used the same measure of moral judgment (the DIT) so that we can aggregate studies in various analyses and subanalyses without confounding the type of test.

CHARACTERISTICS OF SAMPLES

Following the advice of Glass (1977), we did not confine our pool of studies to those published in certain journals, but included as many as we could find that used the DIT to assess the impact of a moral education program. A great help to locating studies were the yearly bibliographies that are listed in the *Moral Education Forum* (Kuhmerker, editor) of both published articles and dissertations on file in *Dissertations International*. Also, many researchers voluntarily sent reports of their studies to the University of Minnesota's Center for the Study of Ethical Development.

The 55 studies included in this review are the only ones with sufficient data that we could obtain.[2] These include 15 studies previously reviewed in Lawrence (1980) and Rest (1979a). Where information was missing (for instance, mean scores on the pretest), an attempt was made to contact the author and/or to search for a more complete report than was sent to us originally. In some cases, we were still unable to obtain the missing information. Some characteristics of the studies are summarized in Table 3.1.

Most of the studies are reported as dissertations (all doctoral dissertations, except for one master's thesis). Subjects were fairly evenly divided across the age spans for which the DIT can be used (the DIT cannot be used with subjects below a sixth-grade reading level). The

Table 3.1 Characteristics of intervention studies using the DIT

Type of publication	Special fields involved
Dissertations: 30*	Social sciences: 7
Journal publication: 18	Law, management: 3
Unpublished manuscript: 7	Nursing: 4
Samples	Teachers: 6
6th-9th grade "junior high school": 12	Treatment duration
10th-12th grade "senior high school": 12	Short interventions: 13
Students, mostly undergraduate: 19	Medium- or long-term
Adults, students over 24 years old: 12	interventions: 42
Types of educational program	Claimed effects
Group discussion of dilemmas: 29	Significant studies: 25
Psychological development programs: 19	Nonsignificant studies: 30
Social studies and humanities classes: 7	Type of designs
	Classical experimental
	designs: 9
	Quasi-experimental design
	with C: 28
	Posttest only or comparison
	group missing: 18
	Type of statistical analysis
	Simple t-test only, pre-post
	comparison: 36
	ANCOVA, two-way
	ANOVA: 19

*Number given is the number of studies having that characteristic.
Total number of studies = 55.
Source: Compiled by the author.

types of educational program (described further, below) were mostly group discussion of dilemmas and "psychological development" programs (that is, programs designed to foster general personality-social development having an experiential component; see dimension, below). About one-half of the studies involved subjects in special fields (social science, law, management, nursing, teachers), the rest of the studies drew more heterogeneous samples. Most of the programs lasted for more than a few weeks. And as has been the case in the previous reviews, about half of the studies claim a significant effect on moral judgment resulting from their interventions.

Many of the studies suffer from a variety of methodological shortcomings:

1. Only nine studies employed a fully randomized, experimental design. Since most of the studies were conducted in existing school settings, quasi-experimental designs with comparison groups were often employed; however, 18 lacked even the features of a quasiexperimental design.

2. Nineteen studies employed ANCOVA or two-way ANOVA in statistical analyses, thus simultaneously testing for treatment effects and controlling for pretest differences. The others compared before and after scores of the experimental group by t-tests without simultaneously correcting for pre-post changes in a control group.

3. Some studies included exposure to and discussion of Kohlberg's stage theory, thereby introducing a possible contamination into the posttesting (because moral judgment tests were developed presupposing a subject untutored in moral judgment theory).

4. A few studies reported that their subjects did not really understand the test, or were too young to take the test, or were given so many tests that motivation to fill out the tests became a problem.

5. Most studies did not include follow-up testing to determine if the gains on the posttest were maintained.

6. Some of the interventions were so brief that it is theoretically unlikely that significant gains could be detected in a broad-gauge instrument like the DIT.

7. Most of the interventions were taught by inexperienced teachers who were trying out the program for the first time without previous piloting.

8. Several studies had such small sample sizes that inferences were difficult to make. Unfortunately, this same list of shortcomings was cited in a previous review (Rest 1979a), and not much progress seems

to have been made since in ameliorating these shortcomings. Nevertheless, our review will examine findings from all the studies, since we are mindful of the conclusions of Glass (1977), which indicate that much useful information still resides in a pool of studies even if the individual studies have some weaknesses. Also we will conduct post hoc analyses that contrast studies with methodological differences, to see if certain design features influence the trends.

Table 3.2 lists the 40 recent intervention studies using the DIT, and Table 3.3 lists the 15 studies reviewed previously (Lawrence 1980; Rest 1979a). The tables give a large amount of information for each study (such information as was available):

1. In the first column is the author's name and year of publication.

2. The "design" is represented by the symbols used by Campbell and Stanley (1963), where R stands for randomization, O stands for observation, and X_1 X_2 X_3 . . . stand for different treatment conditions. Each line represents a different treatment group.

3. The sample is described in terms of total number of subjects, age/education, and other descriptors. Since sex is not a significant factor in DIT scores (Rest 1979a; Thoma 1984), separate analyses are not reported by sex.

4. Treatment duration is given in terms of total time span from beginning to end of the program and/or number of sessions and duration of each session. For instance, "3 X 20 min." stands for three sessions of 20 minutes duration each.

5. Treatment type gives a short characterization for each curriculum or treatment. Where two or more treatment conditions were undertaken in the same study, E_1 designates the treatment most like the effective programs described in previous reviews (e.g., peer discussion of controversial moral dilemmas along the lines suggested by Kohlberg).

6. The column headed "Mean *P%* scores" reports the sample size for each treatment and control group, reports the pretest mean DIT score in terms of the *P%* index (only occasionally is the D index reported when that index was used in place of the *P%* index), reports the posttest mean, and in a few cases reports a follow-up testing mean (designated PT). Note that some studies also reported pre-post scores on variables other than DIT, but those are not considered here.

7. The column headed "Change effect on DIT" reports the statistical analysis (using *t*-tests, ANOVA, and ANCOVA) and probability levels.

Table 3.2 Overview of intervention studies using the DIT, 1977-1983

Author	Design[a]	Sample	Treatment duration
Dilemma discussion interventions			
Bridston (1979)[c]	OX_1O OO OX_2O OO	$N = 69$, nursing students, 1st year, about 23 years old	7 X 30 min discussion of dilemmas
Fleetwood and Parish (1976)	OXO OO	$N = 29$, juvenile delinquents, 16-17 years old	6 X 1½ hrs over 4 wks
Boland (1980)	OXO OO	$N = 52$, Catholic junior high school students	1 hr/wk over 12 wks
Preston (1979)[c]	OXO OO	$N = 69$, black high school students, 7th-9th grade	24 wks
Gallagher (1978)	ROXO ROO	$N = 90$, lower SES metropolitan 11th and 12th grade students	2 X 45 min/wk, over 10 wks
Donaldson (1981)	OXO OO	Bible college, juniors and seniors	1 semester
Shafer (1978)[e]	ROXO ROO	$N = 57$, elementary science education students	10 wks
Hanford (1980)[c]	OXO OO	$N = 32$, nursing students	1 quarter (10 wks)
Riley (1981)[f]	ROX_1OO ROX_2OO RX_1OO RX_2OO	$N = 128$, adults 20-80 years, from Protestant churches, middle class	60 min/wk over 8 wks
Kenvin (1981)	OX_1OO OX_2OO OOO	$N = 30$, private Baptist school, 10th and 11th grades $N = 60$, public high school, 10th and 11th grades, middle class	45 min/wk over 6 wks

Treatment type	Mean $P\%$ scores[b]		Change effect on DIT	Problems with study	Effect size
	Pretest	Posttest			
X_{11} = discussion of dilemmas (Galbraith-Jones) fall class (E_1) spring class (E_2) (linked with discussion of health policy)	$N = 15, E_1$: 43 $N = 16, C_1$: 37 $N = 23, E_2$: 32.1 $N = 15, C_2$: 35.1	47 39.1 32.6 39.3	ANCOVA $F(1, 28) = 1.43$ ns[a] $F(1, 35) = 2.23$ ns	R, F, B, S,	.32 .06 .17 .22
X = discussion of dilemmas (Galbraith-Jones) (E)	$N = 15, E$: 20.9 $N = 14, C$: 56.8	37.7 56.6	$t(14) = 3.31$ $p < .05$ ns	R, A, M, F, S	1.72 −.03
X = discussion of Kohlberg's and Fenton's hypothetical dilemmas. At the end, discussion of real dilemmas. (E)	$N = 22, E_1$: 19 $N = 24, C$: 28	24 26	$t(21) = 1.89$ $p < .05$ ns	R, A, F	.31 −.13
X = dilemma discussion in the health and physical education curriculum (E)	$N = 30, E_1$: 18.6 $N = 38, C$: 18.3	25.4 19.7	two-way ANOVA $p < .05$[d]	R, F, A	.80 .16
X = guided peer discussions of conflicts in high school literature, role plays, dilemmas from newspapers (E)	$N = 60, E$ $N = 30, C$	Not reported	ns ns	A, F	−
X = discussion of dilemmas; clinic approach (Kohlberg-Fenton)	Not available		ns	R, M	−
X = discussion of dilemmas (Galbraith-Jones)	$N = 31, E$: 40.8 $N = 26, C$: 36.98	48.6 42.2	ANCOVA $F(1, 56) = 4.03$ $p < .05$	C, F	.58 .33
X = discussion of dilemmas in bioethics; writing an essay about ethics; teaching of Kohlberg theory	$N = 16, E_1$: 41.6 $N = 16, C$: 46.3	55.1 51.0	$t(15) = 3.36$ $p < .01$ $t(15) = 1.8$ ns	R, A, C F, N, S	.65 .35
X_1 = discussion of dilemmas (Galbraith-Jones) X_2 = control group—lectures about history of church	$N = 28, E_1$: 27.1 $N = 28, C_1$: 24.3 $N = 28, E_2$:[c] $N = 28, C_2$:[c]	31.9 26.5 33.1 25.1	three-way ANCOVA of posttest with education as covariate $F(1, 95) = 11.11$[g] $p < .01$	−	.57 .20
X_1 = discussion of universal values in American history (Fenton) (E_1) X_2 = religious instruction, Bible study, and discussions (E_2)	$N = 30, E_1$: 30.6 $N = 30, E_2$: 29.4	29.8 delayed (32.5) 28.9 delayed (25.5)	two-way ANOVA $F(3, 117) = .13$	R, B	−.06 −.04

(continues)

Table 3.2 *(continued)*

Author	Design[a]	Sample	Treatment duration
Farrelly (1980)	OX_1O OX_2O OO	$N = 191$, 6th grade students	3 hr/wk over 4 wks
Manville (1978)[c]	OX_1O OX_2O	$N = 39$, high school students, 12th grade	45 min/wk over 11 wks
Copeland and Parish (1979)	RX_1O RX_2O RO	$N = 134$, male offenders with a sentence of less than 6 mos confinement	10 hrs over 7 wks
McKenzie (1980)	OX_1O OX_2O OO	$N = 46$, high school students, 11th grade	1 hr/wk over 16 wks
Sachs (1978)[c]	OX_1O OO OX_2O OO	$N = 97$, 9th-12th grade high school students	4 lessons/wk over 20 wks
Codding (1980)	OX_1O OX_2O OO	$N = 147$, high school students, 10th-12th grade	1 semester
St. Denis (1980)[f]	ROX_1O ROX_2O ROO	$N = 120$, nursing students, mean age = 28.5	40 min/wk over 10 wks

Treatment type	Mean P% scores[b]		Change effect on DIT	Problems with study	Effect size
	Pretest	Posttest			
	$N = 15, C_1$: 24.5	28.1 delayed (29.5)	ns		.26
	$N = 15, C_2$	(29.4)	ns		
X_1 = peer group discussion of moral dilemmas (Galbraith-Jones) (E_1)	E_1 X of all stages E_2 reported		P% ns	R, A, F	–
X_2 = individual study of dilemmas (E_2)					
X_1 = discussion of dilemmas (Galbraith-Jones) (E_1). Introduction of Kohlberg theory	$N = 25, E_{11}$: 32.8	33.9 33.5	t-test ns ns	R, A, C, F, S[a]	.09 .00
X_2 = individual study of dilemmas, no group discussion. Introduction of Kohlberg theory (E_2)	$N = 14, E_{12}$: 33.5				
X_1 = discussion of dilemmas (Galbraith-Jones) (E_1)	$N = 50, E_1$[b]	33.3	t-tests	A, M, F	–
X_2 = group counseling program (E_2)	$N = 54, E_2$[b] $N = 30, C$[b]	33.6 34.2	ns		
X_{11} = combination of value clarification strategies and discussion of dilemmas (Kohlberg-Fenton) (E_{11})	$N = 15, E_{11}$: 29.1	34	ANCOVA P: $F = (2, 44) = 4.49$ $p < .05$	R, A, F	.36
X_{12} = discussion of dilemmas (E_{12})	$N = 16, E_{12}$: 34.6 $N = 15, C$: 25.6	29.5 29.2	E_1 vs E_2 posttest $t(30) = 2.02$ $p < .05$ $E_1 = C$: $E_2 = C$		−.37 .46
X_1 = discussion of dilemmas (Kohlberg-Fenton) course in moral issues in literature in parent high school	$N = 20, E_1$: 20.3 $N = 29, C_1$: 20.2	20.4 23.5	ns ns (statistical analysis not available)	R, A, F	.01 .32
X_2 = same program in alternative high school	$N = 35, E_2$: 32.0 $N = 13, C_2$: 35.6	36.1 37.4	ns ns		.26 .17
X_{11} = discussion of dilemmas (Galbraith-Jones) (E_1)	$N = 50, E_{11}$: 39.4	43.6	ANCOVA: E_1 and C	R, F	.51 .28
X_{12} = discussion of common and individual problems (just community) (E_2)	$N = 42, E_{12}$: 44.2 $N = 55, C$: 38.7	46.2 39.2	$F(1, 107) = 6.2$ $p < .01$ ANCOVA: E_2 and C $F(1, 95) = 4.08$ $p < .01$		.06
X_1 = cognitively oriented moral education strategy (Kohlberg-Fenton) (E_1)	$N = 42, E_{11}$: 41 $N = 36, E_{12}$: 44 $N = 42, C$: 47.6	50.5 48.1 42.8	ANCOVA: E_1 vs. C $F(1, 74) = 35.3$ $p < .001$	C, F	.71 .32 −.36

(continues)

67

Table 3.2 *(continued)*

Author	Design[a]	Sample	Treatment duration
Clarke (1978)	OX$_1$O OX$_2$O OX$_3$O	N = 617, 5th grade students	1 hr/wk over 10 wks
Personality development programs			
Cognetta (1977)	OX$_1$O OX$_2$O OO	N = 31, senior high school	2 hr/wk over 10 wks and daily 50 min
Nichols, Isham, and Austad (1977)[c]	ROX$_1$O ROO ROX$_2$O ROO ROX$_3$O ROO	N = 150, junior high school	Daily 50 min over 9 wks
Wong (1977)[f]	OX$_1$OO OO OX$_2$OO OO OX$_3$O OO	N = 29, public school teachers, women	32 hrs over 8 wks Over 4 wks for E$_2$
Tucker (1977)[c]	OXO OO	N = 53, undergraduate students, 20-29 yrs old	2 hrs/wk over 12 wks
Oja (1977)[c]	OXO OO	N = 48, elementary and secondary schoolteachers inservice	3½ hrs/day over 16 days
Whiteley et al. (1982)	OXO OO OO	N = 187, student volunteers	8 mos

Treatment type	Mean $P\%$ scores[b]		Change effect on DIT	Problems with study	Effect size
	Pretest	Posttest			
X_2 = affectively oriented moral education strategy (Rogers) (placed as E_1 under personality development program)			E_2 vs. C: $E(1,74)$ = 13.51 $p < .05$		
X_1 = discussion of dilemmas with role plays (E_1)	not reported		ANCOVA	R, F	–
X_2 = direct instruction program (E_2)			ns		
X_3 = spontaneous program, no formal lessons (E_3)					
X_1 = DPE, Sprinthall-training: self-reflection, communication	$N = 15$, E_1: 28.6	35.1	$t(14) = 2.31$ $p < .05$	R, A, F, S, C	.35 −.13
training, feedback for own counseling (E_1)	$N = 7$, $E_2 = 39.5$	36.7	ns		.05
X_2 = psychology course (E_2)	$N = 9$, C: 37.4	38.5	ns		
DPE curriculum on	$N = 48$, E_1: 8.8	10.31	$t(47) = 1.89$ $p < .05$	R, A, F, T	.26
X_1 = the individual: needs, values, and behavior for	$N = 48$, C_1: 9.6	9.8	ns		.03
7th grade	$N = 46$, E_2: 7.7	11.1	$t(45) = 3.48$ $p < .005$		.55
X_2 = the group: values and behavior for 8th grade	$N = 46$, C_2: 9.6	9.6	ns		.00
X_3 = society: issues and decisions for 8th grade (all DPE	$N = 41$, E_3: 11.3	13.5	$t(40) = 1.93$ $p < .05$		.33
treatments)	$N = 41$, C_3: 11.6	11.7	ns		.01
DPE curriculum focusing on women roles	$N = 11$, E_1: 56.3	65.6	$t(10) = 4.21$ $p < .01$	R, A, C, S	1.17
X_1 = with Kohlberg theories and communication skills	$N = 9$, C_1: 52.3	51.8	ns		−.03
X_2 = with communication skills	$N = 8$, E_2: 51.8	53.8	ns		.13
X_3 = without communication skills	$N = 7$, C_2: 45.1	41.6	ns		−.25
	$N = 10$, E_3: 44	54	$t(10) = 4.07$ $p < .01$		.91
	$N = 9$, C_3: 47	45	ns		−.16
X = DPE curriculum on counseling skills, empathic	$N = 31$, E: 19.1	22.1	$t(30) = 2.04$ $p < .02$	R, A, F, N, T	.40
training with racial and gender emphasis	$N = 14$, C: 18.1	20.7	ns		.24
X = DPE curriculum on communication skills, indi-	$N = 27$, E: 56.3	63.1	t-test on posttest	R, A, C, F, T	.59
vidualized teaching, application of theories in classroom	$N = 21$, C: 46.3	51.5	$t(46) = 2.08$ $p < .02$		.32
X = courses in psychological training and experience in	$N = 83$, E adjusted gains	+6.2	ANCOVA	R, F	.46
special residential college, discussion of social and	$N = 58$, C_1 adjusted gains	+3.1	$F(2, 185) = 3.0$ $p < .05$		.23
individual problems (E)	($P\%$ mean difference pre-, posttest)	+1.2			.08

(continues)

Table 3.2 *(continued)*

Author	Design[a]	Sample	Treatment duration
Avise (1980)[e,f]	OXO OO	N = 22, students of a rural area 15-17 yrs old	1 semester
Wilson (1978)	OX_1O OX_2O OX_3O	N = 41, 9th-12th grade high school students	2 hr/week 20 hrs over 1 yr
Reck (1978)[f]	OX_1O OX_2O OX_3O OO	N = 135, high school students, 11th, 12th grade X_1 = juniors X_3 = seniors	X_1 : 15-18 hrs over 9 wks X_2 : 42 hrs over 9 wks X_3 : 105 hrs over 4 wks, full time
Olson (1982)	OXO OO	N = 27, undergraduate resident students and nonresident students	5 mos

Academic courses

Author	Design[a]	Sample	Treatment duration
Boyd (1980)	OXO OO OO	N = 262, undergraduate business students	1 hr/wk over 11 wks
Finkler, personal communication (1980)[c]	OX_1O OX_2O OX_3O	N = 99, criminal justice students, sophomore level, philosophy students and doctoral students	1 hr/wk over 1 semester
Willging and Dunn (1982)	OXO OO	N = 104, law students, first and last yrs	30 hrs over 10 wks
Redman (1980)	OXO OO	N = 33, student volunteers upper middle class	2 hrs/wk over 2 semesters
Stevenson (1981)[c]	OX_1O OX_2O OO	N = 56, college students in social science, humanities, and English	1 hr/wk over 1 quarter

Treatment type	Mean $P\%$ scores[b]		Change effect on DIT	Problems with study	Effect size
	Pretest	Posttest			
X = improvement of the communication in class, self-reflection (E)	$N = 7$, E: 25.0	25.44	ns	R, A, F, N,	.06
	$N = 7$, C: 19.6	18.29	ns	S, T	−.18
X_1 = WAY: self-reflection and discussion of job and school (E_1)	$N = 12$, E_1: 26	23	ns	R, A, F, N	−.25
X_2 = academic program on career in public health (E_2)	$N = 14$, E_2: 33	30	ns		−.23
X_3 = alternative program on public health (E_3)	$N = 15$, E_3: 31	28	ns		−.20
$X_{1\,2\,3}$ = service program in order to help needy people ($E_{1,2,3}$)	$N = 34$, E_1: 31.6	32.9	ns	R, A, M,	.13
	$N = 19$, E_2: 30.1	35.8	$t(18) = 2.65$ $p < .05$	F, N, T	.43
X_3 = teaching children with learning disabilities	$N = 71$, E_3: 32.8	37.3	$t(70) = 3.06$ $p < .001$		.31
X = leadership training and leadership experience	$N = 11$, C: 28.18	32.0	ns		.34
	Not available		ns	R, A, F, N,	−
			ns	S, T	
X_1 = social-political issues (E_1)	D scores		$t(180) = 3.08$ $p < .02$	R, A, F	.19
	$N = 181$, E_1: (22.0) (23.2)				
X_2 = organizational behaviors course (C_1)	$N = 41$, C_1: (21.1) (22.1)		ns (E and C: post-test $p < .05$)		.15
	$N = 40$, C_2: (20.4) (20.4)				.00
X_1 = humanities and criminal justice (E_1)	$N = 24$, E_1: 44.6	47	ANCOVA $F(1, 92) = 4.59$ $p < .02$ problems: data not described properly	R, M, F, N, A	.17
X_2 = humanities (art, religion) (E_2)	$N = 44$, E_2: 37.1	37.1			.00
X_3 = introductory criminal justice course (C)	$N = 31$, C: 36.8	33.5			−.32
X = legal ethics related to professional responsibilities of lawyers toward society, case studies (E_1)	$N = 41$, E_1: 52.22	52.78	t-test	R, A, M,	.04
	$N = 63$, C: 49.5	52.13	ns	F, N, T	.22
	from longitudinal study (first and last years)		ns		
X = discussion of our values; reading of Skinner, Freud, values in different cultures (E_1)	$N = 19$, E_1: 34.6	45.2	$t(18) = 3.18$ $p < .005$ C: ns	R, A, M, F, N, S, T	.63
	$N = 14$, C: 38.5	44.6			.46
X_1 = social studies, discussion of problems in literature (E_1)	$N = 29$, E_1: 50.1	53.8	t-test ns	R, F, N, T	.25
X_2 = humanities (E_2)	E_2 and C: DIT not applied				
X_3 = English course (E_3)					

(continues)

Table 3.2 *(continued)*

Author	Design[a]	Sample	Treatment duration
Short-term			
Goddárd (1983)[f]	ROX_1O ROX_2O ROX_3O ROO	$N = 68$, students in psychology, sociology, history, and economics	3 X 20 min
M. Greene, personal communication (June 1980)	OXO OO	$N = 62$, associate degree nursing students	Very brief treatment
Holley (1978)	OXO	$N = 37$, students, 24 years old	1-13 counseling sessions
Oberlander (1980)	$ROX_{11}OO$ $ROX_{21}OO$ $ROX_{12}OO$ $ROX_{22}OO$ $ROX_{13}OO$ $ROX_{23}OO$	$N = 100$, introductory psychology course middle class students	50 min film, 50 min discussion of dilemmas
Adams (1982)	ROXO ROO	$N = 72$, teacher students	9 hrs over 1½ days
Clark (1979)[c]	OXO OO	$N = 36$, private school, 8th grade	5 hrs
Laisure and Dacton (1981)	OXO OO	$N = 18$, male students, residence assistants	15 hrs over 2½ wks

Key: R, Subjects not randomly assigned to treatments; A, inadequate statistical comparison of experimental gains with gains of control group or no pretest or no C; C, contamination of posttesting by exposure to Kohlberg stage descriptions; M, subjects not motivated to take test or too young to understand it; F, no follow-up testing to determine if posttest gains are stable; B, treatment was too brief; N, treatment was conducted for first time or taught by inexperienced teacher; S, sample was too small (experimental group fewer than 20); T, no relation explained between Kohlberg theory and treatment; ns, not significant.

[a]R in the design indicates subjects randomly selected. An R does not appear if only treatments are randomly assigned.

[b]Only results related to the DIT scores are reported.

Treatment type	Mean P% scores[b]		Change effect on DIT	Problems with study	Effect size
	Pretest	Posttest			
X_1 = film about didactic principles in Rogerian theory (E_1)	$N = 16, E_1$: 43.3	53.5	$t(15) = 3.57$ $p < .01$	A, F, B, S, T	.69
X_2 = film about didactic principles of assertiveness theory (E_2)	$N = 16, E_2$: 37.8	43.6	$t(15) = 2.54$ $p < .05$		.49
X_3 = placebo film (E_3)	$N = 16, E_3$: 41.3	43.8	ns		.33
	$N = 16, C$: 42.8	44.3	ns		.11
X = empathy instruction	Not available		Two-way ANOVA: ns	R, F, B, N	–
X = short individual counseling for personal problems (E)	$N = 37, E$: 55.1	54.4	ns	R, H, F, B, T	.19
X_{11} = film input: neutral, individual decision	$N = 14, X_{11}$: 42.29	38.50	Two-way ANOVA all ns	C, B, N, S, T	−.15
X_{21} = film input: moral, individual decision	$N = 15, X_{21}$: 46.88	42.40			−.26
X_{12} = film input: neutral, general discussion	$N = 30, X_{12}$: 44.77	40.93			−.19
X_{22} = film input: moral, general discussion	$N = 31, X_{22}$: 49.77	50.55			.03
X_{13} = film input: neutral, consensus	X_{13} no indication				
X_{23} = film input: moral, consensus	X_{23}				
X = workshop: discussions of dilemmas (Galbraith-Jones)(E)	No indication		ANCOVA ns	F, B	–
X = discussion of dilemmas (Galbraith-Jones) (E)	$N = 17, E$: 26.2	25.1	t-test	R, A, F, B, S	−.22
	$N = 16, C$: 25.1	23.0	ns		−.34
X = discussion of dilemmas, case studies about sex, minorities, etc. (E)	$N = 10, E$: 42	46	t-test	R, A, F, B, N, S	.35
	$N = 8, C$: 55	54	ns		−.08

[c]Raw scores were computed into P% scores.

[d]Mistakes in ANOVA.

[e]Means were computed with data supplied by the individual authors.

[f]These scores were not defined within the report, but they gave the appearance of raw scores and were transformed into P% scores.

[g]Degrees of freedom lost by interactions.

[h]No pretest scores available.

Source: Adapted from Schlaefli, A., Rest, J.R., and Thoma, S.J. 1985. "Does Moral Education Improve Moral Judgment? A Meta-Analysis of Intervention Studies Using the Defining Issues Test." *Review of Educational Research* 55, no. 3: 319-52. Reprinted with permission.

Table 3.3 Overview of intervention studies using the DIT, 1972-1977

Author	Design*	Sample	Treatment duration
Dilemma discussion interventions			
Coder (1975)	OX_1O OX_2O OO	N = 87, adults: church members, age 22-55	6 wks 2 hrs/wk
Panowitsch (1975)	OX_1OO OX_2OO	N = 152, college students	1 quarter
Piwko (1975)	OX_1O OX_2O OO	N = 68, college students	10 X 2 hrs over 1 quarter
Siegal (1974)	ROX_1O ROX_2O ROX_3O ROO	N = 358, 8th, 9th, 10th grade, high school	1 semester
Troth (1974)	OXO OO	N = 42, college students	1 semester
Personality development programs			
Balfour (1975)	OXO OO	N = 84, senior high school	1 semester 1 hr/wk and 4 hr/wk practicum
Erickson, Colby, Libbey, and Lohman (1976)	OXO	N = 20, junior high school	1 semester
French (1977)	OXO OO	N = 117, senior high school	1 quarter
Hurt (1974)	OX_1O OX_2O OO	N = 54, college students	1 quarter
Allen and Kickbush (1976)	OXO OO OO	N = 117, 9th grade students	8 mos.
Sprinthall and Bernier (1977)	OXO	N = 18, in-service teachers	6-wk workshop + 1 quarter consultation

	Mean $P\%$ (D) scores		Change effects	Problems with study	Effect size
Treatment type	Pretest	Posttest			

Treatment type	Pretest	Posttest	Change effects	Problems with study	Effect size
X_1 = dilemma discussions X_2 = lecture, no discussion, academic course	$N = 33$, E_1: 46.0 $N = 13$, E_2: 47.0 $N = 13$, C: 43.0	56.0 58.0 41.0	E_1 and E_2 differ from C on post-test: $F = 5.69$ $p < .005$ ns between E_1 and E_2	R, C, F, N	.76 .62 −.13
X_1 = applied ethics course X_2 = course in logic	$N = 72$, E_1: 41.6 $N = 22$, E_2: 40.1	46.5 40.5	E_1 $t(72) = 3.21$ $p < .002$ E_2 $t(22)$ = ns	R	.60 .05
X_1 = moral development workshop, moral values, commitment X_2 = human development course	E_1: 44.72 C_1: 45.55 C_2: 39.44	52.77 47.08 38.61	E_1 $t(33) = 6.89$ $p < .05$ C_1 = ns C_2 = ns ANCOVA	R, A, C, F, N	.54 .06 −.12
X_1 = dilemma discussion X_2 = meux treatment X_3 = aver treatment X_4 = control	E_1: 25.72 E_2: 20.78 E_3: 21.03 C: 23.78	26.75 23.33 21.32 23.53	ns ns ns ns	A, F, N	.08 .24 .03 −.02
X = course on moral values (to integrate personal values and behavior)	$N = 20$, E: 51.3 $N = 19$, C: 49.3	56.3 50.3	t-test ns ns	R, A, F, N, S	.71 .47
X = humanities outreach course, community experiences seminar	$N = 54$, E: 36.08 C: 37.71	39.41 41.35	$t(53) = 2.01$ $p < .05$ ns	R, A, F, N, T	.35 .47
X = DPE curriculum for personal development, within school classes	$N = 20$, E: 19.12	25.97	$t(19) = 2.27$ $p < .02$	R, A, C, F, N, S, T	.62
X = classes in English and history with values clarification	$N = 79$, E: 14.8 $N = 38$, C: 16.9	15.5 17.7	t-test ns ns	R, F, N, T	.14 .26
X_1 = DPE counseling, empathy training in educational psychology course X_2 = active C	$N = 15$, E: 47.78 $N = 19$, E_2: 51.13 $W = 20$, C_1: 52.17	53.45 54.65 54.92	$t(14) = 1.94$ $p < .037$ $t(18) = 1.80$ $p < .045$ ns	R, A, F, N, S, T	.42 .29 .27
X = confluent education course with a semester unit on moral education	Not available		t-test ns	R, M, F, N, T	–
X = intensive workshop in personal, professional development, plus seminar while teaching	$N = 18$, E: 56	65	$t(17) = 2.91$ $p < .01$	R, A, C, F, N, S, T	.53

(continues)

Table 3.3 *(continued)*

Author	Design*	Sample	Treatment duration
Academic courses			
Rest, Ahlgren, and Mackey (1972)	OXO	$N = 61$, junior high school students	12 wks
Morrison, Toews, and Rest (1973)	OXOO OOO	$N = 103$, junior high school students	6 mos
Short-term studies			
Walker (1974)	OX_1O OX_2O OX_3O OX_4O OX_5O	$N = 70$, 8th graders	One lesson treatment
Geis (1977)	OX_1O OX_2O OX_3O	$N = 90$, college students	4 × 50 min per wk over 2 wks

Note: This table was adapted after Rest (1979a).

Key: R, subjects not randomly assigned to treatments; A, inadequate statistical comparison of experimental gains with gains of control group or no pretest or no C; C, contamination of posttesting by exposure to Kohlberg stage descriptions; M, subjects not motivated to take test or too young to understand it; F, no follow-up testing to determine if posttest gains were stable; B, treatment was too brief; N, treatment was conducted for first time or taught by inexperienced teacher; S, sample was too small (experimental group fewer than 20).

*R in the design indicates subjects randomly selected. An R does not appear if only treatments are randomly assigned.

8. The column headed "Problems with study" reports which of the methodological problems already mentioned above pertained to the particular study. Types of problems are designated by letters, and the key to the letters is given at the end of the table.

9. The last column, "Effect size," is an indicator of the power of the treatment effect, relative to within-group variance. The customary

Treatment type	Mean *P%* (*D*) scores		Change effects	Problems with study	Effect size
	Pretest	Posttest			
X = social studies instructional unit to change attitudes toward police	$N = 61$, E: 22.67	24.17	*t*-test ns	R, A, M, F, N, T	.12
X = course in civics and social studies involving discussion and projects	$N = 74$, E: 11.73	10.23	*t*-test ns	R, M, N, T	−.18
	$N = 39$, C: 10.13	11.72	ns		.19
Narrative modeling of pro-, con-reasoning,	$N = 17$, E_1: 21.97	21.87	ANOVAS all ns	F, B, N	−.01
X_{11} = own stage (preconventional subjects)	$N = 17$, E_2: 22.65	18.63			−.39
X_{21} = +1 stage modeling (preconventional subjects)	$N = 12$, E_3: 21.25	24.72			.37
X_{31} = −1 stage modeling (conventional subjects)	$N = 12$, E_4: 20.56	23.75			.29
X_{41} = own stage (conventional subjects	$N = 12$, E_5: 16.12	19.58			.31
X_{51} = +1 stage (conventional subjects)					
X_{11} = consensus discussion group	$N = 15$, E_{11}: 32.9	37.9	All ns	M, F, B, N	.36
X_{21} = open-ended discussion group	$N = 15$, E_{21}: 32.9	32.2			−.06
X_{31} = individual decision + reflection	$N = 15$, E_{31}: 30.2	32.6			.19

method for computing effect size is based on the difference between the experimental group mean and the control group mean, divided by the within-group standard deviation. We modified this method somewhat because many studies had more than two treatment groups, and because many studies reported results in terms of *t*-tests (pre to post changes for each treatment group, not comparisons on posttests across treatment groups controlled for initial pretest scores). Effect size in this review was computed in the following way:

(a) For each independent treatment group, effect size for that treatment is represented by the difference between the mean of pretest and posttest, divided by the pooled standard deviation (that is, the weighted average standard deviation within the groups of the study).

(b) If the pooled standard deviation was not directly given in the report of the study, it was estimated from statistics provided in the study. In one case information for this was lacking and standard deviations were estimated from data for norm groups in the DIT manuals. When mean scores were not even reported, no estimate of effect size could be made, and a blank appears in the table.

(c) In grouping the effect sizes from various studies, the size of the samples was taken into account in determining average effect size for a group of studies. For instance, in comparing the average effect size of moral education programs for high school students with programs for adults, one study of adults might have 20 subjects and another study of adults might have 100 subjects. The larger sample was weighted five times as much in calculating the average effect size for programs for adults. In addition to providing an estimate of each group's effect size, we also include a 95 percent confidence interval (cf. Hedges 1981). Following convention, these intervals will be used to determine the statistical significance of each effect size. If, therefore, an interval brackets zero, then we must consider the possibility that the effect in question is actually nonexistent. Thus, for example, we expect intervals computed on control groups to bracket zero, suggesting no effect over testings. As for practical significance, we will rely on Cohen's (1969) generic interpretation of effect sizes. He suggests effect sizes of .20, .50, and .80 be considered the cut points for small, medium, and large effects.

META-ANALYTIC RESULTS

Treatment Effect in General

Table 3.4 presents the average effect sizes for all treatment groups (E_1) without regard to type of program, subject characteristics, duration of the program, and so on. The effect size of these moral education programs can be compared to control groups (C) that did not receive any deliberate educational intervention, and to the comparison groups (E_2) that received some sort of educational intervention but not of the sort usually thought to be especially germane to moral thinking (e.g., a course in ancient history). As expected, only the E_1 treatments unambiguously suggest a significant effect. The fact that E_2 and C show positive trends can be attributed to the time interval

Table 3.4 Treatment effects in general

Group	Number of samples	Average effect size[a]	95% C.I.
E_1	68[b]	.28	(.20 $< d <$ .36)
E_2	15	.08	(-.11 $< d <$ .27)
C	40	.11	(-.01 $< d <$ .23)

[a]Averages are weighted according to sample size.

[b]The number of samples exceeds the number of studies because some studies provided two or more treatments.

Source: Compiled by the authors.

between testings (in some cases about a year) and to natural development. Previous research (Rest 1979a) indicates little testing effect per se from merely taking the test repeatedly. Thus we conclude from Table 3.4 that the overall power of moral education programs taken together without regard to type of program is statistically significant, but is, according to Cohen, in the small range. The kinds of treatments that have been shown to be effective in the past also are effective here, whereas the alternative treatments (i.e., the E_2 group) are not effective as a group in promoting moral growth. This brings us to the question of finer analyses that regroup the treatments and samples into more homogeneous groupings.

Effects of Different Kinds of Programs

While every program is different in some ways from every other, there are some family resemblances that can be drawn across the studies. Four major groupings seemed to capture the resemblances for us, and the studies in Tables 3.2 and 3.3 are grouped according to these four types:

1. There are programs that emphasize peer discussion of controversial moral dilemmas according to the suggestions of Kohlberg (e.g., Blatt and Kohlberg 1975). Frequently the reports of the programs cite Galbraith and Jones (1976) as the specific guide for their "Kohlbergian" programs. These guides give specific suggestions for setting up the group discussion, selecting dilemmas for the stimulus material, and for the role of the teacher as discussion leader. We label these treatments as "dilemma discussion." Presumably the effective condition for facilitating development in this type of treatment is providing concentrated practice in moral problem-solving, stimulated by peer give-and-take

(challenging one another's thinking, reexamining assumptions, being exposed to different points of view, building lines of argument, and responding to counter-argument).

2. There are programs that emphasize personal psychological development and involve some experiential activity and intense self-reflection. Initiated by Mosher and Sprinthall (1970), these programs are intended to promote personality and social development in general, of which moral development is a major strand. The programs involve subjects in diverse kinds of activities (e.g., cross-age teaching, empathy training, communication skill training, cooperation simulation games, volunteer service work, keeping logs about one's personal thoughts and feelings), but the activities all have the objective of promoting reflection about the self and self in relation to others. What one learns about oneself in these concrete activities is blended with learning the general theories of developmental psychology through assigned readings and class discussions. Frequently, one of the theories that subjects encounter is Kohlberg's theory of moral judgment development. We label these programs as "personality development" (a modification of the name given by Sprinthall and Mosher, "deliberate psychological education," and labeled DPE in the tables).

3. There are programs that emphasize the academic content of humanities, social studies, literature, or contemporary issues. These programs do not focus as much as the previous two groupings of programs on extended practice in moral problem-solving or personal development activities. While value issues are discussed and related to real-life events, emphasis is placed on learning bodies of information and the basic tenets of academic discipline. The contents of these programs are varied (criminal justice and U.S. law, great books, various topics in social studies). We label these programs as "academic course," even though there were many innovative and nontraditional features of these programs that distinguish them from the typical high school, college, or professional course. In some cases, we included in this classification treatment groups that used regular academic courses as a comparison to dilemma discussion groups or personality development treatments.

4. In this last group are programs where duration was short-term— only three weeks or less. These programs are characterized not by type of activity in the intervention but by the shortness of the intervention. In previous reviews of educational studies using the DIT, short-term educational programs have not been effective, regardless of the type of treatment. We label this group "short term."

Table 3.5 Effects of different types of treatments

Treatment type	Number of samples	Effect sizes	95% C.I.
Dilemma discussion			
E_1	23	.41	(.28 < d < .56)
C	17	.09	(−.11 < d < .28)
Personality development			
E_1	38	.36	(.20 < d < .52)
C	17	.09	(−.09 < d < .27)
Academic courses			
E_1	9	.09	(−.09 < d < .27)
C	7	.16	(−.11 < d < .43)
Short-term			
E_1	15	.09	(−.15 < d < .33)
C	3	−.11	(−.74 < d < .52)

Source: Compiled by the authors.

In Table 3.5 the effect sizes of the different treatments are compared. This table indicates that the dilemma discussion programs have on the average the greatest impact, followed by personality development programs. Both of these programs have modest to small effect sizes. The academic course and short-term programs, on the average, do not have an effect on moral judgment development.

EFFECTS OF EXPOSURE TO KOHLBERG'S THEORY

What is the effect of being exposed to Kohlberg's theory, especially to descriptions of the higher stages of moral judgment? The impact of this exposure might be explainable in two ways. One explanation is that reading the stage descriptions in effect instructs the subject how to perform on a test of moral judgment. A subject learns how to make a favorable impression by learning the theory. And so exposure to the theory contaminates the posttesting. On the other hand it might be argued that exposure to the theory is a powerful educational tool for actually changing a person's moral thinking. In this view, the theory facilitates restructuring of thinking, and the increase in posttest scores is not an artifact of an invalidated test, but a true indication of development. At this point, we cannot say which explanation is correct, and the issue deserves further research.

Table 3.6 Effect of exposure to Kohlberg's theory

Exposure	Number of samples	Effect size	95% C.I.
Exposed to theory			
E_1	12	.56	(.32 < d < .81)
C	8	.02	(−.29 < d < .33)
Not exposed			
E_1	56	.25	(.16 < d < .34)
C	36	.10	(−.03 < d < .23)

Source: Compiled by the authors.

Table 3.6 leads us to conclude that exposure to Kohlberg's theory does have a relation to treatment effect size. However, it should also be pointed out that groups without exposure to the theory also show treatment effects. Effect size in the interventions with exposure is about twice that of groups without exposure. Considering only the adult groups, four of nine adult samples were not exposed to theory (Riley 1981; St. Denis 1980; Wong 1977). The effect size of the non-exposed adult sample is 0.23, but the effect size of the five exposed samples is 0.71—about three times the size. Obviously it is important to learn whether exposure to theory produces a testing artifact or facilitates true development.

EFFECTS OF DIFFERENT SUBJECT AGES

Subject ages were divided into junior high (13 to 14 years old), senior high (15 to 17 years), college (18 to 23 years), and adult (24 years and older).

Table 3.7 indicates that treatment effects were most powerful for the adult group (.61) and least for the junior highs (.22). Several explanations for this disparity in subject groups might be suggested. First, the programs for adults involved mostly volunteer subjects, people who showed a willingness to participate in a moral education program. In contrast, junior high and senior high subjects tended to be captive audiences. Also, an educational program with adults might be more powerful because they can draw on more previous experiences and hence may find greater personal meaning in an educational intervention. A third explanation is that the DIT employs an index (the P score) that is more sensitive to higher-stage reasoning than to reasoning

Table 3.7 Effects of different subject ages

Age group	Number of samples	Effect size	95% C.I.
Junior high school			
E_1	14	.22	(.03 $< d <$ .41)
C	7	.02	(−.23 $< d <$ .27)
Senior high school			
E_1	20	.23	(.08 $< d <$ .39)
C	12	.17	(−.07 $< d <$ .41)
College students			
E_1	25	.28	(.14 $< d <$ .42)
C	15	.19	(−.01 $< d <$ .39)
Adults			
E_1	9	.61	(.34 $< d <$ .88)
C	6	−.13	(−.52 $< d <$ .26)

Source: Compiled by the authors.

at lower stages. Hence, if the effects of moral education programs on younger subjects are to cause shifts from stages 1 and 2 into stages 3 and 4, the DIT might be relatively insensitive to these effects. Last, the age effect in treatments might be due to complex interaction with other variables that also correlate with the size of treatment effects (for instance, direct exposure to Kohlberg's theory happened more in adult samples than in younger samples; this might explain why adults show greater gains than younger subjects).

EFFECTS OF TREATMENT DURATION

We already have seen that short-term treatments were ineffective. However, the duration of treatments in the total set of educational studies varied from one hour to one-half year. After some minimum period, do longer treatments cause bigger effects? We divided the groups into short-term (0-3 weeks duration), medium-duration (4-12 weeks), and longer-duration (13-28 weeks and very intensive interventions of 8 weeks and longer).

Table 3.8 indicates that the longer-duration treatments have no more effect than the medium-duration treatments. Perhaps the longer-duration treatments were weaker than the medium treatments. Perhaps subjects grow tired of moral education past 12 weeks, and the

Table 3.8 Effect of program duration

Duration	Number of samples	Effect size	95% C.I.
Short-term			
E_1	15	.09	$(-.15 < d < .33)$
C	3	-.11	$(-.74 < d < .52)$
Medium-term			
E_1	36	.32	$(.21 < d < .43)$
C	25	.08	$(-.08 < d < .24)$
Long-term			
E_1	17	.30	$(.13 < d < .46)$
C	12	.19	$(-.02 < d < .39)$

Source: Compiled by the authors.

impact of intervention falls off. Perhaps interventions need to shift gears after 10-12 weeks and attempt something very different from what goes on in the first part. Perhaps artificial stimulation is effective for just limited periods, and a subject needs to rest and consolidate after intensive stimulation and growth.

EFFECTS OF "GOOD" VERSUS "POOR" STUDIES

In reviewing studies, one often finds some studies are intuitively more convincing and more tightly constructed than others. Therefore, analyses were conducted to check the advice of Glass (1977) that all studies should be included in a meta-analysis because by and large even

Table 3.9 Effects of randomized versus nonrandomized studies

Study type	Number of samples	Effect size	95% C.I.
Randomized			
E_1	12	.35	$(.15 < d < .54)$
C	7	-.01	$(-.25 < d < .22)$
Nonrandomized			
E_1	56	.27	$(.17 < d < .37)$
C	33	.16	$(.01 < d < .30)$

Source: Compiled by the authors.

Table 3.10 Effects of subjective impression of study quality

Impression	N	Group	Effect size
"Good" studies	17	E_1	0.40
	16	C	0.05
"Less convincing" studies	40	E_1	0.35
	39	C	0.13

Source: Compiled by the authors.

a group of poor studies contributes useful information. The first analysis of "good" or "bad" studies employed an objective, straightforward criterion: namely, whether subjects were assigned to treatment groups on a randomized basis.

Table 3.9 shows that the design features of randomization did not make a difference. Classifying studies as "good" or "bad" only by their using random or nonrandomized designs is a narrow criterion (although a fairly objective one). Therefore, we also classified studies as good or bad in terms of multiple criteria, relying more on an overall "clinical judgment" as to how convincing the study was to us. We are uncertain about how our overall judgments would compare with those of other judges, but we wanted to check out the effects of using multiple criteria.

Table 3.10 shows the same general trends as Table 3.9—namely, that the overall trends are similar in both the good or bad studies, and therefore aggregating all studies is warranted.

GENERAL DISCUSSION OF MORAL EDUCATION PROGRAMS AND THEIR EFFECTS

These are the major conclusions of the meta-analysis:

1. Moral education programs emphasizing dilemma discussion and those emphasizing personality development both produce modest but definite effects, with the dilemma discussion method having a slight edge.

2. Academic courses in the humanities and social studies do not seem to have an impact on moral judgment development.

3. Programs with adults (24 years and older) seemed to produce larger effect sizes than programs for younger subjects; however, several artifactual explanations may account for this trend.

4. Effect size is related to exposure to Kohlberg's theory. Whether this is test contamination or true developmental change needs to be determined.

5. Interventions longer than 12 weeks have no more impact than interventions of 3-12 weeks; however, durations less than three weeks tend to be ineffective when measuring moral judgment by the DIT.

6. Similar trends are obtained when studies are aggregated as "good" or "bad" studies. Although the aggregate of "good" studies gave a general picture similar to that of the aggregate of "bad" studies, we would urge researchers to avoid the methodological shortcomings listed in Tables 3.2 and 3.3. Had the studies been free of such limitations, we could have pressed the analysis much further, asking more pointed questions (e.g., do older subjects profit more from dilemma discussion when the intervention is nine weeks or longer?). In other words, with more reliable individual studies, we do not have to resort to aggregating large numbers of studies in order to have confidence in the conclusions; greater confidence could be placed in the individual studies and more precise conclusions could be warranted. Had the studies been more robust, we could have attempted in this meta-analysis further subanalyses that untangle some of the confounding variables. We are interested in pursuing more specific questions: For whom does what specific program work best, and under what conditions? This further level of specificity can only come from more precisely crafted studies. Further, we would urge the reporting of more detail in reports, at least enough to be able to fill out the entries of Tables 3.2 and 3.3. The attempt to benefit from the experience of many studies was frustrated by incomplete reporting. This review leaves many important questions unanswered, including the following:

1. *What are the critical conditions in the moral discussion interventions and the personality education programs that are responsible for facilitating development?* Perhaps the minute analysis of discussion transactions as carried out by Berkowitz in experimental settings (1980) could be extended to the analysis of educational interventions. Perhaps the identification of cognitive and role-taking prerequisites to moral judgment development would help explain who gains and who does not (Walker 1980). Perhaps simply finding out which subjects begin the program with positive expectations or negative expectations, and who maintains interest would clarify the effects.

2. *What impact does studying the formal moral and psychological theories have on moral judgment development?* The question here is

not simply whether exposure to Kohlberg's writings has contaminated posttesting. The question is whether exposure to moral reasoning of philosophers and other experts can facilitate transformations in one's own moral decision-making. Must all exposure to new ideas come from discussions with peers, or can one profit from reading the classic philosophers? If academic courses in the humanities and social studies (with the more traditional format of lecture and readings) do more than train people in surface verbalisms, why did they not show more impact on moral judgment development?

3. *If people change in tests of moral judgment because of a moral education program, do they also change in their real-life behavior?* To date, no studies have demonstrated directly that changes wrought by these moral education programs have brought about changes in behavior. Instead, some studies are cited that show that moral education produces gains in moral judgment, and other studies are cited that show that moral judgment is linked with behavior, and indirectly it is presumed therefore that this moral education produces changes in behavior. This question is particularly vexing because it presupposes that we know how moral judgment is related to behavior, and this relationship is a matter of considerable controversy even among cognitive developmental theorists (for instance, see various statements by Blasi, Damon, Kohlberg and Candee, and Rest; all chapters in Kurtines and Gewirtz 1984).

Assuming the four-component model (discussed in Chapter 1), then it follows that educational programs that foster development in moral judgment may or may not have affected the other processes that determine moral behavior in concert with moral judgment. Thus it would be quite difficult to assess how gains in one component process affect a behavioral result that is codetermined by four processes. By and large, aggregating results from many subjects, over many situations, from many studies, we would expect there to be at least some modest correlation between moral judgment and behavior (which is what we do find—see Blasi 1980). And hence our expectation would also be that educational programs that foster moral judgment development would likewise have this general modest effect, given sufficient aggregation so that the other important variables would cancel themselves out. But in order to achieve precision and power in our predictions of behavior, this view implies that we have to assess all four component processes simultaneously in the given behavioral situation. It follows also that in order to assess the impact of moral education programs on behavior, we have to assess its impact on all four processes as they operate in the behavioral situation. Hence, the evaluation of moral education needs to include ways of assessing its impact on all four processes, not only moral judgment. In short, multiple measures need to be considered for evaluating the benefits of a moral education program. While this requires a tremendous development effort in constructing new measures, the good news may be that some moral education programs that do not produce significant gains in moral judgment may nevertheless be effective in fostering some other component process. Some moral education interventions may be effective in stimulating moral judgment, others may be more effective in stimulating moral motivation, and so on. This more complex view of the psychological processes of morality would give many people a lot to do for a long time.

NOTES

1. Although some reviewers describe the amount of gain through interventions to be one-fourth to one-half a stage, using a metric of portions of a stage has special problems. A major problem is that movement of one stage means different things in different systems. Whereas a one-stage movement in Kohlberg's 1958 scoring system took on the average three to four years to accomplish, a one-stage movement in his most recent scoring system averages over 10 years. Furthermore, the DIT and some other measures of moral judgment do not express development in terms of stage-typing algorithms, but instead in terms of a continuous index ($P\%$ or D). Another problem in expressing change in terms of portions of a stage is that transition to some stages is more difficult than shifts to others (e.g., a shift from stage 3 to 4 is easier than from stage 4 to 5). Therefore, a less problematic metric that allows comparisons across various measures is in terms of equivalent number of years of growth as indicated in longitudinal studies (a rough analogy is expressing academic achievement in terms of school grade equivalents).

2. "Sufficient" data means that the report contained enough description about the intervention so that we could classify it, enough information about subjects that we could classify them, and enough information about DIT change that we could tell whether the intervention had some impact or not.

4
Different Cultures, Sexes, and Religions

James Rest, Stephen J. Thoma, Yong Lin Moon, and Irene Getz

Almost all individuals in all cultures go through the same order or sequence of gross stages of moral development, though varying in rate and
terminal point of development. [Kohlberg 1971, 176]

The above quote by Kohlberg raises the central issue in studies of
people with different life circumstances: Do all people develop in the
same order of stages? However, rather than stating the issue in terms
of "moral development" (which in our view is an ensemble of several
processes), we would restate the question in this way: Do all people—
the world over—base their judgments of moral right and wrong upon
concepts of cooperation and justice; and do all people develop concepts of cooperation and justice in the same way (i.e., in the developmental order described by Kohlbergian stages)? The issue, therefore,
is whether or not a single description of a developmental course accurately represents all humans on earth or whether different descriptions of various developmental courses are necessary to characterize
the moral judgment process of people with different life circumstances
and social histories.

To some social scientists, it is preposterous to propose a single developmental course that represents moral development for all people.
Morality is notoriously controversial, diverse, and conditioned by particular experience and circumstance. A central theme in anthropology
is how cultures and subcultures evolve in adaptation to their particular
ecological niche and history. Innumerable instances could be cited
in which an act considered morally right in one culture is considered

morally wrong in another time and place. Moreover, one becomes all the more suspicious if it appears that the researcher's own group (white, liberal, male Americans) are obtaining the highest developmental scores, and that other groups (nonwhite, conservative, female, non-American) are getting lower scores. Such a theory appears to be a thinly disguised exaltation of the researcher's own particular view and interests—ethnocentrism at its worst. Some social scientists sense a danger in such theories giving rise to imperialism, racism, and sexism. They oppose on moral grounds any psychological theory that portrays one group as superior and another group as inferior, especially morally inferior.

To consider this question, we will examine research findings from 20 cross-cultural studies, from a meta-analysis of 56 studies on sex differences, and from 24 studies on religious differences. Comparisons of people in different countries (particularly comparisons of Western with non-Western countries) provide the most dramatic data on the effect of different life circumstances. Presumably, life in different countries represents different cultural histories, different ways of adapting to social and economic contingencies, and different opportunities for creating the meaning and value structures that pervade a group of people. Sex differences provide another kind of contrast—males and females are within the same culture and interact with each other, yet the opportunities and socialization experiences can be so different that they may foster different paths of development for the sexes. Differences in moral judgment that are associated with religious differences provide a third way of addressing the universality issue. Here we shall regard religion as representing a particular ideological environment. Religious ideology is a particularly apt starting point for finding differences due to ideology, since religions speak quite directly to definitions of ethical conduct.

Before moving on to consider the empirical findings, let us consider the type of argument that cognitive developmentalists make in support of a theory of cultural universals. Piaget began talking about universals in human cognitive development in his analysis of how people build up representations and knowledge of the physical world. Of course, the physical world that one person sees can be strikingly different in appearance from the physical world that others can see, particularly if one considers the differences between the world of the Eskimo in contrast to New York City or the Amazon River. There are, however, certain basic conceptions that people use in all these environments to interpret their experience of the physical world: dimensions such as the length and volume of objects, weight, density; locating objects in space; using causal concepts to represent relations between events. Such concepts are basic to mental representations of one's experience of the physical world and are common underlying categories of meaning that a person in any physical environment develops in order to structure experience. Of course the objects may vary in appearance from location to location (ice floats, skyscrapers, mango trees), but the basic concepts (weight, density, space, causality) are common.

Likewise, one might argue that there are certain basic conceptions and categories in the social world that are common throughout various cultures. The cognitive developmentalist is not unaware of cultural and subcultural differences, but these are superficial in comparison with more fundamental commonalities. Just as one can distinguish "surface" physical features (ice floats, skyscrapers, mango trees) from more fundamental conceptions (density, space, causality), so also one might contend that there are fundamental conceptions that structure human understanding of the social world. Instances of fundamental conceptions of the social world are the following: awareness of individual differences in social power and capacity; awareness that each self has an internal consciousness, along with his/her own point of view, desires, interests; awareness of human relationships of affection, loyalty, mutual caring; awareness of group expectations and norms, social roles, customs, and laws. The cognitive developmentalist would argue that these kinds of conceptions are fundamental to representing and organizing social experience in every culture and are equally relevant in every society. While each culture may have distinct group expectations, the individual must come to understand that there are such things, whatever they are. While people in one culture may form intimate relationships different from those of people in another, nevertheless, bonds of affection are established in all cultures, and this is a fundamental concept relevant to understanding of the social world in all cultures. Therefore, the cognitive developmentalist does not deny the cultural diversity apparent to everyone (just as the cognitive developmentalist does not argue that ice floats look like skyscrapers or mango trees). However, the cognitive developmentalist proposes a level of analysis that is more fundamental than surface appearances. Supposedly, at this "deeper" level, one finds certain basic conceptions that are critical to making sense of social experience and are common to the way humans represent and interpret the social world. Kohlbergian stages of moral judgment are supposedly pitched at this level, and that is why it is not preposterous (at least before gathering empirical data) to propose that they are universal.

An analogy might help illuminate the kind of argument that is being made here. Let us consider a computer analogy (those readers who have not been smitten by the computer mania may wish to skip to the next paragraph). Computer hardware and its power potential have an analog in the human brain and its power. The less intelligent among us are operating on an 8-bit system at 3 megahertz; the more intelligent are operating on a 32-bit system at 12 megahertz. But raw brain power accomplishes no more than a computer without a program. While there might be some ROM in the human-brain-computer (i.e., genetically fixed behavioral patterns, perhaps in the expression of certain emotions, perhaps in guiding the acquisition of language, etc.), nevertheless it is clear that most of human behavior must be acquired through the development of software programming. One critical difference between computers and the human brain is that computers need to have someone write the software for them, whereas the human brain is a self-programming computer—that is, it operates on its own experience to develop its own software. And (pushing this analogy a little further) the study of cognitive development is the study of the successive programs that humans are writing for themselves. Now, as everyone knows who has suffered the joys and tribulations of working a home computer, there are different levels of software: roughly we may say there are the application programs (like word-processing packages, graphics, statistics, games) and there are the basic programs called "operating systems" (CP/M, MS-DOS, UNIX), which underlie the application programs. It is the operating system software that provides the interface between the mechanicals and circuitry of the hardware and the specific operations of the application programs. All the application programs are based on the operating system and are enabled to do their various jobs within the capacity of the operating system. Application programs are many and varied; a single operating system for a computer underlies the various application programs. Now to bring the analogy directly to bear on the central issue of this chapter: cognitive developmentalists can be portrayed as attempting to study something like the basic operating systems of human thinking, not attempting to study the application programs or the particular variables that are entered into the application programs. This is why cognitive developmentalists can accept the findings of anthropology about cultural diversity, yet also assert without contradiction that there are cultural universals. Translating the universality issue into a computer analogy, we can then restate the central question in the following way: Are all human brains so fundamentally alike and is human experience so fundamentally similar that the basic categories of meaning-making that evolve in human understanding turn out to have essentially the same operating system?

Having put forth an argument for the plausibility that there might be universals, however, does not establish its truth. Much research has been devoted to exploring the universality of Piaget's features, and to date the evidence still seems to be ambiguous (Laboratory of Comparative Human Cognition 1983). Similarly, in other fields of psychology (language, for instance) the debates continue over whether there are universals in development or not (Maratsos 1983).

For me, the answer to the question of universals in moral thinking can be argued logically either way, and hence this question is an empirical one. What is critical to the cognitive developmental theory is the distinction between "surface behavior" and "deep structures" (that is, the distinction comparable to application program software and operating system software). It is not critical to cognitive developmental theory that there be only one developmental path of "deep structures." If, for instance, it turns out that Kohlbergian stages represent the deep structures for making moral judgments of only 2 billion people in the world, then the theory doesn't apply to the other 2 billion people of the world, but it still would be a tremendously useful representation for understanding how many people organize their thinking for making moral judgments. What would be devastating to a cognitive developmental theory is evidence that their accounts of deep structures are not illuminating nor helpful in representing the moral judgment process for any sizable, definable group. Therefore we move into the literature on cultural differences (and sex and religious differences) not so much in order to defend the validity of the theory or the DIT instrument, but rather to explore a fascinating empirical question.

One other issue deserves comment before we move on to the studies: Is it moral to do comparisons among cultures if the possiblity exists that one culture might be characterized as superior and another inferior? Some researchers take the position that such research is evil in principle and can only lead to imperialist, racist, or sexist outcomes, and furthermore, if any differences are found between cultures (races, sexes), then that fact in itself invalidates the measurement procedure.

There are several curious assumptions in such a position that one could spend a long time discussing; however, I will attempt to deal with these arguments with dispatch. First, the idea that group differences on some measure prove the measure's invalidity is absurd because it gratuitously presupposes a conclusion (namely, that there are no differences). Suppose, for instance, that we use the foot-ruler to measure heights of Japanese adult men and American adult men, and find a significant difference in average heights. This does not invalidate the foot-ruler as a measurement device.

Second, let us consider the idea that differences in group scores on a moral judgment test lead to imperialism, racism, or sexism. It is true that imperialists, racists, and sexists have used the argument that some alleged sort of inferiority justifies treating members of the allegedly inferior group in a prejudicial manner. But just because imperialists, racists, and sexists use the argument does not make it valid. If, for instance, it turns out that there is clear evidence that some culture has lower average scores on the DIT than some other culture, there is no logical way to get to the conclusion that the lower-scoring culture should be denied rights, has less of a claim to secure their interests, or should be treated shabbily (see Brandt 1959). Concern for the welfare and integrity of all cultures does not entail that one argue that comparisons cannot be made among cultures. The possibility of cross-cultural comparisons on some measurable characteristic is an empirical and methodological issue of social science, not a moral issue.

Lest the reader suspect that my defense of comparative studies will nevertheless lead to the exaltation of white, American males, let me jump ahead a bit in our story to point out that the cross-cultural studies do *not* put Americans as the highest scorers in moral judgment at any age, nor do the sex difference studies put males ahead of females. In fact, the evidence is just the opposite. And so on logical and empirical grounds, hopefully, the charge will be dismissed that our group comparison studies are the work of the devil.

CROSS-CULTURAL STUDIES USING THE DIT

There are now some 20 studies using the DIT in 15 different cultures (Moon 1984). These 15 cultures are represented by samples collected in: Australia (3), Brazil (1), Greece (1), Hong Kong (2), Taiwan (2), Iceland (1), India (1), Israel (1), Japan (2), Korea (1), Mexico (1), Philippines (1), Saudi Arabia (1), South Africa (1), and Trinidad and Tobago (1). All of these studies were cross-sectional, and all but one study attempted to address the question of the universality of moral judgment development as measured by a translated version of the DIT. The one remaining study (Villanueva 1982) used the same procedure for measuring moral judgment development as that used by the DIT; however, the moral dilemmas and stimulus items were rewritten to maximize the cultural familiarity and acceptance of the task. Thus, in Villanueva's study no attempt was made to provide a translation of the DIT.

Of the 19 studies that used translations of the DIT, seven measured two or more culturally distinct samples in order to directly assess cultural differences. The remaining 12 studies compared their results on a single sample to typical American findings presented in the DIT manual (Rest 1979b). Table 4.1 presents a summary of the 20 cross-cultural studies.

Review of the Findings

Perhaps the most difficult task in performing cross-cultural research is ensuring the equivalence of test stimuli across cultures. It makes little sense to address the issue of cultural differences when the presence or absence of such differences is confounded by nonequivalent tests. As presented in Table 4.1, column 8, most of the studies employed translations of the DIT into languages other than English, but provide little information on the procedures used to arrive at a translation. Only three of these studies describe the method used to arrive at a translation of the DIT (Thornlindsson 1978; Benor et al. 1982; Hau 1983). Of these three, only one systematically attempted to identify translation error (Hau 1983).

Researchers seem to underestimate the problems of translation and cultural adaptation. There is evidence suggesting that even slight differences in translations can have rather dramatic effects on the resulting scores. For instance, recent work by Moon (1984; see also Hau 1983) shows that differences in word choices, without any perceived difference in meaning, can significantly affect average P score values. Moon created three Korean versions of the DIT using the bilingual method; that is, bilinguals in the target culture translated the English version into their own language. Moon added two additional steps to this procedure. First, the bilingual translators were given each other's translation to critique. In addition, the three translators came together as a group to discuss any of the difficulties found in each translation. The result of this process was three Korean versions of the DIT, which, according to the translators, all adequately represent the English DIT,

Table 4.1 Summary of cross-cultural studies using the DIT

Culture (country), authors, study type	Sample description	n	Age/grade	P(%) score	SD	Major variables	Forms of DIT,[a] language, methods of translation	Validity/ reliability	Cultural adaptation
Australia Dickinson (1979)[i], Etic, cross-sectional	HS students[b]	14	15			Religion, sex, family, and friends	Long,[a] English	Test-retest $r = .98 \sim .99$ Cronbach = .66	Words
	HS students	761	16						
	HS students	334	17	32.2	12.7				
	HS students	19	18						
Watson (1983)	Study I Anglo-Australian (age 14-58)	10	14.7	19.2	6.2	Age, sex, education, non-students	Long, English	NA[c]	Dilemmas, phrases, words
		10	16.8	32.7	11.2				
		10	18.7	43.8	7.0				
		10	21.2	47.5	8.0				
	Study II Anglo-Australian[d]	20	18.8	43.7	7.0	Culture, sex, religion	Long, English	NA	Names, concepts (e.g., God)
	Miscellaneous Australian[d]	10	18.6	41.8	13.5				
	Greek-Australian[d]	10	18.5	34.0	9.2				
	Asian Chinese[d]	20	19.11	32.6	12.7				
Clarke (1978)[e], Etic, cross-sectional, intervention	PR pupils[b]	617	5th	–		Teacher, familial, societal, and intervention effects	Long, English	–	–
	Teachers	24	–	41.7	–				
Brazil Bzuneck (1978)[i], Etic, cross-sectional	Adolescents					Delinquency, father-absence	Short,[a] Portuguese	Test-retest $r = -.13 \sim .32.$ $r = .0 \sim .51$	
	Delinquents	40	12-18	20.2	9.3				
	Non-delinquents	39	12-18	18.7	7.8				
Greece Fox (1982)[i], Etic, cross-sectional	HS students					Culture and sex	Short, Greek	NA	NA
	English	33	17	33.9	–				
	Greek	18	17	32.3	–				

Study	Sample	N	Grade			Variables controlled	Instrument	Reliability	
Hong Kong									
Ma (1980), Etic[i], cross-sectional	HS students					Age, sex, culture, item-analysis	5-story form, Chinese	NA	NA
	English	108	15.2	26.1	14.0				
	Chinese	78	17.1	27.9	12.5				
Hau (1983)	Students					Age, education, IQ, sex, fakability, item-analysis, translation	Long, Chinese, bilingual	Test-retest $r = .32$ $= .50$	
	JR students[b]	68	7th-8th	25.2	—				
	JR students	71	9th-10th	29.3	—				
	SR students[b]	69	11th-12th	34.5	—				
	University students	34		37.9	—				
Iceland									
Thornlindsson (1978)	Students					Familial-societal, urban-rural, role-taking, language, mother-child interaction	Short, Icelandic; Multiple translation	NA	M-items
	JR students	27	8th	21.6	—				
	College and graduate students	19	—	56.0	—				
India									
Prahallada[e] (1982), Etic[i], cross-sectional	HS students	16	—	—	—	IQ, SES, personality (Bell Inventory),[f] school-speciality	NA; Indian (Kannada); NA	NA	NA
		17	—	—	—				
		18	—	—	—				
		19	—	—	—				
Israel									
Benor et al. (1982)	Applicants for medical school					Admission interview	Short, Hebrew, back-translation	NA	Name, nationality, occupation
	School I[g]								
	Accepted	44	—	39.4	12.4				
	Rejected	135	—	40.0	13.2				
	School II[g]								
	Accepted	38	—	50.0	17.0				
	Rejected	161	—	39.4	12.8				
Japan									
Jacobson (1977), Etic[i], cross-sectional	Americans living in Japan					Sex, ethnic background	Long, English	NA	NA
	U.S. teachers[h]	30	—	42.6	10.0				
	U.S. mothers[h]	63	—	34.8	14.1				

(continues)

97

Table 4.1 *(continued)*

Culture (country), authors, study type	Sample description	n	Age/grade	P(%) score	SD	Major variables	Forms of DIT,[a] language, methods of translation	Validity/ reliability	Cultural adaptation
	Japanese-born mothers,h	24	–	28.6	12.0				
	Children of Japanese-born mothers,	24	–	24.5	8.3				
	Children of U.S. mothers	63	–	18.5	6.9				
Deyoung (1982) Etic,[i] cross-sectional	Japanese teachers and students, U.S. teachers,					Culture, school type, teacher/students	NA	NA	NA
	Jr college students	47	–	–	–		NA		
	University students	47	–	–	–		NA		
	Jr college teachers,	10	–	–	–		NA		
	University teachers,	17	–	–	–				
	U.S. English teachers living in Japan	30	–	–	–				
Korea Park and Johnson (1983) Etic,[i] cross-sectional	Students	60	6th	25.0	–	Age, education, sex, urban-rural	Short, Korean	Test-retest $r = .69$	NA
	JR students	60	8th	30.2	–		NA		
	SR students	60	11th	37.4	–				
	College students	60	–	41.5	–				
Mexico Miller (1979)	Mexican and U.S. students					Sex, age, career interests	Long, English	NA	NA
	Bilingual Mexican students	37	11th-12th	19.6	–				
	U.S. students living in Mexico	35	11th-12th	22.5	–				

Country / Study	Sample	N	Age	Mean	SD	Covariates	6-story form	Test-retest	Emic
Philippines Villanueva (1982) Emic,[1] cross-sectional	Students					Age, education, sex, urban-rural, familial factor	NA NA	$r = .74 \sim .91$ DIT and EEI[j] $r = .83$	
	HS students	77	13.8	21.3	7.5				
	HS students	70	15.3	21.8	9.6				
	College students	42	20.4	22.3	7.5				
	Graduate students	16	32.9	23.5	7.2				
	Seminarians	23	26.0	31.6	8.9				
Saudi Arabia Ismail (1976) Etic,[1] cross-sectional	U.S. and Saudi students in U.S. colleges					Culture, length of stay in U.S., urban-rural	Long, English	NA	NA
	American								
	Undergraduate	20	28	22.0	8.4				
	Graduate	20	28	29.5	7.5				
	Saudi-Arabian								
	Undergraduate	21	28	15.7	4.7				
	Graduate	19	28	18.5	6.2				
South Africa Heyns et al. (1981) Etic,[1] cross-sectional	Delinquents (boys)	57	11th-12th	21.1	12.7	Demographic data and Quay Scale[k]	Long, English	NA	NA
Taiwan Tsaing (1980) Etic,[1] cross-sectional	Students					Age, education, sex, SES, family size, birth order, child-rearing	Long, Chinese, group discussion	NA	NA
	JR students	160	13						
	JR students	165	14	20.4	6.8				
	SR students	158	16						
	SR students	172	17	26.8	6.2				
Gendron (1981) Etic,[1] cross-sectional	Catholic school students					Age, education, religion	NA Chinese NA	NA	M-items
		41	16-18	31.7	11.5				
		37	16-18	28.9	10.7				
		36	20-26	37.9	10.7				
		40	23-63	33.4	14.6				
		16	22-30	44.4	15.8				

(continues)

99

Table 4.1 *(continued)*

Culture (country), authors, study type	Sample description	n	Age/grade	P(%) score	SD	Major variables	Forms of DIT,[a] language, methods of translation	Validity/ reliability	Cultural adaptation
Trinidad & Tobago Beddoe (1981) Etic,[i] cross-sectional	4 teachers' college students					Age, education, religion, school type		NA	NA
	College I[l]			35.1	—		Short		
	College II[l]			25.0	—		NA		
	College III[l]	210	20-39	26.2	—		NA		
	College IV[l]			26.7	—				

[a]Long, 6 dilemma story DIT; short, 3 dilemma story DIT.

[b]PR, Primary school; JR, junior high school; SR, senior high school; HS, high school.

[c]No information or information not available.

[d]Anglo-Australian students: Students whose parents were born in Australia or who migrated from Britain. Greek-Australian students: Students' parents were of Greek descent and at least one parent grew up in Greece and came to Australia after 18 years of age. Miscellaneous Australian: Students who had at least one parent who was of non-English-speaking background and did not meet the criteria for inclusion in one of the Anglo- and Greek-Australian groups. Asian-Chinese: Students whose parents were both of Chinese descent.

[e]Only the synopsis or abstract of the study was used in this review.

[f]Bell's Personality Adjustment Inventory.

[g]School I: The Sackler School of Medicine, Tel Aviv University (STA), where applicants are selected only on the basis of previous scholastic achievement and performance on a psychometric test. School II: The faculty of Health Sciences, Ben-Gurion University (BGU), where applicants are selected on the basis of personal characteristics, interpersonal skills and orientation toward the community as expressed by previous behavior with down-played scholastic achievement.

[h]U.S. teachers: American teachers employed by a Department of Defense Overseas school located in Japan, a Middle School. U.S. mothers: American-born women who are wives of American enlisted men or officers or Department of Defense civilians serving in Japan. Japanese-born mothers: Japanese-American women who are wives of American soldiers or DOD civilians serving in Japan.

[i]Emic: Refers to an anthropological approach in which cross-cultural comparison is ruled out. Etic: An anthropological approach comparing one culture to another.

[j]EEI: The Exercise in Evaluating Issues.

[k]Quay Scales: 3 lists and questionnaires were used: (a) the Behavior Problem Checklist—B list; (b) the Checklist for the Analysis of Life History Data—A list; (c) the Personal Opinion Study—P list.

[l]College I: Catholic Women's Teacher's College (CWTC). College II: Government Training College (GTC)—Coed. College III: POSTC—Coed. College IV: Mausica—Coed.

Source: Compiled by the authors.

and have no differences in meaning between them. Moon then randomly administered the three supposedly parallel Korean versions to a class
of Korean high school students. His results indicate significant P score
differences between the three forms. Thus, even when a stringent translation process was followed, differences between seemingly identical
versions of the Korean DIT were observed.

Since most of the DIT cross-cultural studies do not provide detailed descriptions of the procedures used to either translate or culturally adapt the DIT for the target culture, one must look for indirect indication of translation equivalence. One set of indicators is the
psychometric properties of the translations. Here we expect that the
degree to which translations provide similar patterns of reliability and
validity coefficients, the more appropriate are the translations. The
reasoning is a little convoluted here, but it goes like this: *if* the translations are adequate, and *if* our theories of moral judgment apply to
other cultures, then the translated DIT given in other cultures should
behave in foreign samples as it does in U.S. samples.

Table 4.2 provides the reliability data from the four studies providing this information. In addition, Table 4.2 provides reliability data
on the original DIT (Rest 1979a). In general, test-retest coefficients
tend to be lower in non-Western cultures. Using the D score, Hau
(1983) found significant but weak stability coefficients in his sample
of Chinese students (age/education range: high school through university). Bzuneck (1978) also found weak stability in a sample of Brazilian

Table 4.2 Reliability and internal consistency (*P* score)

Study and country	Test-retest reliability		Internal consistency	
	6-story	3-story	6-story	3-story
Rest (1979b) United States	.82	.77	.77	.76
Dickinson (1979) Australia	.98		.66	
Bzuneck (1978) Brazil		.39		
Park and Johnson (1983) Korea		.69		
Hau (1983) Hong Kong	.32 .37 (*D* score)		.50	

Source: Compiled by the authors.

adolescent delinquents. This result, however, may be attenuated by the extreme homogeneity of the sample. Park et al. (1983) obtained a test-retest coefficient comparable to those found with the original DIT in a heterogeneous sample of Korean students. Not surprisingly, the most stable adaptation of the DIT was obtained by Dickinson (1979), who used an almost identical version of the original DIT with a large Australian sample.

Internal consistency coefficients were also provided by two of the studies. Again the Western (and English) adaptation of the DIT showed higher internal consistency than the Chinese version; however, both coefficient alphas are in the satisfactory range.

Hau's (1983) study offers some additional insight into the psychometric properties of a translated version of the DIT. In addition to the data mentioned above, Hau replicated Davison's interstage correlational analysis on his Chinese version of the DIT—that is, each stage score is correlated with every other stage score. Like Davison (in Rest 1979a), Hau found a simplex pattern in the correlation matrix (the stage scores correlate highest with adjacent stages, and then systematically decrease for more distant stages). Further, in factor analysis Hau found the same two factors in his data that Davison found on data from a U.S. sample. Thus, the internal structure of Hau's Chinese version of the DIT is much like that found in the original version.

Table 4.3 Correlations of DIT with Kohlberg's Test (MMS) and Law & Order Test (Pearson r)

Study	DIT (*P* score) & MMS		DIT (*P* score) & Law & Order	
	6-story DIT	3-story DIT	6-story DIT	3-story DIT
Thornlindsson (1978)				-.4498
Tsaing (1980)	.486			
Ma (1980)	.196			
	.286			
Rest (1979b)	.43[a]		-.60	-.58
	.70[b]			

[a]Homogeneous group
[b]Heterogeneous group
Source: Compiled by the authors.

Hau also replicated McGeorge's (1985) fakability study. Like Mc-George, Hau's Chinese subjects could not increase their scores when asked to "fake good." However in the "fake bad" condition, subjects reduced their scores.

Table 4.3 presents correlations between translated versions of the DIT and the Moral Maturity Scale (MMS; derived from Kohlberg's interview). Also presented is the one correlation between the Law and Order Measure (Rest 1979a) and DIT translated into Icelandic. These correlations represent an aspect of convergent validity (that is, we expect positive, significant correlations). If these translations are equivalent to the original, then they should resemble the correlations derived from the original DIT (provided in the last row of the table). Tsaing (1980), in a somewhat restricted sample of Chinese (Taiwanese) students (ages 13-17), obtained correlations between his DIT and MMS equivalent to the U.S. average for homogeneous samples. Ma (1980), using a restricted sample of Chinese (Hong Kong) students (age 17), found a weak relationship between these same variables. Thornlindsson (1978) found a moderate relationship between Icelandic versions of the DIT and Law and Order test. This latter correlation is roughly equivalent to those found in U.S. samples.

Effects of Cultural Differences

The effect of cultural differences on moral judgment scores was tested in two ways: (1) by comparing the scores from a foreign culture using a translated DIT with American scores using the original DIT, and (2) by comparing the scores from various foreign cultures using the same translated DIT (for instance, Watson [1983] gave his DIT translation to Greek-Australians, Anglo-Australians, and Asian Orientals in Australia). Seven studies compared various cultures (or subcultures) on a translated DIT, and are presented in Table 4.4.

Of the seven studies shown in Table 4.4, only three show evidence of significant cultural differences. Note that in these studies, cultural difference is indicated by differences in the average DIT score (not by correlational patterns with other variables or differences in internal structure). Since some studies supplied multiple cultural comparisons, the number of comparisons is a total of ten independent contrasts between cultures. Six of these contrasts are between Western and non-Western samples. Five of the six contrasts show significant differences. In comparison, only one of the remaining four Western versus non-Western contrasts is significant. These findings suggest that average *P*

Table 4.4 Cultural (ethnic background) effect

Study/sample		Age	n	P (%) score	SD	Significance
Watson (1983)						
1 Anglo-Australian[a]	CS	18.8	20	43.75	6.97	1 & 2, NS
2 Misc-Australian	CS	18.6	10	41.84	13.55	1 & 3[b]
3 Greek-Australian	CS	18.5	10	34.00	9.17	1 & 4[b]
4 Asian Chinese	CS	19.11	20	32.73	12.73	
Miller (1979)						
American HS		17	35	37.6	–	NS
Mexican HS		17	31	32.8	–	
Fox (1982)						
English HS		17	33	33.9	–	NS
Greek HS		17	18	32.3	–	
Jacobson (1977)						
1 American-born mothers[c]		–	42	43.83	14.14	1 & 2[b]
2 Japanese-born mothers			15	28.26	12.0	
3 Children of Japanese-born mothers		10-14	39	18.51	6.90	3 & 4[b]
4 Children of American-born mothers		10-14	21	24.57	8.36	

104

				P score: NS
				(D score)[b]
Ma (1980)				
English HS	15.2	108	26.11 (16.6)	14.0 (4.2)	
Chinese HS	17.1	78	27.9 (18.3)	12.5 (3.2)	
Ismail (1976)					
U.S. undergraduates	28	20	22.00	8.40	25.58 (8.70)[b]
U.S. graduates	28	20	29.15	7.46	
Saudi undergraduates	28	21	15.71	4.74	16.95 (5.64)[b]
Saudi graduates	28	19	18.52	6.22	
Deyoung (1982)					
U.S. English teacher	—	30	—	—	NS
Japanese college teachers	—	17	—	—	

[a]See Table 4.1 for detailed explanation.
[b]$p < .05$.
[c]See Table 4.1 for detailed explanation.
CS, College students; NS, nonsignificant.
HS, High School.
Source: Compiled by the authors.

scores are more likely to diverge when the contrast is between Western and non-Western samples. It is important to note, however, that the three studies contributing four of the six Western/non-Western contrasts (all of which were significant) used an English version of the DIT (e.g., Watson 1983; Jacobson 1977; Ismail 1976). In each case native English speakers were compared to bilinguals; thus it is difficult to know the extent to which the obtained significant effects were confounded with the subjects' English fluency. It is interesting that Watson (1983) found that Greek and Asian immigrants living in Australia had very similar responses on the English DIT, a finding inconsistent with the cultural difference hypothesis. In short, while differences exist between cultures (particularly Western and non-Western) it is unclear from the present data set whether these differences are due to cultural milieu or fluency with the test language.

Age/Education Trends

Nothing is more crucial to a cognitive developmental explanation of moral development than evidence of change over time from less advanced modes of thinking to more advanced forms. In American samples it is now well documented that DIT scores increase with age/education shifts (Rest 1979a)—38 percent of the variance in DIT scores can be accounted for by age and/or education level. Furthermore, by using longitudinal data (Rest and Thoma 1985; this book, Chapter 2) and cross-sectional analyses, we see that the element most strongly associated with moral judgment development is education.

Table 4.5 presents the six cross-cultural studies providing age/educational comparisons. In each study, with the exception of Beddoe et al. (1981), average moral judgment scores increase with age/educational levels. The Beddoe study can be discounted because the data used for comparison is so unbalanced (194 subjects in their twenties are contrasted to 18 subjects in their thirties), and because the educational range is restricted, as both age groups are in college.

A second observation of interest is that U.S. samples are not always the most advanced within age/educational levels. As Figure 4.1 indicates, in the younger age/educational groupings most of the six samples are equal to or greater than the U.S. averages. This pattern holds until the college years, when U.S. as well as the two other Western samples climb at faster rates than the non-Western groups. In addition, the flatter developmental profile of non-Western data suggests that age/education may not be as powerful a correlate of moral judgment

Table 4.5 Age-education trends of the DIT *P%* score

Study	Junior HS (1)			Senior HS (2)			College			Graduate			Adults			Significance
	n	P%	(SD)	n	P%	(SD)	n	P%	(SD)	n	P%	(SD)	n	P%	(SD)	
Rest (1979b)	1322	21.90	(8.5)	581	31.80	(13.50)	2479	42.30	(13.20)	183	53.30	(10.90)	1149	40.0	(16.7)	1-4[a]
																1-3[a]
Hau (1983)	68	25.27	(–)	71	29.35	(–)	34	37.88	(–)							b
				69	34.47	(–)										
Tsaing (1980)	325	20.16	(6.78)	330	26.84	(6.16)										
Park and	60	25.00	(–)	60	37.40	(–)	60	41.5	(–)							a
Johnson (1983)	60	30.20	(–)													
Thornlindsson (1978)	27	21.6	(–)										19	56.0	(–)	a
Gendron (1981)				37	28.92	(10.7)	40	33.42	(14.86)				16	44.38	(15.8)	
				41	31.71	(11.5)	37	37.87	(14.64)							
Watson (1983)				10	19.2	(6.2)	20	43.8	(7.0)							a
				10	32.70	(11.2)	10	47.5	(8.5)							
Beddoe (1981)							194[c]	27.80	(–)							NS
							18[d]	32.68	(–)							

[a] P < .001.
[b] P < .05.
[c] Age range 20-29.
[d] Age range 30-39.
NS, Nonsignificant.
Source: Compiled by the authors.

Figure 4.1 Cross-cultural age-educational trends in DIT scores

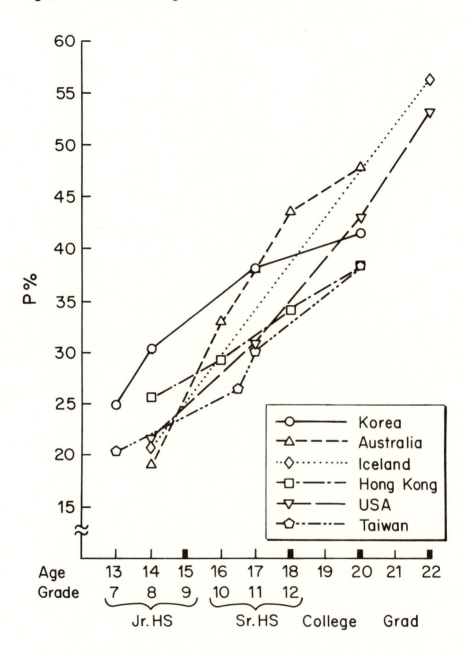

development in non-Western countries. Hau (1983) also noted this possibility. He computed the variance accounted for by age/education and found this relationship to be less than the typical U.S. finding (12 versus 38 percent). Like U.S. results, however, education and not age was identified as the primary correlate with moral judgment development.

In summary, various studies were conducted in foreign countries that parallel the original reliability and validity studies performed on U.S. samples with the original DIT. In general, the patterns of results in foreign countries are more often similar than dissimilar to the U.S. studies. While the magnitude of the obtained relationships is somewhat lower than that obtained in U.S. studies, these differences are as likely to have been caused by translation error as they are by true cultural variation. It is interesting to note that at no time were the critical data trends nonsignificant or of a direction different from the data trends in U.S. samples. If this type of finding had occurred, then cultural variability as the cause for these differences would have been much more probable. The age trend comparisons also suggest more similarity in moral judgment development across different cultures than differences. While non-Western samples tend to show a flatter rate of developmental increase than Western samples, all samples showed increasing levels of moral judgment in higher age/educational levels.

Conclusions from Cross-Cultural Studies

The question of interest in viewing these cross-cultural studies is whether the theoretical assumptions and predictions derived from a U.S. population are applicable in other Western and non-Western populations. Specifically, does the DIT (or translations of the DIT) yield findings in non-U.S. samples that are similar to the original results? At least three general shortcomings in the existing data set limit the conclusions that can be drawn. First, the number of both studies and cultures assessed is small. For instance, in some cases we must determine trends based on four or five studies, representing three cultures, and comprising college students. Thus the range in both within-culture age/educational levels and between-culture comparisons are only marginally addressed by the 20 studies. Second, many of the translations were derived using unknown methods and with untested results. Therefore, a majority of these translations must be assumed to be of questionable equivalence to the DIT. Finally, all 20 studies are cross-sectional.

With the absence of longitudinal data we are without the primary evidence for assessing the developmental properties of moral judgments in other cultures.

In spite of these limitations, the 20 studies do provide support for the generality of our view on how moral judgment works and suggest that the DIT methodology is portable. We find the similarities between cultures much more striking than the differences between them. The results of the DIT studies could have produced data trends that were so discrepant with data from U.S. samples that they indicated the nongenerality of our view of moral judgment or of the limits of DIT methodology; but they did not, and that provides some support. Of course, we are also aware of the cross-cultural research using the Kohlberg test (see the impressive review by Snarey 1985), and those results and our results corroborate each other in support of the cognitive developmentalist's approach, with the emphasis on justice concepts. At this point, however, we cannot rule out the possibility that some concept other than justice, or some process other than the one we have described (Chapter 1) could be identified, and when put to the empirical test, would produce stronger data trends. There has simply not been enough research to make us confident of the universality of our theory. And in principle, one cannot rule out the possibility that some alternate theory may be forthcoming in the future that will be better. At present, however, there are no alternative theories that account for how people arrive at their judgments of moral right and wrong which have sufficient theoretical elaboration and empirical support. From time to time people mention some possibilities, but the theoretical and empirical work remains to be done on these alternatives.

A second implication of these findings relates to the often encountered criticism that Kohlberg's interview measure fails to identify principled reasoning in non-Western populations, and thus a major portion of his theory has not been validated (cf. Simpson 1974). It is interesting to note that the DIT is not affected by this criticism since all of the results mentioned earlier are derived from subject's responses to principled items (*P* score). The capacity of the DIT and its translations to identify principled reasoning where Kohlberg's interview test does not is most likely due to the difference in task requirements (see Appendix for discussion). Therefore, like their U.S. peers, non-U.S. subjects may be able to recognize the superiority of principled concerns, and yet not be able to formulate a response scorable at that level.

SEX DIFFERENCES

Males and females, it is argued, experience the social world differently, with the result that a systematic difference develops in social skills, orientations, and attitudes. While it is clear that male and female stereotypes are prevalent in our society (Broverman, Vogel, Broverman, Clarkson, and Rosenkrantz 1972), it is a matter of some controversy whether these views in turn influence social problem-solving and behavior.

Dr. Carol Gilligan published a very widely read book in 1982 (originally an article in 1977) that focused a great deal of attention on sex differences within the study of moral judgment development. Although some of her recent statements seem to retract and contradict her 1977/1982 position on sex differences, it is the 1977 statement that is most widely known and widely discussed, and which presents the boldest challenge to moral judgment research in the tradition of Piaget, Kohlberg, and other cognitive developmentalists. Therefore we will focus on the 1977 statement. Gilligan starts with the premise that male social development highlights a growing sense of individuality, while female development stresses connectedness between individuals. Gilligan then contends that these markedly different social pathways result in the development of two moral orientations: a justice orientation (predominantly male), and an ethic of care (predominantly female). When women are assessed under justice-defined measures of moral judgments (i.e., Kohlbergian measures), she argues, what is particular to the care orientation is overlooked and misscored. Existing measures of moral judgment (she focuses on Kohlberg's) force upon women a foreign system, and therefore when women are assessed by a male-defined system (i.e., justice concepts rather than the care orientation), women are short-changed and misscored. This results in the downgrading of female moral judgment, and women appear to be morally inferior to men because of the male bias in the scoring system. Gilligan contends that the male bias in justice-oriented scoring systems came about (at least partly) because Kohlberg is a male, used only males for subjects in his dissertation and longitudinal sample, and uses male protagonists in his hypothetical stories.

Gilligan makes many assertions about the proper way to assess moral development in males and females, but the one major testable assertion is that current, justice-oriented scoring systems of moral judgment downgrade women, and make women's development appear inferior to men's. Readers of Gilligan come away with the impression that the Kohlbergian, justice-oriented approach to studying moral judgment is invalid for half the world's population (i.e., women).

Many readers of Gilligan's 1982 book are surprised to hear that she did not actually do a systematic review of the moral judgment literature on sex differences before making the bold statement that justice-oriented scoring systems downgrade women. Such a data base is there, waiting for analysis, and systematic reviews are now available. In 1985 Walker published a review of studies using various versions of Kohlberg's test, and the results are unambiguous: it is a myth that males score higher on Kohlberg's test than females. If justice-oriented scoring systems downgrade women, it doesn't show in differences between the sexes on Kohlberg's test. Recent major studies that use Kohlberg's most recent scoring system also show no sex differences (Snarey, Reimer, and Kohlberg 1985; Gibbs and Widamon 1982; Nisan and Kohlberg 1982).

Recently, Thoma (1984) has applied both meta and secondary analyses procedures to a representative sample of 56 DIT studies and over 6000 subjects, in order to estimate sex differences on the DIT. Thoma's meta-analysis procedure is an improvement over previous treatments of this subject (cf. Rest 1979a; Walker 1985), because unlike the prior reviews, it offers precise information on the size and significance of the gender effect. To perform the meta-analysis of the 56 DIT studies, Thoma chose two measures to represent the magnitude of gender differences in each independent study: effect size d (Cohen 1969; Hedges 1981), and W (Hays and Olkin 1980; Fleiss 1969). The d statistic represents the difference between mean DIT scores for females and males divided by the within-group standard deviation. This ratio expresses the difference between means in a standard score form (therefore, $d = .5$ would indicate that two means differed by half a standard deviation). Cohen (1969) suggests that sizes of .2, .5, and .8 be considered small, medium, and large effects, respectively.

In Thoma's adaptation of the d statistic, the sign of d was set to be positive if the study found differences consistent with the hypothesis that males score higher than females on the DIT. Therefore, a negative d value suggests that females have higher scores than males.

The second statistic used by Thoma was W. This statistic estimates the proportion of variance in the dependent variable accounted for by the independent variable(s). In Thoma's application, W represents the proportion of DIT score variance attributable to gender groupings. W has a meaningful range of 0-1.0.

The 56 studies selected for the meta-analysis were the result of a screening process to ensure stable estimates of gender effects. The major screening criteria were: (a) comparable age ranges of both sexes. For example, a study comparing mothers' moral reasoning with their sons' scores would not be included. (b) For statistical concerns, the proportion of subjects falling within the gender groupings had to be roughly equivalent (i.e., the proportion of one sex had to fall within the range $.3 \leqslant p \geqslant 0.7$ of the total sample). (c) Sample sizes of a gender grouping had to be greater than 10.

The results of Thoma's analyses are presented in Table 4.6. It shows each of the 56 studies sorted within one of five groups. The first four groups correspond to major age/education levels, and the fifth represents those studies that present subject data at more than one age/educational level. Thoma reports that group five, labeled "mixed," is overly represented by older age subjects.

Of particular interest in Table 4.6 is the consistent pattern of negative d values. This finding indicates that gender differences favor females—that is, that females actually score higher on the DIT than males. In addition to the direction of the effect, each d value, while statistically different from zero, lies within the small range according to Cohen's recommendations mentioned earlier. Furthermore, the W values indicate that gender accounts for no more than .9 percent of the variance in DIT scores. Across all studies less than one-half of 1 percent of the variance in DIT scores is attributable to gender. In short, sex difference on the DIT is trivial.

Thoma also compared the magnitude of effects due to gender with those due to age/education. Table 4.7 presents the descriptive data for a subset of the 56 studies providing the necessary information. Using the information presented in Table 4.7, Thoma was able to perform a two-way unweighted means ANOVA (sex by age/education levels). His finding estimates that age/education is over 250 times more powerful than gender in accounting for DIT score variance (variance due to gender $W = .002$; due to age/education $W = .525$). The interaction between gender and age/education was nonsignificant.

Thoma's analyses suggest that a very slight gender difference on the DIT exists ($d = .21$). Unlike current expectations, however, females consistently score higher than males. While these findings are important with respect to charges of a gender bias on measures of moral judgment, the size of the effect is trivial, both in comparison to age/educational effects, and in terms of Cohen's interpretive guidelines.

Table 4.6 Summary of the meta-analyses

	Jr. high school	High school	College	Adult/graduate students	Mixed	Total group
$\bar{d}$	-.152	-.167	-.213	-.279	-.238	-.207
95% C.I.[c]	$(-.27 \leq \delta \leq -.04)$	$(-.29 \leq \delta \leq -.05)$	$(-.32 \leq \delta \leq -.11)$	$(-.50 \leq \delta \leq -.07)$	$(-.32 \leq \delta \leq -.16)$	$(-.26 \leq \delta \leq -.16)$
median ω^2	.001	<.001	.004	.007	.009	.003
Range[b]	.014	.090	.150	.107	.029	.150
Number of samples	8	16(14)[a]	19(18)[a]	4	9	56(53)[a]
Number of subjects	1255	1249(1107)[a]	1539(1468)[a]	370	2450	6863(6650)[a]

[a]Three samples left unreported the direction of gender differences. In these cases ω^2 was the only measure computed.
[b]Range = (highest value − lowest value).
[c]C.I. = Confidence interval.
Source: Compiled by the authors.

114

Table 4.7 Descriptive statistics for the major age/educational levels

Statistic	Jr. high school	High school	College	Graduate school*	Adult*
Males					
$\bar{x}$	19.068	28.685	44.106	60.97	42.78
SD	6.229	11.770	12.212	14.04	11.77
n	528	424	449	52	90
Females					
$\bar{x}$	19.789	30.361	45.875	62.97	46.04
SD	6.332	10.851	12.190	10.87	12.85
n	519	436	436	42	183
Number of samples	8	12	14	2	2

*The descriptive data for these groups was not included in the secondary analysis due to their relatively small sample sizes.
Source: Compiled by the authors.

115

Recently, Moon (1986) completed a dissertation examining sex differences in the DIT on the individual item level. Moon used several techniques from research on aptitude and achievement testing which had been developed to detect sex bias at the item level, not only the summary score level. His findings also indicate that sex differences are trivial on the item level as well as in the general indexes (the P and D score).

From these findings we can conclude that there exists little evidence in DIT data to suggest that males are better able to reason about hypothetical dilemmas, or that justice reasoning is in some way a male domain. While males and females may indeed have different social experiences, the resulting development of justice reasoning is remarkably similar. Since the amount of variance accounted for by sex differences is so trivial, it would seem that other variables present a much more promising avenue for investigation to researchers.

Apparently in the face of such overwhelming contradiction of her original position, Gilligan lately has attempted to shift focus away from sex differences to the contention that the care orientation exists in both men and women, and is more likely to be found in self-produced moral dilemmas than in hypothetical dilemmas. We have to wait for the evidence before determining the validity of this assertion. However, the available evidence does not support this claim either. Walker (1985) recently reported a study comparing "justice" orientations and "care" orientations in both spontaneous and hypothetical moral dilemmas, and found no difference.

The enormous theoretical and methodological problems with Gilligan's views fly in the face of their popularity in some circles. One problem is in the lack of a coherent theoretical definition of the care orientation and how it differs from a justice orientation. At different times the care orientation is characterized in terms of moral sensitivity (Component 1), of judging what is morally right (Component 2), of a person's values and what a person is most invested in (Component 3), and at times the care orientation seems to be a theory about the entire organization of personality. It is difficult to know what the care orientation is. On those occasions when the care orientation is talked about as an alternative and parallel course of development to the justice orientation, then it seems to be a theory about Component 2 processes. Accordingly, we expect to have a description of the conceptual tools used to judge which course of action is the morally right one (since that is the function of Component 2 processes). But it isn't clear how the care orientation, which provides directives for action choices in conflictive social situations, is different from the justice orientation (as Kohlberg defines justice, or as justice is defined in Chapter 1). It isn't enough to claim that the care orientation is *really* concerned about people and is an orientation that emphasizes connectedness. Those characteristics are also characteristics of a justice orientation and are presupposed if a person senses that a social situation poses a *moral* dilemma (in which the decision-maker is concerned about various parties and various interests but realizes that the situation prevents giving everything to everybody). The crux of a Component 2 construct is to describe the decision-making tools for deciding how to balance or prioritize conflicting interests in situations where the person cares about people and their interests (if the decision-maker only cared about one person or one interest, then there wouldn't be a moral dilemma). Instead of elucidating the logic for deciding moral conflicts, Gilligan seems to characterize the concept of justice in terms closer to a portrayal of macho ideology and male chauvinism, while characterizing the care orientation as the alternative to macho ideology. Given the option between macho ideology and the care orientation, the care orientation comes off well. But the concepts of justice are misrepresented. For instance, Gilligan links justice with individualism, and care with "connectedness" between individuals. In contrast, recall the discussion of justice in Chapter 1. There, the central problem of justice is discussed in terms of arranging cooperative networks among people, to organize reciprocal systems of mutual benefit; these are hardly themes of individualism and separateness.

The empirical problems with Gilligan's position are even more devastating. Although the care orientation is said to be an alternative and parallel path of moral development, there is not one longitudinal study or any cross-sectional data to support the claim. In fact, other researchers have difficulty in even obtaining a copy of a scoring system for scoring developmental stages of the care orientation. The research program for the care orientation as an alternative path of development to the justice orientation has not made it to first base yet. Although interesting anecdotes and bold claims are plentiful, these do not provide a substantial empirical base.

Are we arguing then that justice concepts are the only determinants in people's judgment of what is morally right or wrong? While the cross-cultural research and the sex difference research has not yet produced a serious alternative to the justice concept, we do not believe that only concepts of justice determine people's judgment of what is morally right. In fact, as the reader will see in the next section and in the next chapter, there is convincing evidence (not just bold claims and speculation based on a handful of anecdotes) that some other processes are involved in some people some of the time in their judgment of what is morally right. Although the research now at our disposal does suggest that justice concepts are a pervasive and powerful determinant of moral judgment, there is convincing evidence that concepts of justice are not the only determinant. We now turn to research relating religion to moral judgments and will develop these points.

RELIGION AND MORAL JUDGMENT

If one thinks about people such as Albert Schweitzer, Mahatma Gandhi, Martin Luther King, Mother Theresa, or Jerry Falwell, it seems obvious that religious ideology has a lot to say about their judgments of what is morally right and wrong. For these people it would be difficult to separate religious thinking from moral thinking. What then is the connection between religion and the development of concepts of justice (such as are described in Chapter 1), and how does religious ideology influence one's moral judgment?

Dr. Irene Getz has recently reviewed the psychological literature on these questions (Getz 1984). She points out that psychologists have collected various kinds of information in order to study and index religion. She identifies seven ways that researchers have measured or assessed religion as a psychological variable:

1. Affiliation or membership in congregations or religious groups.
2. Religious behavior such as attending worship services, reading religious literature, praying, and contributing money or resources.
3. Religious knowledge: ability to recall information on religious topics.
4. Religious ideology (belief): for example, the belief that all are sinners; belief in the truth of the Bible, life after death, and so forth. Often religious ideology is characterized on a conservative-liberal dimension.
5. Religious experiences such as conversion, visions, near-death experiences, and the like.
6. Intrinsic-extrinsic motivation, which tries to identify people whose motives for religious participation are status and self-justification (extrinsic), or a source of value and direction (intrinsic).
7. Religious education: attendance at church-affiliated educational institutions.

We will follow Getz's seven classes in summarizing this research. In addition to the seven classes, Getz includes an eighth that is a miscellaneous category, including studies for which religion was not the primary focus but was included in the analysis. A brief description of the studies as they fall into these eight groupings is presented in Table 4.8.

Religious Affiliation

One of the most straightforward procedures for assessing whether religion influences moral judgments is to focus on religious affiliation. Without much difficulty a researcher can obtain moral judgment information on subjects of different religious organizations and contrast these results. If differences between these groups are found, than all other things being equal, one may assume that the associated religious experiences influence moral judgment development. Of course, the assumption that all other "things" are equal is usually not the case. For example, many of the other religious variables such as degree of commitment and involvement, and religious knowledge, among others, are confounded in contrasts based on simple affiliation. Thus it is not surprising that studies of this type often produce quite meager results.

Wahrman (1981) found no significant differences between religious affiliation and scores on the DIT for a sample of college students. It is interesting that these same subjects produced a significant correlation between dogmatism (a measure of the nature of their beliefs) and DIT scores. In a study of 1,228 Australian high school students, Dickinson and Gabriel (1982) found that religious affiliation, along with three other variables, predicted 5.2 percent of the variance in DIT scores (two of the other three variables are conceivably correlated with religious affiliation—e.g., occupation, and education of the father—and therefore the unique effect due to affiliation is unknown; the final variable was sex). In a second Australian sample, Radich (1982) found no relationship between religious affiliation and moral judgment among young adolescents. Finally, McGeorge (1976) found a difference between church members (of all types) and nonmembers in the second testing of a longitudinal sample of New Zealand undergraduates. Specifically, two years after the first testing in 1973, nonmembers scored significantly higher than church members. Post hoc analyses showed that the church members' DIT *P* scores did not increase over the two-year period. Moreover, those subjects who indicated that their first interest was church and religion had the lowest

Table 4.8 Studies on the relation of moral judgment and religion categorized by type of religious variable

Study	Sample	What was being assessed	Results
Religious belief Ernsberger (1977); Ernsberg and Manaster (1981)	169 adult church members	Assessment of four churches as conventional or principled, and of moral judgment of members and leaders. Relation of moral judgment to religious orientation.	Members of conservative churches preferred Stage 4; leaders showed even greater preference. Members of liberal churches preferred principled reasoning; leaders showed even greater preference.
Lawrence (1979)	29 ninth-graders, 30 philosophy doctoral students, 16 fundamentalist seminarians	Assessment of moral judgment of three divergent groups, assessment of thinking behind choice of arguments among the seminarians.	Typical levels of P scores for ninth-graders and doctoral students, but low for seminarians who chose responses compatible with their church's stance.
Brown and Annis (1978)	80 college students	Relation of moral judgment to religious behavior and belief (also intrinsic-extrinsic orientation; see below).	Significant relationship between high P scores and low literal belief. Nonsignificant relation of P scores and religious behavior.
Clouse (1979)	371 college students	Relation of moral judgment to religious belief and political ideology.	Significant relationship between high P scores and liberal religious and political thinking.
Cady (1982)	57 clergy	Relation of moral judgment to liberal and conservative affiliation and belief.	Significant differences in P scores; higher for liberal clergy and clergy with flexible beliefs.
Harris (1981)	438 11th-grade students	Relation of moral judgment to belief, knowledge, and practice.	Nonsignificant relation of moral judgment to belief and practice, significant relation of moral judgment to knowledge.

Intrinsic-extrinsic orientation

Study	Sample	Focus	Results
Ernsberger (1977); Ernsberger and Manaster (1981) Walters (1981)	169 adult church members 224 volunteer religion teachers	In addition to that listed above, assessment of intrinsic-extrinsic orientation of members and leaders. Relationship of teachers' orientation to level of moral judgment.	Intrinsically oriented members reflected congregational moral level more than did extrinsic members. Nonsignificant relation between intrinsic-extrinsic orientation and moral judgment.
Brown and Annis (1978)	80 college students	Relation of intrinsic-extrinsic orientation to moral judgment.	Nonsignificant.
Religious affiliation			
Wahrman (1981)	124 college students	Assessment of moral judgment and dogmatism of orthodox, liberal, and nondenominational students.	Nonsignificant correlation of religious affiliation and moral judgment. Dogmatism weakly correlated with moral judgment.
Dickinson and Gabriel (1982)	1,228 senior high school students	Assessment of factors that may predict principled moral judgment.	(153, $p < .04$). Religion was one of five sample characteristics that together accounted for 5.2% of variance in P scores; variance attributed to religion was minimal.
Radich (1982)	60 adolescents, ages 15 to 17	Relation of conservatism, altruism, religious orientation, and moral judgment to religious affiliation (Roman Catholic, Brethren Christian, and nonreligious).	Significant differences among the three affiliations on conservatism, altruism, and religious orientation. Nonsignificant relation of religious affiliation and moral judgment.
McGeorge (1976)	1973: 140 college students 1975: 92 college students	Relation of moral judgment to church membership.	P scores of non-church members significantly higher than those of church members at second testing (nonsignificant at first testing).

(continues)

121

Table 4.8 *(continued)*

Study	Sample	What was being assessed	Results
Religious education Stoop (1979)	390 9th- and 12th-grade students	Relation of religious education (three types) and public education with moral judgment.	Nonsignificant *P* scores at grade 9 in all schools. Significant difference in *P* scores of Lutheran students at grade 12. Stage 4 scores were significantly higher in the conservative religious school.
Wolf (1980)	76 college students	Relation of religious education, level of commitment to religion, and conversion to moral judgment.	Students with high exposure to religious education had significantly lower *P* scores. Students with high exposure to religious education and high commitment had lower *P* scores. Nonsignificant relation of conversion to moral judgment.
Blackner (1975)	160 students grade 9 to post-high school	Relation of degree of involvement in religious education to moral judgment.	Nonsignificant relation of religious education to moral judgment.
Killeen (1977)	7th- and 12th-grade students	Relation of Catholic religious education to moral judgment and to abstract reasoning.	Catholic students had significantly higher *P* scores and scored higher in abstract reasoning than did public school students.

O'Gorman (1979)	199 9th-grade students	Relation of religious knowledge to moral reasoning.	Significant relation between high P scores and high religious knowledge.
Harris (1981)	438 11th-grade students	Relation of moral judgment to religious knowledge, belief, and practice.	Significant relation of moral judgment to religious knowledge. Nonsignificant relation of moral judgment and belief and of moral judgment and practice.
Miller (1979)	40 female college students	Relation of moral judgment to high, medium, and low levels of overall religiosity, including knowledge.	Significant chi-square distribution: students with high P scores tended to register low on religiosity.
Other studies Hay (1983)	149 conscientious students	Relation of basis for conscientious objection to level of moral judgment.	Those basing decision on personal code had significantly higher P scores than did those basing decision on religious grounds (college and graduate, not high school, students).
Meyer (1977)	40 private and state college students	Assessment of changes in intellectual development by analysis of religious content, and changes in moral judgment.	Nonsignificant differences in P scores. Significant differences in intellectual development between freshmen and seniors at both colleges. Significant differences in religious beliefs between freshmen and seniors, not between colleges.

(continues)

Table 4.8 *(continued)*

Study	Sample	What was being assessed	Results
Volker (1979)	36 college students	Relation of kinds of college experiences to level of moral judgment.	Significant negative correlation between high *P* scores and conservative religious beliefs. Nonsignificant relation between *P* scores and religious experience. Nonsignificant but positive relation between high *P* scores and low level of religious activity.
Schomberg (1978)	289 university freshmen	Relation of college experiences (including religious activities) to level of moral judgment.	Nonsignificant relation between participation in religious activities and level of moral judgment.

Source: Adapted from Getz, I. 1984. "The Relation of Moral Reasoning and Religion: A Review of the Literature." *Counseling and Values* 28:94-116. Reprinted with permission.

P scores of any of the eight interest groups. Thus in this case, religion seems to hinder moral judgment development.

Religious Ideology (Liberal-Conservative Belief)

Simply looking at religious affiliation does not produce very clear trends, and there are hints that affiliation is an insensitive way to represent religion. Both Wahrman's finding that dogmatism relates to moral judgments and McGeorge's findings that commitment is influential suggests that an individual's interpretation of the religious experience may be a more sensitive variable. One such measure focuses on a subject's religious ideology.

Seven studies using the DIT assess the relationship between moral judgment development and religious ideology. Six of these studies find liberal religious thinking is associated with higher *P* scores than is conservative religious thinking. Let us first present the empirical findings, and then discuss the theoretical implications. Brown and Annis (1978) found high *P* scores related to low scores on a scale measuring a literal belief in the Bible ($r = .44$, $p < .01$). Similarly, Cady (1982) found that liberal responses to a scale measuring flexibility in Biblical interpretations related positively to *P* scores ($r = .58, p < .01$). Cady also found conservative clergy scored lower than liberal clergy on *P* scores ($t(31) = 5.72, p < .01$). Using college students Clouse (1979) found religious liberals had higher *P* scores than their conservative peers. This same pattern was found with measures of political orientation.

Ernsberger (1977; Ernsberger and Manaster, 1981) surveyed factors which conceivably could account for the religious conservative and liberal difference on moral judgment development. After matching four congregations on locale and SES, they replicated the finding that conservative (Baptist and Misssouri Synod Lutheran) congregations differed from liberal church members (Methodist and Unitarian). They did not rely on denominational reputation for determining liberalism or conservatism, but they analyzed the religious curriculum and official statements from the four churches. The two conservative churches showed significantly less preference for principled moral thinking in these materials than the two more liberal churches. Finally, the found the leaders of the conservative churches had significantly lower *P* scores than the liberal church leaders. Interestingly, the difference in the leader-group was more pronounced than differences found in the random sample of church members. That is, conservative church leaders scored below the random sample of conservative church members, while liberal church leaders scored higher than their own congregations. This suggests that religious commitment may intensify existing moral orientation, and that the church leadership is more extreme in their views than the congregation in general.

In the one study using younger subjects (11th grade high school students), Harris (1981) found no relationship between moral judgment scores and religious belief.

An ingenious study by Dr. Jeanette Lawrence (1979) presents an in-depth investigation into the process by which religious ideology influences moral judgments and provides insights into why the liberal-conservative dimension of religious ideology is related to moral judgment scores. Lawrence collected DIT data on three groups: students in a graduate program in philosophy, students in a radically fundamentalist seminary, and ninth-graders in a liberal suburban high school. The mean *P* scores for these groups were 55, 22, and 31, respectively. For the philosophy students and ninth-graders these scores are fairly typical; however, for the fundamentalist seminarians the scores were extremely low, considering the level of education of the seminarians (that is, with education past the college degree, we would expect much higher DIT scores). Lawrence also assessed the three groups on moral comprehension as well as on the DIT, and found that the groups were ordered in line with expectation: philosophy students highest, then the seminarians, and the ninth-graders last. Therefore, the seminarians had comprehension of higher-stage concepts of justice, but they were not using these concepts in rating the DIT items. Then Lawrence conducted an intensive interview in which the subjects were asked to talk about how they were thinking as they filled out the DIT. In Lawrence's analysis of these protocols, she shows that the ninth-graders dealt with DIT items in this way: they did not understand the high-stage items, but they did understand the lower-stage items and tended to endorse them. In contrast, the philosophy students understood the high-stage items and the low-stage items, but endorsed the high-stage items because they seemed to present a more adequate way of thinking about the problem. However, the seminarians understood the low-stage items, and they understood to some extent the high-stage items, but deliberately chose to endorse the Stage 4 items. These fundamentalist seminarians obtained the highest Stage 4 scores we have seen on the DIT. The seminarians explained their thinking process in this way: they understood that they were being asked to make moral judgments. A tenet of their religious faith is that moral values come from divine revelation and that mortals should not depend on their own intuitions for making decisions about such matters. Therefore they deliberately suppressed their own personal notions about what was fair or just, and rated the DIT items in terms of whether the item was consonant with some biblical passage, or some part of church doctrine that they could remember. And so in solving the DIT dilemmas, they self-consciously discounted their own concepts of justice (their own intuitions of fairness), and deliberately derived a judgment of what was right by substituting religious ideology. The high Stage 4 scores comes from advocating external authority for the solution of moral dilemmas. The Lawrence study gives clear demonstration that people may have certain concepts of justice, yet they may not use them. In the case of the fundamentalist seminarians, it is conservative religious ideology that overrides their own intuitions of justice. Parenthetically, we might note that there is no reason to believe that only ideologies of the right (or conservative ideologies) preempt concepts of justice; ideologies of the left and other ideologies (such as nationalism and political ideologies) can also preempt concepts of justice in judging what is morally right.

In summary, we would offer this interpretation of the consistent finding that liberal religious ideology is associated with higher moral judgment scores on the DIT: conservative religious ideology tends to highlight adherence to church doctrine and external religious authority in judging moral dilemmas, whereas liberal religious ideology tends to foster an orientation toward moral decision-making that emphasizes the subject's own sense of how the various interests can be fairly balanced. Generally it seems that a liberal religious ideology would place more responsibility on the problem-solving capacities of the individual and less reliance on external authority, thus encouraging more self-struggle with moral dilemmas and fostering more practice in working out just solutions. However, in the case of the fundamentalist seminarians, their lower DIT scores were not due simply to the incapacity to conceptualize higher-stage notions of justice, but to the deliberate decision not to use them, in deference to a higher authority.

Now we will continue our review of literature pertaining to the relation of religion with moral judgment.

Intrinsic-Extrinsic Religious Motivation

As applied to religious motivation, an intrinsic individual tends to be devout, and internalize the teachings of his/her congregation. In contrast, extrinsically religious individuals are described as participating in religious organizations for instrumental reasons such as status and social connections. The instrument most often used to measure intrinsic/extrinsic religious motivation is the Religious Orientation Scale (ROS) developed by Allport and Ross (1967).

Studies incorporating intrinsic-extrinsic religious measures do so for two basic reasons. The first use is to address the question of whether development in moral judgment is related to a particular religious motivation. Second, scales like the ROS are employed to assess whether systematic differences in the motivation to participate in religious organizations influence existing relationships between other religious and dependent variables like the DIT. That is, religious motivation may act as a moderator variable between religious belief and the DIT.

Two studies offer information on the relation of extrinsic/intrinsic religious motivation with moral judgment development. These studies do not test the potentially more interesting question of whether differences in orientation moderate an existing relationship between a religious variable and the DIT. Both of these studies obtained nonsignificant correlations (Walters 1981; Brown and Annis 1978). Getz (1984) points out that these samples were homogeneous on factors that may limit the ability to realize the expected outcome (e.g., only one religious group selected).

Ernsberger (1977; Ernsberger and Manaster 1981) did test the moderator hypothesis. As mentioned earlier, these studies contrast conservative and liberal congregations on moral judgment development. Using the ROS, they found that intrinsically religious members tend to attach greater importance to principled moral considerations if their denominations do so, or, similarly, to conventional considerations if the church highlights conventional thinking. Like the previous two studies, the simple correlations between DIT and ROS scores were nonsignificant.

Taken together, these findings suggest a complex relationship between moral judgment and extrinsic/intrinsic religious motivation. While simple relationships between these variables are not found, there is evidence that religious orientation intensifies existing relationships between moral judgment and religious beliefs.

Religious Education

Several studies have attempted to examine whether formal religious instruction influences moral judgment development. Typically, these studies compare high school students at religious institutions to same-aged subjects in the public school. Unfortunately, these studies pay little attention to the nature of instruction or to the ideology being promoted. Some religious schools, for instance, instill a sense of obedience in their students. Others expose students to divergent viewpoints and encourage independent thought. In the absence of any information on the orientation of formal religious training, we are left with contrasts similar to the affiliation comparisons mentioned earlier. At worst, we have a simple secular/nonsecular contrast.

Stoop (1979) used four different school samples: Roman Catholic, Lutheran, conservative Christian, and a public school. Subjects were selected from the ninth to twelfth grades. On the P score, there were no differences between schools at ninth grade. By twelfth grade, however, the Lutheran students scored significantly higher than the other three groups. Stoop interprets this latter finding as due to the religious training offered in the Lutheran school; however, other differences between these groups may be the causal factor (e.g., SES). Blackner (1975) related the DIT scores of young adults to their degree of involvement in weekday religious education. The results were nonsignificant.

Wolf (1980) investigated the joint effect of religious education and religious commitment. In a sample of 76 college students, those subjects with high exposure to religious education had significantly lower P scores in comparison to those subjects with low exposure. Wolf also asked subjects to record their level of commitment to their religion and any experiences of conversion. Contrary to Wolf's hypothesis, subjects indicating high exposure to religious education and high commitment scored significantly lower on the DIT than a group defined by high exposure and low commitment. Thus religious education may be an inhibitor of development in concepts of justice. In apparent contrast, Killeen (1977) argues that religious training can foster moral judgment development. Killeen obtained scores on the DIT and measure of concrete and abstract religious thinking. Results indicate that Catholic high school students scored higher on the religious thinking and the DIT measures. Thus those students with formal religious training tended to be more abstract thinkers on religious topics, and achieved higher DIT scores. While significant differences between groups on SES and IQ (Catholics were higher on both) reduces the strength of Killeen's conclusions, together with the Wolf study these results suggest that the impact of formal religious education depends on the quality of that education. As with moral intervention studies (presented in Chapter 3), the success of religious educational programs in promoting moral judgment development is perhaps best understood as an interplay of the educational environment and student character-istics. Until studies incorporate both sources of information, our knowl-edge of whether religous training influences moral development will be limited.

Religious Knowledge

Several studies have assessed the relation of religious knowledge and moral judgments, some combining knowledge with other religious dimensions such as belief, practice, and experience. The typical mea-sure of religious knowledge used by these studies contains short-answer items about church doctrines or biblical information.

O'Gorman (1979) studied the relationship between religious knowl-edge and moral judgments in a high school sample of both Catholic and public school students. Findings indicate that religious knowledge and DIT scores were positively related. Type of school did not affect the obtained relationship. Unfortunately, O'Gorman did not assess the influence of cognitive ability on this relationship. It may be, therefore, that cognitive ability is the causal factor in the relationship.

Similarly, Harris (1981) found religious knowledge related to DIT scores ($r = .36, p < .01$) in a sample of eleventh-grade students. While Harris points out that grade point average (a proxy variable for cogni-tive ability) was related to DIT scores, no information was provided on whether this cognitive variable could account for the DIT and reli-gious knowledge relationship.

Miller's (1979) findings suggest a negative effect of religious knowl-edge. In a sample of Wellesley College women, low P scores were re-lated to high scores on a measure of religiosity that included religious knowledge (other facets of this measure were belief, practice, and ex-perience). Due to the confounding of components in the religiosity measure, the meaning of this finding is unclear.

Studies that Include Religious Measures

In addition to studies focusing on religion, there are a number of studies that include some measure of religion in their assessment bat-tery.

Hay (1983) identified three groups within a sample of conscien-tious objectors, ages 15 to 35, one-third female. The first group ($n = 81$) based their attitude toward military service on a personal moral code, which they considered valid apart from any belief in God or reli-gion. A second group ($n = 40$) stated their primary basis for objection was a belief in a supreme being and in religious teachings. The final group (n = 28) based their position on a rejection of the government's right to require military service and other political arguments. The first group had significantly higher P scores than did the second group at both the college and graduate school levels, but not at the high school level. Hay also noted that religious affiliation was not meaningfully related to moral judgment scores. This finding is consistent with the results of studies directly assessing affiliation and moral judgment development (see above).

Meyer (1977) compared 10 freshmen and 10 junior college students on a number of developmental measures. Results indicated that seniors had higher P scores and were more religiously liberal than the freshmen subjects; however, due to small sample sizes both differences were nonsignificant.

Volker (1979) attempted to identify college experiences that relate to moral judgment development. In a sample of 36 college students, he found a tendency for low religious activity to relate to high DIT scores. A significant and negative relationship was found between DIT scores and religious belief. Those subjects who characterized their religious beliefs as conservative had lower P scores. Volker also found religious experiences and DIT scores to be unrelated.

Schomberg (1978), in a study much like Volker's, found religious activities (e.g., attending worship services, contributing money to religious groups, reading the Bible and other religious material) unrelated to DIT scores in a sample of 289 university freshmen.

Conclusions About Moral Judgment and Religion

The most striking finding from the literature relating religious measures to moral judgment development is the consistent relationship between DIT P scores and religious beliefs. Those who are described as religious conservatives tend to have lower P scores than their liberal peers. The relationship between other dimensions and moral judgments is less striking. Affiliation has little relation to moral judgment; religious education shows an unclear, mixed relationship; and religious knowledge tends to correlate significantly with moral reasoning, but both may be related in part to cognitive ability. While the conclusion is still tentative, intrinsic motivation appears to serve as a moderator variable intensifying the relationship between moral judgments and religious beliefs.

GENERAL CONCLUSIONS WITH REGARD
TO UNIVERSALITY

The basic theme of this chapter has been that similarities in moral judgment development are more pronounced than differences across a variety of groups. Our interpretation of these findings is that moral judgment development as concepts of justice is a universal component in the social decision-making "tool box" for individuals of quite different environmental backgrounds. While differences between religious conservatives and liberals seem to contradict this statement, the research of Lawrence (1979) and Ernsberger (1977; Ernsberger and Manaster 1981) suggests that these findings are not simply due to differences in the capacity for justice concepts, but represent the use of alternative decision-making criteria. From this latter finding and related research suggested by the four-component model (see the next chapter), we contend that justice concepts may not have a universal utility for all people all of the time. Specific groups may systematically utilize alternative criteria in solving moral dilemmas. One practical implication of this claim is for the future study of group differences. When group differences are expected, researchers should obtain further information on moral comprehension (one such measure is described by Rest 1979a). By observing the pattern of group differences on both measures, a determination can be made as to whether these results are due to true group or utility differences. True group differences would be indicated when both moral judgment and comprehension levels differ, whereas differences in the utilization of justice concepts are implicated by group differences on the DIT in the absence of comprehension differences. In particular, cross-cultural researchers should be sensitive to potential differences in the cultural utility of justice concepts and should design their procedures accordingly.

5

Moral Judgment, Behavior, Decision Making, and Attitudes

Stephen J. Thoma and James Rest
With Robert Barnett

Landing a man on the moon, producing a vaccine that eliminates polio, exploding a nuclear bomb, transplanting a human heart—these are dramatic demonstrations of the power of science. Accomplishments such as these give an immediate credibility to the theories and research methods underlying them. Psychology does not have any demonstration so dramatic as these, and perhaps it never will. The long-term goal of the psychology of morality, nevertheless, is to understand (and perhaps predict) moral behavior in real-life contexts. If we can ever do this with any precision, the psychological theories and research methods that underlie that result will have a compelling validation. This accomplishment, of course, will not just happen. It can happen only with a determined campaign of research, with many theoretical breakthroughs, and some luck. In this chapter we describe some next steps in our campaign to reach the eventual goal of understanding moral behavior. We start from these assumptions: (1) Moral behavior results from the interplay of the four component processes described in Chapter 1. (2) One of the critical processes is how a person judges which course of action is morally right (Component 2). (3) Moral judgment is largely influenced by a person's understanding of the possibilities of social cooperation (i.e., their concepts of justice). However, as argued in the previous chapter, the concepts of cooperation and justice do not always determine moral judgment. (4) Currently the DIT is a useful tool in representing how concepts of justice determine the moral judgment process. (5) A reasonable next step is to study the linkages of the DIT to moral decision-making and to behavior.

Two questions make up the theme of this chapter. First, what is the evidence that moral judgment as measured by the DIT has anything to do with a person's behavior, attitudes, or actual decision-making? In other words, what does filling out the DIT questionnaire have to do with anything outside the questionnaire? Second, if a relationship exists, what is the nature of this relationship? What is the specific role of a person's concepts of justice in the determination of behavior?

One answer to the first question is that words have little to do with deeds. That is, there is no relation between moral judgment and behavior; the development of verbalisms (moral and otherwise) follows a track different from that of behavior. Mischel and Mischel (1976) exemplify this point of view with a theatrical statement:

> History is replete with atrocities that were justified by involving the highest principles and that were perpetrated upon victims who were equally convinced of their own moral principles. In the name of justice, of the common welfare, of universal ethics, and of God, millions of people have been killed and whole cultures destroyed. In recent history, concepts of universal right, equality, freedom, and social equity have been used to justify every variety of murder including genocide. [p. 107]

Without disputing that people sometimes attempt to excuse and cover up dastardly deeds with high-sounding justifications, the evidence has gone against the view that words have nothing to do with deeds. Blasi, in 1980, reviewed studies relating moral judgment to behavior. Most of these studies had used some form of Kohlberg's method of assessment, and Blasi's review shows that 57 of 75 studies reported a significant relationship between moral judgment and behavior. Blasi, however, points out that although there seems to be a consistent relationship, the strength of the relationship is only moderate (typically, correlations in the .3 range). He urges researchers to move on to the next question: that of determining the nature of the relation between moral judgment and behavior.

Thoma (1985) recently compiled a review of studies that relate DIT scores to behavioral measures. As Table 5.1 shows, the measures of behavior are quite varied over about 30 studies. Roughly half of the studies use such naturally occurring phenomena as the behavioral criterion (delinquency/nondelinquency, conscientious objectors/nonobjectors, voting for different presidential candidates, ratings of medical interns, etc.). The other half use controlled "lab" simulations for measuring behavior (cheating behavior, distribution of rewards, co-operative behavior, etc.). The great variety of approaches to measuring behavior constitutes the strength of the present data base. Since we observe a consistent pattern of significant relationships between DIT scores and the behavior measures, it seems safe to conclude that generally there is a link between moral judgment and behavior.

In addition to noticing that the link is pervasive, we also notice that the strength of the relationship is only moderate (similar to Blasi's finding of a correlation on the order of .3). The picture from the two reviews is similar: a pervasive and consistent association between moral judgment and behavior, but at only a moderate level. This suggests that other variables (variables not accounted for nor measured in the present studies) are also determinants. Therefore, along with Blasi, we agree that the next phase of research should be in clarifying the nature of the relationship.

It seems reasonable to assume further that moral judgment is linked to behavior insofar as moral judgment represents the different ways of construing the situation. That is, different scores on the DIT represent different ways that people define situations; the differences in situational definition lead to differences in judging what is important, and consequently to differences in judging what course of action is appropriate. We can test this assumption empirically in several ways. One way (although indirect and somewhat rough) is to relate DIT scores to tests of attitudes. Although the construction of attitude scales follows a rationale and methodology different from that of cognitive developmental measures, we can regard attitude scales as indicative of different perceptions of and conceptions about reality. It is important, however, to keep in mind that moral judgment measures are designed to represent how different conceptions of justice influence the process of moral judgment, whereas attitude tests are designed to represent the different conclusions or outcomes of judging. In other words, moral judgment is intended to measure the process of reasoning, whereas attitude tests are intended to characterize the conclusions of the reasoning process. We therefore look to studies that relate DIT scores to attitude tests. We have this question in mind: Does the way that a person constructs his/her perceptions about situations (as indexed by the DIT) have anything to do with the person's conclusions or advocacy of particular viewpoints (attitudes)?

One set of studies, using the "Law and Order Test," related DIT scores to positions on a set of controversial public policy issues. The Law and Order Test asks questions about free speech, due process,

Table 5.1 Studies relating DIT scores to a measure of behavior

Study	Subjects	Measure of behavior	DIT relationship tested	Outcome
Marston (1978)	18 Predelinquent[a] 18 Matched comparison (52 partial information) Adolescents	School drop out/in status School behavior profile One-item adjustment scale	Group differences on P score in school > dropouts $t(50) = 2.33$; correlation with overall scale score, high P associated with fewer behavioral problems, $r(35) = -.34$;[b] Correlation with P $r(36) = -.13$, NS	Yes Yes No
Kagarise (1983)	Delinquents (age range, 12-19), $n = 82$	Delinquent status Type of crime Socialized versus solitary offenders Victimless versus other offenders	Comparison to nondelinquent norms, delinquent < nondelinquent Comparison by person versus property crimes, NS Comparison by socialized versus solitary offenders, NS Victimless versus person, $t(16) = 1.92$, $P < .05$ Victimless versus property, $t(43) = 2.0$, $P < .05$	Yes No No Yes Yes
McColgan et al. (1983)	Predelinquent, $n = 26$[c] Matched comparison, $n = 26$; Adolescents	Delinquent status	Group difference $t(25)$[d] $= 3.58$, delinquent < comparison $P < .05$	Yes
Cain (1982)	Delinquent group $n = 20$ Adolescents	Delinquent status	Group comparison to age equivalent norms, 5.8	Yes
Nitzberg (1980)	Delinquent types 26 Psychopaths 11 Neurotics 22 Subcultural delinquents	Delinquent subgroup status	Group comparisons[e] Psychopaths > neurotics = subcultural delinquents; $F(2,56) = 5.82, P < .01$	Yes Yes

Hay (1983)	21 High school students 101 College students 27 Graduate students, all belonging to a conscientious objector organization; one-third female	Conscientious objector status	C.O. group averages compared to DIT norms; all three groups differ from norms	Yes
Cooney (1983)	22 Married male age $\overline{x} = 33$ 25 Married female age $\overline{x} = 32$ 24 Cohabiting male age $\overline{x} = 29$ 24 Cohabiting female age $\overline{x} = 26$	Traditional versus non-traditional lifestyles	Married = cohabiting subjects No sex differences or sex by life style interaction	No
Steibe (1980)	171 Full-time college or graduate students; 74 female, 94 male; average age, 36	Attendance at social justice meetings, 0-3	Correlation between attendance rate and DIT Sig $r(169) = .23, P < .05$	Yes
Benor et al. (1982)	199 Medical school applicants at Ben-Gurion University 179 Medical school applicants at Sackler School of Medicine	Admitted versus not admitted into program	Group difference for Ben-Gurion University; $t(197) = 4.35, P < .01$ For Sackler School; $t(177) = -.57, P > .05$	Yes No
Leming (1978)	152 College under-graduates	Cheating on a spatial recall task	High/Low DIT levels on cheating rates; $x^2(2) = 10.4; P < .05$ High P, lower rates of cheating	Yes

(continues)

Table 5.1 *(continued)*

Study	Subjects	Measure of behavior	DIT relationship tested	Outcome
Sprechel (1976)	43 Seventh-graders[f]	Cooperative responses in a version of the prisoners' dilemma procedure	Correlation between DIT and cooperative moves, NS; $r(41) = -.03$	No
Jacobs (1977)	60 Adult females	Cooperative responses on the prisoners' dilemma procedure	High versus low P comparison; $F(1,50) = 31.74$g	Yes
Brabeck (1984)	32 Undergraduates	Whistle-blowing in laboratory setting	Moral judgment level and rates of whistle-blowing for experimental groups,[h] $\text{chi}^2(1) = 5.94, P < .05$	Yes
Malinowski and Smith (in press)	53 Male undergraduates	(1) Cheating behavior number of trials S's cheated	P score correlation with (1), $r(51) = -.48$, $P < .01$	Yes
		(2) Number of seconds S's inflated their scores	P score correlation with (2), $r(51) = -.39$, $P < .01$	Yes
		(3) Latency before cheating began	P score correlation with (3), $r(51) = .43$, $P < .01$	Yes
Lupfer (1982)	240 College students 120 High P 120 Low P	Degree of severity of sentencing in mock juries in a mild and severe consequence condition	Main effect for MJ level NS	No
			Significant interaction between MJ and intentions of perpetrator (e.g., high P); better able to interpret case information	Yes
Lupfer et al. (1982)	66 College students split into 11 juries	Number of guilty votes per jury	High P juries significantly lower guilty votes	Yes
	126 College students split into 21 juries	Leadership in mixed P juries (ratings)	Correlation between P and leadership ratings in mixed juries $r = .47, P < .01$	Yes

138

Study	Sample	Measure	Results	
Clark (1983)	253 High school students	Leadership in small group discussions	In mixed MR groupings high MR member chosen as leader more often than expected by chance chi²(1) = 4.54	Yes
Keller (1975)	37 Unmarried couples, college aged, grouped into 4 groups, both high P mixed high low, both low P	Behavioral measure of communication style, 15 scales		
Gunzburger et al. (1977)	49 High school students Age range, 13-18	Distribution of money for different levels of work output	Distribution styles different[i] by P levels; F(3,39) = 5.10, P < .01	Yes
Carella (1977)	48 College students, 16 high P, 16 middle P, 16 low P	Ratings of disruptive classroom behavior		
		(1) Individual ratings of the severity of the disruptions	Low P ratings were more severe than high P subjects	?
		(2) Dyad judgment of severity	High P subjects made more appropriate judgments	Yes
		(3) Change from individual to dyad ratings	Low P dyads were more severe than high P dyads	?
		(4) Appropriateness of subjects' disciplinary judgments	No differences in change scores by dyad configuration	?
Sauberman (1978)	107 College students; 56 females, 51 males	Judgments of responsibility in two stories differing in consequences and age of protagonist	No effect of consequences on judgment	No
			Low P subjects affected by less appropriate sources of information	Yes

(continues)

Table 5.1 *(continued)*

Study	Subjects	Measure of behavior	DIT relationship tested	Outcome
Eberhardy (1982)	39 Medical practitioners	Division choice on two experimental situations: (a) Newborn situation (b) Terminally ill situation	Correlation between P and decision on (a) Sig $r = .35$ Decision on (b) $r = .06$, NS	Yes No
Dispoto (1977)	140 College students: 87 science majors, mostly male; 51 humanities majors, mostly female	Self report measure of activity in environmental courses	Correlation between P and activity rating for science majors, NS Between P and activity ratings for humanities majors, $F = .27$, $P < .05$	No Yes
Charles (1978)	105 College students	Predictive ability judgments	Correlation between measures reported significant	Yes
Cook (1976)	196 Adult pediatricians	Performance ratings based on at least a year of observations	Correlation between measures reported significant	Yes
Sheehan et al. (1980)	133 Medical interns	Performance ratings 1 = top rating	Correlation between measures, $r = -.22$	Yes

| G. Rest (1977) | 72 College under-graduates 43 Adults | 1976 Presidential preference measures | Curvilinear relationship between P and preference measure Sig | Yes |
| Bredemeier and Shields (1984) | 24 Male, 22 female college basketball players | (1) Coaches' ratings of aggression (2) Coaches' ratings of aggression among peers (3) Recorded fouls adjusted for playing time | Correlation between P and measure 1: $r = -.23, P < .10$ Correlation between P and measure 2: $r = -.30, P < .05$ Correlation between P and measure 3: $r = -.28, P < .10$ | Tendency Yes Tendency |

MJ, moral judgment.
NS, no significance.
[a]Measured in 1975. See McColgan (1975).
[b]Partial correlation between P and scale scores controlling for IQ is significant $r(35) = -.35, P < .05$.
[c]Comparison group matched to predelinquents on 14 factors including IQ, SES, age, home composition, school location.
[d]Matched pairs t-test.
[e]Study used d scores.
[f]Questionable use of DIT with these subjects.
[g]Data from "partner defection" condition.
[h]Results unaffected by GPA, sex, age, assertiveness.
[i]Age effect was nonsignificant.
Source: Compiled by the authors.

civil disobedience, and so on. The questionnaire is scored by counting the number of items on which a subject gives almost limitless power to authorities, or advocates that existing social institutions be maintained even at high cost to individual welfare and freedom (hence the label "law and order"). There are theoretical reasons for believing that concepts of justice at Stage 4 would be congenial with a "law and order" position on these controversial issues, and that a principled (Stage 5 and 6) way of thinking would lead to a low score on the Law and Order Test (Rest 1979a, 161-65). And indeed, what we do find is that the DIT and the Law and Order Test are significantly correlated (the *P* score being negatively correlated with the Law and Order Test, the Stage 4 score being positively correlated with the Law and Order Test). In the 1979 book, seven of eight studies reported significant statistical correlations. In the recent retesting of 102 longitudinal subjects (discussed in Chapter 2), the correlation was -.61 between the Law and Order Test and the *P* score. Recall also that Thornlindsson (1978) found a correlation of -.45 on his translation of the DIT with the Law and Order Test in his Icelandic study. And so this set of studies shows a consistent relationship between the DIT and one political attitude test, the Law and Order Test.

In a recent review of other measures of political attitudes, Barnett (1985) found consistent positive correlations of liberal political positions with the DIT *P* score and consistent correlations of conservative political positions with Stage 4 scores. Table 5.2 summarizes the studies.

Table 5.2 reveals that the DIT is related to political liberalism/ conservatism in a way similar to that of religious liberalism/conservatism (as discussed in Chapter 4).

In a recent doctoral dissertation, Irene Getz (1985) explored the idea that subjects scoring higher on the DIT not only endorse more liberal views with regard to human rights issues, but also that the structure of their thinking is different from more conservative, lower-scoring subjects on the DIT. She reasoned that people with high *P* scores on the DIT structure their moral thinking in terms of general principles for organizing society—for that is what a "principle" is (a general guideline or feature of organizing human interactions so as to optimize certain human values). Accordingly, a person with a high *P* score understands that endorsing a certain principle entails that social relationships are generally to be structured in certain ways. In contrast, a person with a low *P* score may view a statement espousing a moral principle as expressing a nice sentiment but not recognize its ramifications.

Table 5.2 Summary of studies of moral judgment and political attitudes

Study	n	Age/education	Attitude measure	Principled stages 5 and 6
Clouse (1979)	371	College	Libs/Cons.	$F = 2265.53$
Coder (1975)	58	Adult	Rad/Cons.	.13
Crowder (1978)	70	Adult	Political toleration	.04[a]
Elmer, Renwick, and Malone (1983)	73	College	New lift scale	
			Traditional moralism	-.49***
			Machiavellian tactics	-.42***
			Machiavellian cynicism	-.04
			New Left philosophy	.39***
			Revolutionary tactics	.09
Eyler (1980)	135	College	For Maj rule: Hi MJ = 56% yes; Low MJ = 18% yes 27.8**b	
			For Min rights: Hi MJ = 88% yes; Low MJ = 61% yes: 3.8*b	
			For Partisan conflict: Hi MJ = 52% yes; Low MJ = 21% yes: 4.7*b	
Fincham and Barling (1979)	55	College	Wilson's conservatism	-.22*
Forsyth (1980)	221	College	Idealism	-.01
			Relativism	.01
Getz (1985)	105	Adults	Attitudes toward human rights	$r = .66$***
	67	College		$r = .52$***

(continues)

Table 5.2 (continued)

Study	n	Age/education	Attitude measure	Principled stages 5 and 6
Gutkin and Suls (1979)	284	College	SEA	-.27*
Lonky, Reilman, and Serlin (1981)	287	Secondary and college	For Maj rule	.45*
			For Min rights	.52
			For Equal opp	.37*
			For Civil libs	.42*
			For Soc welfare	.20
Nardi and Tsujimoto (1978)	179	College	SEA	-.32
G. Rest (1977)	111	College and adult	Lib/Cons.	-.46*
			Lib self-ratings	-.20
Rest, Cooper, Coder, Masanz, and Anderson (1974)	329	Secondary, college, and adult	Law and order	-.23*
			Libertarianism	.37*

[a]Tests of significance were not reported.
[b]Chi-square analyses were conducted.
[c]Analyses of variance were conducted.
*$p = .05$.
**$p = .01$.
***$p = .001$.
Source: Compiled by the authors.

Presumably people who do not think in terms of principles for organizing society in general, conceptualize morality in more concrete terms, involving the maintenance of certain rule and role systems, of certain relationships, and of certain promises and agreements.

With these ideas in mind, Getz devised two types of attitude items about human rights: one type was a highly general statement such as, "Freedom of speech should be a basic human right," and "People should have freedom of worship and freedom of belief." The second type was a statement about rights of particular people in a particular setting, such as, "Laws should be passed to regulate the activities of religious cults that have come here from Asia." The hypothesis was that all people would endorse the first type of platitudinous, "apple pie" statements. But the implications and applications of the first type of items would be best recognized by subjects with high P scores and not recognized by subjects with low P scores. Therefore, Getz hypothesized that high P subjects would be consistent in their endorsement of the two types of items, whereas lower P subjects would be inconsistent across the two types of items, but not realize it. This hypothesis was confirmed. Consistency/inconsistency was significantly related to P score ($r = -.41$). And so, in addition to there being an association between the DIT and liberal political positions on human rights, there is furthermore a relation between the DIT and the structure of thinking about human rights (i.e., principled subjects realize the ramifications of a moral principle). Moreover, Getz found in multiple-regression analyses that both consistency in beliefs and DIT scores contributed distinctive and significant predictability to attitude scores on human rights, above and beyond that accounted for by self-declared political liberalism/conservatism ("I am a liberal," "I am a conservative"). Therefore, the DIT and the consistency-in-belief measures are not reducible simply to liberal/conservative attitudes, a point to which we shall return below.

The previous discussion has centered on the relationship between DIT scores and basically a conservative/liberal dimension within religious and political attitudes. In addition to these studies there is now a growing body of studies that assesses the relationship between moral judgment development and more general social issues. These studies are presented in Table 5.3.

The first four studies deal with the issue of authority. Smith (1978) assessed the understanding of college students concerning their own difficulties with the governing body of a university. Bloom (1978) and Deal (1978) both relate a measure of attitudes toward the use of an

Table 5.3 DIT and general social attitudes

Name	Sample	Measure	Results
Smith (1978)	55 College students	Interview ratings of subjects' interpretation of their own discipline experience (composite score)	$r = .62$
Bloom (1978)	189 Undergraduate education students	Pupil Control Ideology Scale	$r = -.18$
Deal (1978)	28 Graduate students	Pupil Control Ideology Scale	$r = -.60$
Lapsley et al. (1976)	65 College females	Attitude to authority scale	$r = -.29$
Bidwell (1982)	Adults (age range, 27-65)	Death Anxiety scale (scale measures complexity of thinking, and attitude toward death)	$r = .68$
Malloy (1984)	64 Medical technologists	Attitude toward the study of medical ethics	$r = .44$
DeWolfe and Jackson (1984)	113 College students	Attitude toward capital punishment	$r = -.41$
Letchworth and McGee (1981)	24 College students	Reasoning about the Equal Rights Amendment	$r = .55$
Walgren (1985)	49 Lower-division college students	Minnesota Importance questionnaire (needs and values related to work satisfaction)	$r = .37$
Felton (n.d.)	102 Graduate and 209 undergraduate nurses	Attribution of responsibility scale	r = n.s.
Corcoran (n.d.)	20 Female college students	Attitude toward a noncooperative other in the prisoners' dilemma procedure	F = n.s.

n.s., not significant.
Source: Compiled by the authors.

authority position within the classroom to DIT *P* scores. Lapsley, Sison, and Enright (1976) relate *P* scores to a general measure of authority. While the magnitude of the correlations varies, all of these studies show significant relationships between different features of authority and moral judgments.

The next two studies, Bidwell (1982) and Malloy (1984), assess the relationship between current medical issues and moral judgments within medical populations. Following these studies, DeWolfe and Jackson (1984) and Letchworth and McGee (1981) relate moral judgment scores to more general social issues using college student populations. All four studies suggest that different stands on current issues are related to moral judgment development.

Walgren (1985) relates DIT scores to college students' perceived needs and values relevant to work adjustment and satisfaction. She found a significant nonlinear relationship between the summary score of these values and *P* scores. Walgren suggests that researchers are too quick to assume that the appropriate form of the relationship between moral judgment and other measures is linear. We would agree that in some cases, subjects at different reasoning levels may respond similarly to specific attitude measures and behavioral situations, resulting in nonlinear relationships. The most clear-cut example of this possibility is with political preference. Here, G. Rest (1979a) found that a curvilinear relationship best described the relationship between moral judgment and preference in the 1976 elections (Jimmy Carter was preferred by high and low reasoners, while Gerald Ford was the preference of subjects falling in the middle range). Although the DIT provides continuous indices of moral judgments, researchers should retain the notion of qualitative differences (and nonlinear relationships) when developing hypotheses concerning relationships with other variables.

The final two studies assess the relationship between moral judgments and attitudes toward specific situations within a laboratory setting. Felton (n.d.) found moral judgments unrelated to a measure of responsibility within nursing dilemmas based on real-life situations. Similarly, Corcoran (n.d.) found *P* scores unrelated to attitudes about a noncooperative confederate in the Prisoners' Dilemma procedure. Given that there is little overlap in the topics covered by these studies, it is difficult to determine whether the lack of significance is due to the laboratory setting or the highly specific nature of the attitude assessment, among other potential causes.

Mention should also be made of some pioneering work done by Marilyn Johnston at the University of Utah (1984a, 1984b). In exploratory work using a clinical, case study method, Johnston has found linkages between DIT scores and the way teachers understand school discipline and curricular issues. Functioning as a teacher in a classroom involves many complex social interpretations and value judgments, and DIT scores seem to tap into the conceptualization of these professional matters by teachers. Johnston's work (moving the study of moral judgment into real-life professional settings) parallels our interests here at Minnesota in moving into examination of decision-making in the health professions.

Taken together, the studies focusing on behavior, law and order, political attitude, conservative-liberal religious ideology, and miscellaneous social attitude (70 studies) consistently show a significant relationship with DIT scores. Therefore, it is safe to conclude that moral judgment as measured by the DIT relates to something outside the questionnaire itself. In fact, the variety of things that it does relate to is striking. Consequently, the question of interest becomes, What does it all mean? That is, what is the nature of the relationship?

IS MORAL JUDGMENT THE SAME AS LIBERAL/CONSERVATIVE ATTITUDE?

Before moving on to our own approach to dealing with this question, let us consider a rival interpretation. Recently, Emler, Renwick, and Malone (1983) have claimed that moral judgment is reducible to liberal/conservative attitudes. In their view, cognitive developmentalists have been mistaken all these years in theorizing about the development of concepts of justice, because all that is really there is a dimension of individual differences in liberal and conservative attitudes. One need go no further than simply recognizing that some people are conservative, others are liberal, and all other theorizing about moral judgment development is superfluous. Emler et al. (1983) state:

> We believe that individual differences in moral reasoning among adults—and in particular those corresponding to the conventional-principled distinction—are interpretable as variations on a dimension of politico-moral ideology and not as variations on a cognitive-developmental dimension [p. 1075]

> Kohlberg's conventional-principled distinction as applied to the moral reasoning of adults is one of ideological content rather than structural complexity. [p. 1079]

> These findings must raise doubts about the DIT as a developmental measure but also about the developmental status of Kohlberg's principled

level of moral reasoning. Of all the stages that Kohlberg has claimed have been identified in research samples, evidence for the developmental basis of a fifth stage is the weakest. [p. 1079]

A little history of this dispute may help put these arguments in some context. Emler's claims are echos of his mentor, Dr. Robert Hogan, who has been arguing this point of view for over a decade. In the early 1970s Hogan developed his measure of moral judgment, the Survey of Ethical Attitudes (SEA), which was essentially a measure of liberal-conservative attitudes (1972). At that time, however, Kohlberg's research completely eclipsed all other approaches to moral thinking. Hogan argued that the liberal end of his SEA represented Kohlberg's Stage 6, and the conservative end represented Kohlberg's Stage 5. Hogan further claimed that there are really no developmental differences between Stage 5 and Stage 6, but each is an equally advanced alternative ideology and is measured effectively by the SEA. Research, however, by Gutkin and Suls (1979) and by Nardi and Tsujimoto (1978) indicated that the liberal pole of the SEA was not at all related to Stage 6 (but instead had at most a weak correlation with Stage 5), and that the conservative pole of the SEA was most related to Stage 4. Since these investigators used the DIT for measuring structural development, and since the DIT has consistently shown strong developmental shifts from Stage 4 to Stage 5 (represented by increases in the *P* score, the most used index of the DIT), the evidence has not been very supportive of Hogan's claims.

Then, in 1979, Meehan, Woll, and Abbott found that the SEA was highly susceptible to response dissimulation under instructions to subjects to fake a conservative or liberal profile. That is, Meehan et al. found that subjects' responses on the SEA varied enormously when they were asked to create a favorable or unfavorable impression or were asked to fake political conservative or liberal answers. A subject who originally scored as a conservative on the SEA could easily fake a liberal score. Between 55 and 78 percent of the variance of SEA items could be explained by social desirability. Meehan et al. concluded that the SEA was ineffective as a measure of moral reasoning and, like previous researchers (Lorr and Zea 1977; Woll and Cozby 1976), suggested that the SEA be more appropriately considered as a measure of political attitudes.

In response to these criticisms, Hogan and colleagues (Johnson and Hogan 1981; Mills and Hogan 1978; Hogan and Emler 1978) reinterpreted the meaning of the findings of Meehan et al. Instead of disputing that the SEA was highly correlated with social desirability, they agreed that social desirability was a large part of political attitudes. They argued that a person takes a political stand on some issue in order to convey a certain self-image to others. So, for instance, taking a conservative stand on some issue, they argued, indicates that a person believes that appearing as a conservative will favorably impress those he/she wants to impress—the converse is true for liberals. Therefore, one's score on a political attitude test tells more about the person's attempts at self-presentation and impression manipulation than it tells about how the person sees the sociopolitical world. "People use their responses to items on tests as a means of telling an audience . . . how he or she wants to be regarded; people's responses to items on any psychometric device are organized in terms of their underlying self-images" (Johnson and Hogan 1981, 62).

Thus, in meeting Meehan's criticism of the SEA, the meaning of all "psychometric devices" was reinterpreted to reflect impression management and attempts by the test-taker to appear socially desirable. It was not a large step to apply this same logic to the DIT. Emler et al. therefore followed the path of Meehan et al. and manipulated test-taking instructions to the DIT. Emler et al. found the usual relationship between DIT scores and liberal/conservative political attitudes (liberals tend to have higher P scores on the DIT). Subjects were also asked to complete the DIT twice—once from their own perspective and another time from the political perspective opposite from their own (in other words, subjects who had been classified as conservatives were asked to take the DIT a second time as a liberal; subjects who had been classified as liberals were asked to take the DIT a second time as a conservative). Emler et al. found that the test-taking manipulation (i.e., to fake a liberal or a conservative score) was successful in shifting the DIT scores of subjects. That is, when liberals were asked to fake conservative answers, their DIT scores (the P score) went down, and when conservatives were asked to fake liberal answers, their DIT scores went up.

It is the increased DIT scores of the conservatives that present the challenge to cognitive developmentalists. (That the liberals can fake downward is consistent with cognitive developmental theory.) Finding that the conservatives' scores go up, Emler drew the following conclusions:

1. There is no difference in conceptual capacity between conservatives or liberals or between high P scores and low P scores on the DIT. Rather, there are only differences in how a person chooses to

present himself/herself. In short, DIT scores are a matter of preference for self-presentation, not cognitive capacity. This follows from the fact that subjects can change their scores upward or downward.

2. The notion of a developmental sequence in moral judgment is likewise false. If every subject can have a high *P* score or a low *P* score, depending on personal preference, then it makes no sense to talk about a developmental order based on cognitive development.

3. Since the manipulation to fake a liberal or conservative score was so powerful in shifting DIT scores around, this indicates that the variance in DIT scores must primarily reflect the person's intention to appear like a liberal or appear like a conservative. In other words, the power of the manipulation is evidence that the usual process in taking the DIT is a process of self-presentation and the subject's attempt at impression manipulation. Therefore, all the previous studies that have interpreted variance in DIT scores in terms of cognitive development and conceptions about the social-political world must be reinterpreted in terms of self-presentation.

The findings of the study by Emler et al. do present a challenge to the cognitive developmental view. But this one study hardly puts the whole cognitive developmental research program out of business. A response to this challenge involves two elements: (1) putting the Emler findings alongside other evidence and (2) looking more closely at what the Emler manipulation really involves, and examining the logic of deriving the conclusions from the study's findings.

The Emler interpretation is at odds with a number of well-established findings:

1. There is clear and consistent evidence that DIT scores move upward over time and with more education (cf. the longitudinal and cross-sectional studies discussed in Chapter 2). It is difficult to dispute the orderly changes that occur in DIT scores. And since the main index of the DIT is the *P* score (i.e., Stages 5 and 6), Emler is simply wrong in asserting that evidence for principled morality is scantier than for the lower stages. As mentioned before, the shift from conventional morality (Stages 3 and 4) to the principled stages is the mainstay of the DIT. How does a self-presentational view account for the facts of developmental change? Emler does not even mention the age-change data in his article, nor does he deal with this body of evidence in any way.

2. There are about a dozen studies that link moral judgment scores with comprehension (see the review in Rest 1979a; also see Walker,

deVries, and Bichard 1984). Since Emler did not even assess comprehension in his study, it is difficult for him to contradict the many studies that did directly assess comprehension and have found strong relationships with DIT scores.

3. To equate DIT scores with attitude scores on liberalism/conservatism overlooks the studies that show that moral judgment scores have unique information above and beyond the variance accounted for by measures of liberalism/conservatism. For instance, Rest (1979a) found that in multiple-regression analyses, after partialing out liberal/conservative attitudes, the DIT still added predictability to views on the 1976 presidential election. Getz (1985) found that after partialing out liberal/conservative attitudes, the DIT still added predictability to views on human rights issues. This is not to say that liberal/conservative attitudes and DIT scores are unrelated—the previous section has reviewed many studies that show that there is a consistent, although moderate connection. Rather, this is to say that they are not identical constructs, and that neither reduces to the other. If moral judgment as measured by the DIT were really just another measure of liberal-conservative attitudes, we would expect other measures of liberal-conservative attitudes to have the same data trends as the DIT exhibits. But measures of liberal-conservative attitudes do not show the same data trends as the DIT (see discussion in Rest 1979a). Therefore, the DIT cannot be empirically reduced to liberal-conservative attitudes.

Theoretically, the DIT is designed to measure how concepts of justice influence the process of moral judgment; in contrast, attitude measures are characterizations of the conclusions of judgments. The DIT is related to attitudes because the process by which people think about moral matters is related to the outcome of the thinking process. even if the DIT were reducible to liberal/conservative attitudes, social scientists would still be left with the question, Why do some people prefer liberal thinking and why do others prefer conservative thinking? Emler acknowledges that his position does not lend any light to that problem ("Why some individuals should define themselves as left wing, others as right wing, and yet others as moderates remains to be determined"; 1983, 1079). This, however, is precisely the problem that moral judgment research addresses—to explain how people's intuitions about right and wrong works, why some people prefer conservative positions and why other people prefer liberal positions.

The most compelling evidence against Emler's view, however, involves a reanalysis of his findings, probing what they really mean, and presenting another new study that exposes the flaw in his chain of reasoning. There are two critical issues in Emler's interpretation of his findings: (1) By what process are the conservative subjects increasing their P scores under the "fake like a liberal" condition? (2) Does the instruction manipulation reflect the normal process that accounts for variance in DIT scores?

Consider how manipulations of test instructions can affect our interpretation of a test. Imagine the following (Scenario no. 1): a test purporting to measure mathematics ability is given to a group of subjects, and some of them score very low. Then we give the test again, but offer $1000 rewards to everyone making a perfect score. We find that all the subjects make perfect scores, including the subjects who received low scores on the first testing. Were this to happen, we would doubt that the original test given under the no-incentive condition was a good test of mathematics ability, because with incentives, those who scored low can score just as high as the others. The manipulation suggests that variance on the first testing is mostly attributable to motivation to perform on the test rather than to capacity. In short, the shift in scores due to test manipulation invalidates the test.

Now imagine Scenario no. 2: We first give a test purporting to measure mathematics ability. Then we give the test again, but offer an answer key to subjects scoring low on the first testing. We find on the second testing that subjects scoring low on the first testing now score very high. Does this shift in scores also invalidate the test?

We would say the test manipulation in Scenario no. 2 does not invalidate the test. Giving some subjects the answer key actually directed them to fill out answers without really working the problem. The performance of subjects with the answer key does not really reflect anything about their mathematics ability. Every test assumes some set of normal conditions, and giving some subjects the answer key is not one of these normal conditions. Just because some subjects with an answer key received higher scores does not entail that they have greater mathematics ability; it just means that they took the test under invalid conditions.

In essence, we would contend that Emler's manipulation was more like Scenario no. 2 than Scenario no. 1. The first tip-off for this comes from an examination of his own data. Although Emler did not report this result, a reanalysis of his data shows that the strongest effect of asking the conservative subjects to fake like a liberal (or actually, as a "radical," to use the exact phrasing that Emler employed) was to increase the A score, and only secondarily the *P* score. The A score on the DIT represents items that espouse an angry, antiauthoritarian, antiestablishment viewpoint. For instance, in the Heinz dilemma, the following item is an A item: "Whether the druggist is going to be allowed to hide behind a worthless law which only protects the rich anyway." Other A items on the DIT for other stories are: "Wouldn't we be better off without prisons and the oppression of our legal systems?" or "People would be much better off without society regimenting their lives and even their deaths." When Emler asked conservatives to fake like radical liberals, they primarily went for the A items, selecting items on the feature of sounding angry and antiestablishment. The subjects were not working the moral problem by trying to find a fair and just solution, but instead were guided by the new instruction to select items on the basis of how angry the item sounds. When they ran out of A items, they had no place to go but to *P* items. The conservative subjects would eliminate Stage 4 items because those were the ones they had chosen for themselves; they would eliminate lower-stage items (Stages 2 and 3) since they could recognize that Stages 2 and 3 were lower than their own stage and childish—thus leaving the *P* items as a second resort with nowhere else to go. Therefore, the shifts in *P* score that Emler obtained by his test instructions to subjects is actually due to an artifact of violating test conditions and to the limited item pool on the DIT. We would contend that Emler's instructions to fake like a radical have the effect of instructing subjects (like Scenario no. 2) to select items on a basis different from the normal conditions presupposed in the testing conditions, and is not evidence that low-scoring subjects on the DIT could, if they wanted, use principled moral thinking. Rather, in effect, the Emler manipulation provides an external answer key to the test: instead of working through the moral problem and trying to render the person's best judgment of what is just and morally right, Emler's instruction directs the subjects to select items on the basis of what sounds angry, antiestablishment, and antiauthoritarian. Attending to these features of items rather than to the different concepts of justice, subjects first pick out the *A* items, then only resort to the *P* items when there is nothing else left to choose from.

If our interpretation of Emler's manipulation is correct, how could one obtain evidence to substantiate or refute our interpretation over

Emler's? Actually, it is rather simple. Dr. Robert Barnett (1985) conducted an elegant study that is unambiguous in its findings and exposes the flaw in Emler's reasoning. If it is the case that the shift in P scores was really due to the fact that subjects had nowhere else to go, then if we provide more A items in the DIT item pool, they will have somewhere else to go. Barnett simply expanded the number of A items in the DIT from 5 to 21 (equal to the number of P items), so that when subjects were asked to pick four items for each story from a set of 15 items, they did not have to choose P items as a last resort (although they could still choose P items if they wanted to). Our interpretation of Emler's test manipulations is that he changed the task from one asking about a subject's concepts of justice into a task to discriminate items that sound angry. Therefore Barnett wrote A items such as the following: "Whether the 'establishment' unfairly controls every aspect of our lives," "Whether the solution for contemporary problems lies in striking at their roots, no matter how much destruction might occur," "Whether society only serves to perpetuate evils rather than solve problems."

Barnett then followed Emler's procedures and instructions, but this time with an expanded DIT with the additional A items. Table 5.4 presents Barnett's data alongside Emler's. As in Emler's study, subjects were grouped into liberals, moderates, and conservatives on the basis of their own labels of political ideology. So each study looks at three groups of subjects. Each study has two conditions: the "self" condition (in which subjects take the DIT under the usual instructions), and the "radical" condition (in which subjects take the DIT so as to fake like a liberal radical).

We note that Barnett's study has about four times the number of subjects in the critical conditions than Emler's study used (e.g., 49 versus 12 subjects). We note that in the "self" condition, Barnett's subjects scored virtually identically to Emler's subjects on Stage 4 and P, although the A score in Barnett's study was higher due to the increased number of A items in the expanded DIT. The most interesting contrasts are in the shifts in P score from the self condition to the radical condition in the conservative groups. In Emler's study, the P score went from 30.80 to 52.58, but in Barnett's study the P score went from 30.94 to 26.53. In Barnett's study, where there were more A items to choose from, the effect of Emler's manipulation was to increase the A score, but not to increase the P score. (In fact, the conservative's P score even goes down when the conservatives don't have to choose the P items.)

Table 5.4 Comparison of mean Stage 4, A, and P scores by self-defined political view from Emler et al. and the present study

Study	Group (n)		Self			(n)*	Radical		
			4	A	P		4	A	P
Emler et al.	Liberals (26)	$\overline{X}$:	16.60	7.12	52.12	(12)	12.50	15.00	45.50
		SD:	8.72	5.53	13.37		8.57	8.78	15.45
	Moderates (24)	$\overline{X}$:	30.06	2.43	35.07	(11)	13.33	16.06	46.97
		SD:	12.12	3.61	10.58		8.03	10.15	7.95
	Conservatives (23)	$\overline{X}$:	46.62	2.46	30.80	(11)	12.12	16.37	52.58
		SD:	12.40	2.60	12.53		11.10	11.10	14.42
Barnett	Liberals (49)	$\overline{X}$:	17.42	15.27	51.91		7.45	42.01	39.16
		SD:	10.57	11.59	12.96		7.65	17.47	14.72
	Moderates (13)	$\overline{X}$:	29.75	10.77	37.31		15.64	27.82	37.44
		SD:	9.10	9.80	12.69		10.01	17.71	11.17
	Conservatives (47)	$\overline{X}$:	45.50	7.60	30.94		13.88	38.95	26.53
		SD:	12.07	6.67	11.43		10.57	16.88	9.25

Note: Only approximately half of the subjects from each political group were placed in the Radical Condition in the Emler et al. 1983 study.

Source: Compiled by the authors.

Clearly, for all three groups, the effect of Emler's instructions to fake like a radical liberal is to increase the angry *A* items, not to increase the *P* items. Table 5.5 gives the results of various analysis of variance computations. Therefore, Emler's increases in *P* scores are artifacts of his procedure, not evidence that everybody can have high *P* scores if they wanted to. Emler's claims about his study disproving cognitive developmental research are a little overstated.

Barnett's study and discussion also suggest a more general caution to researchers who manipulate test instructions. Care should be taken that the manipulation does not fundamentally change the nature of the task given to subjects. In the case of Emler's manipulation, the task in effect changed from requiring subjects to solve a moral problem in terms of their concepts of justice to a task asking subjects to select items on the basis of a stylistic feature (how angry the item sounds). By changing the task so fundamentally, little inference can be made about the moral judgment process. For instance, if instructions are given to choose items on the basis of their alphabetical order, the *P* score may change, but little can be said from this about the subject's moral judgment.

Now we have addressed the first critical question posed by Emler's study: How are we to interpret the shift in *P* scores? Now let us address the second critical question: What is the relation between Emler's manipulation and the process by which subjects normally make moral judgments? Recall Emler's position: Since the manipulation to fake like a liberal or fake like a conservative was so powerful in shifting DIT scores around, this indicates that the variance in DIT scores must primarily reflect the person's intention to appear like a liberal or appear like a conservative. In other words, the power of the manipulation is evidence that the usual process in taking the DIT is a process of self-presentation and the subject's attempt at impression manipulation.

Barnett (1985) again provides an elegant answer. After subjects had filled out the extended DITs under both conditions, Barnett asked subjects to reflect on the process that they had used in filling out each questionnaire. Barnett presented six characterizations of problem-solving strategies in accord with cognitive developmental theory: one strategy maximized interpersonal concordance; a second maintained law and order; a third optimized individual rights; and a fourth was based on general ethical principles. The next two strategies were designed to exemplify those claimed to be the operative ones by Hogan and Emler. One of these strategies reads, "I wish to be regarded as a

Table 5.5 Means and standard deviations for "Self" and "Radical" DIT scores by political view

Condition:				Self					
DIT Index: 2	3	4	5A	5B	6	A	M	P
Liberals (n = 49)									
$\overline{X}$: 2.65	9.49	17.42	30.82	12.01	9.12	15.27	3.47	51.91
SD: 4.15	7.29	10.57[a]	9.21[b]	5.77[b]	5.87	11.59[b]	3.38	12.96[b]
Moderates (n = 13)									
$\overline{X}$: 4.36	13.46	29.75	25.00	7.18	5.13	10.77	3.59	37.31
SD: 4.69	8.86	9.10[a]	10.23[c]	3.93[c]	5.16	9.80	3.53	12.69[c]
Conservatives (n = 47)									
$\overline{X}$: 3.22	8.55	45.50	17.17	4.77	9.11	7.60	3.77	30.94
SD: 3.54	5.56	12.07[a]	8.70[a]	3.69[b]	5.34	6.67[b]	2.98	11.43[b]

[a]Mean is significantly different from two other group means at the .05 level.
[b]Liberals and conservatives differ significantly at the .05 level.
[c]Moderates and conservatives differ significantly at the .05 level.
[d]Liberals and moderates differ significantly at the .05 level.
In a repeated measures analysis of variance, the Radical score differs from the Self score: $*p = .05$; $**p = .01$; $***p = .001$.
All group means are expressed as percentages.
Source: Compiled by the authors.

liberal, so I respond to social issues and problems as I believe a liberal would." The second strategy substitutes the word "conservative" for "liberal." Barnett simply asked subjects to rate the extent to which the subject used each strategy in filling out the DIT under normal conditions and then in filling out the DIT under the "fake like a liberal" conditions. Table 5.6 presents the results.

It shows that none of the groups indicates using the Emler/Hogan strategies in the normal DIT condition. However, all of the groups indicate using the Emler/Hogan strategies in the "fake like a liberal" condition. The subjects indicate that they switched basic strategy in the change from taking the DIT under normal conditions to taking the DIT under the Emler condition (see Barnett 1985 for further discussion). Since subjects report using different strategies for taking the DIT under the different conditions, this is evidence that the strategy evoked by Emler's manipulation condition involves a *different* process from that usually evoked in filling out the DIT under normal condi-

				Radical				
2	3	4	5A	5B	6	A	M	P
Liberals								
1.60*	7.21*	7.45***	26.50*	9.01	6.60	42.01***	2.65*	39.16***
3.23^d	7.28^b	7.65^b	11.15^b	11.88^b	12.07	17.47^d	3.10	14.72^b
Moderates								
4.74	10.26	15.64**	29.92	5.13	5.39	27.82**	4.10	37.44
4.40^d	8.41	10.01^c	11.03^c	3.63	4.09	17.71^d	4.44	11.17^c
Conservatives								
2.94	14.40***	13.88***	17.61	5.18	3.32***	38.95***	3.19	26.53*
3.60^c	8.50^b	10.57^a	7.42^a	3.62^b	3.45	16.88	3.99	9.25^a

tions. The task of finding items that sound angry is different from solving a moral problem in the fairest way conceivable. Emler's manipulation does not illuminate anything about the usual processes of making moral judgments or about how the DIT normally works.

In contrast, consider the fakability studies by McGeorge (1975), Bloom (1977), and Hau (1983). After taking the DIT under the usual instructions, subjects are asked to then take the DIT "so that it records the highest, most mature level of social and ethical judgment possible" (McGeorge 1975). In all three of these studies, the extra incentive to "fake good" did not increase the subjects' *P* score. Why not? We would contend that under the normal conditions, subjects are judging what is morally right by using the most advanced concept of justice that is possible for them. This is what a test of moral judgment is supposed to indicate. The extra incentive and directions in the "fake good" condition do not result in a shift of scores, because we have not directed subjects to choose items in a way that is different from that which reflects their own concepts of moral rightness (we did not direct them to put aside their own notions of justice and look for the angry items, or to choose items on the basis of their alphabetical order, etc.). Therefore, if a researcher is interested in characterizing what notions of justice a person has in making judgments of what ought to be done, the task as set by the usual DIT instructions

Table 5.6 Means and standard deviations for accuracy ratings of "Self" and "Radical" decision-making strategies

	Normal Decision-Making						Radical Decision-Making					
	Intprs. Confrm.	Law and Order	Indiv. Rights	Ethical Prncpls.	Liberal Image	Cons. Image	Intprs. Confrm.	Law and Order	Indiv. Rights	Ethical Prncpls.	Liberal Image	Cons. Image
Liberals (n = 46)												
$\overline{X}$:	3.74	2.76	4.09	4.17	2.33	1.22	2.76***	1.41***	3.91	4.09	3.24***	1.04*
SD:	.93	1.02[a]	.81	.89	1.27[b]	.46[b]	.99	.69[a]	1.13[b]	1.11[b]	1.52[b]	.30[b]
Moderates (n = 12)												
$\overline{X}$:	3.67	3.67	4.33	4.17	2.08	2.50	2.42**	2.50*	2.92**	3.50	4.25**	1.67**
SD:	1.16	.89[a]	.78	.72	.99	.67[c]	.90	1.31[d]	1.08[d]	1.24	1.36	.89[b]
Conservatives (n = 45)												
$\overline{X}$:	3.73	4.40	4.27	3.98	1.33	3.07	2.82***	1.87***	2.58**	3.24***	4.07***	1.30***
SD:	.96	.78[a]	.89	1.03	.77[b]	1.44[a]	1.25	.89[b]	1.16[b]	1.26[b]	1.20[b]	.77

[a]Mean is significantly different from two other group means at the .05 level.

[b]Liberals and conservatives differ significantly at the .05 level.

[c]Moderates and conservatives differ significantly at the .05 level.

[d]Liberals and moderates differ significantly at the .05 level.

In a repeated measures analysis of variance, the Radical score differs from the Normal score: *p = .05; **p = .01; ***p = .001.

The "decision-making strategies" measure used a "very accurate" (5) to "very inaccurate" (1) rating scale.

Source: Compiled by the authors.

160

or in the "fake good" conditions are equivalent, and either can be used.

In summary, Barnett's findings show that subjects do not regard a self-presentational strategy as accurately portraying how they make moral judgments. There is no evidence that Emler's manipulation reflects or illuminates the usual processes whereby people make moral judgments. The evidence provided by the manipulation studies of McGeorge, Bloom, and Hau indicate that subjects are already trying to represent their best concept of justice when filling out the DIT.

AN APPROACH TO INVESTIGATING THE ROLE OF CONCEPTS OF JUSTICE IN BEHAVIOR AND DECISION-MAKING

The Four-Component Model assumes that no single variable will ever predict strongly to behavior. We accept as essentially accurate the conclusions from the moral judgment-behavior studies that indicate a consistent but low-magnitude correlation. The role of concepts of justice in producing behavior must be understood alongside other variables and mediators. Our approach, therefore, is basically the search for the other variables and mediators. To guide the search, we start with hunches about the role of concepts of justice in decision-making.

We start with assumptions about what people learn from social experience. As children develop, not only do they learn more and more concrete social rules, they also come to understand the nature, purpose, and function of forms of social cooperation. Children first come to understand simple forms of cooperation, involving only face-to-face bargaining and concrete, short-term exchanges. Gradually, with development, they come to understand more complicated forms of cooperation involving society-wide networks, institutions and role-systems, law-making and law enforcement, and ideals for guiding the creation of cooperative societies. These concepts or realizations are generally schemes that are abstracted from concrete social experience and become the basis for understanding how people cooperate with each other. These basic schemes of cooperation are the underlying structures in our definitions of moral judgment stages. A moral judgment stage is defined by its notion of how cooperation is organized— in particular, how the benefits and burdens of cooperation are allocated, how rights and obligations are derived. In short, our stages represent different concepts of justice.

A scheme remains in long-term memory as a general knowledge structure. When a person is faced with a concrete social situation involving a moral dilemma, the person attempts to "make sense of it" by identifying what courses of action are available, what the consequences of each course of action would be to the parties involved, what moral claims can be made, which moral claims are most important, and so on. A general scheme aids in construing the concrete situation by guiding attention to the important considerations, by helping to sort out relevant from irrelevant facts, by prioritizing the conflicting moral claims of the various parties, and by integrating information so as to arrive at a judgment of what ought to be done. A basic scheme therefore guides one's understanding of social situations and helps to formulate the crux of decision-making.

Several features of the DIT are worth emphasizing again. First, individual items are not pure representations of a scheme or stage. A DIT item is a story-specific consideration that would be highlighted or prioritized in the application of a general scheme/stage to that story. The existence of general schemes in a person's long-term memory is inferred by a subject consistently giving high importance to the particular set of items keyed to a particular stage over six stories. However, sometimes a subject may attribute high importance to an individual item for idiosyncratic reasons (having little to do with the application of a scheme). But by and large, by aggregating over 72 items in six stories, such idiosyncratic ratings are expected to be randomly distributed and cancel each other out in the aggregated scores. Note then that operationally a stage score on the DIT is not tied to a particular situation (or to advocating particular courses of action) because stage scores come from aggregating across situations. Theoretically, a stage score is a more general structure than any particular situation or particular action—it is a general way of understanding how cooperation should be organized.

Second, notice that DIT items are designed to represent only various fairness considerations in a situation. Other pragmatic and ideological considerations (which may be important to a subject) are not represented in DIT items. In effect the DIT forces subjects to choose between concepts of fairness. No attempt is made to inventory all considerations of every kind.

With this point of view, we have engaged in a series of studies that are reported in an article written in 1984 (Rest and Thoma) and in Thoma's dissertation (1985). The studies represent a persistent pursuit of one of the linkages between moral judgment and behavior, and follow cumulatively, one on the other. There are nine studies in this series, and a detailed report of them takes as many pages as in this entire book, drawing on a stack of computer printout several feet high. In the pages that follow, we will try to communicate the major threads of our investigations, the logic that links one study with the next, the major findings, and our interpretations of those findings. The brevity of this description makes the exposition somewhat dense, but we hope the reader can gain a sense of how we have pursued this question and the outcomes.

We start by looking at subjects' decisions on the six hypothetical dilemmas (e.g., steal, can't decide, and not steal on the Heinz dilemma—see Appendix). These action choices are assumed to represent the outcome of decision-making about the specific hypothetical dilemmas. If we want to understand how concepts of justice (as exemplified in DIT items) are related to decision-making and behavior, we thought it made sense to look at how DIT items relate to subject's action choices on the DIT dilemmas. In the following pages, we will summarize nine studies.

1. While much has been written about the DIT as a measure of moral judgment development, relatively little effort has been focused on the subject's action choice decisions or the relationship between DIT item selection and action choice decisions. Martin, Shafto, and Van Deinse (1977), in a general discussion of the DIT, noted that subjects' action choice decisions were related to the importance rating of Stage 4 items within the same story. Cooper (1972) created an index representing the degree to which a subject's action choice decisions matched the decisions of moral philosophy graduate students. That is, he noticed that an overwhelming majority of moral philosophy graduate students made the same action choice (e.g., Heinz should steal, that the doctor should give the morphine overdose, that Webster should hire the minority mechanic, etc.). This set of action choices over the six dilemmas of the DIT could be used as a standard, and the action choices of other subjects could be indexed in terms of how many of their choices agreed with this standard. Cooper then correlated this index with DIT scores and found a positive but modest relationship ($r = .34$). These studies are consistent with the presupposition that moral judgment structures are related to the outcome of specific moral decisions. However, much like the first-generation research on moral judgment's relationship to specific behaviors, these studies provide little additional information concerning the nature of this relation-

ship (i.e., why and how they are related). Our work in this area represents the first in-depth inquiry into the relationship between item endorsement and action choice.

Unlike any of the previous studies, we began by collecting descriptive data on action choices. This data was necessary to address two questions: first, do the action choices of a large group of subjects suggest a diversity of selections or do subjects tend to choose the same action choice? If virtually all subjects pick the same action choices then any search for relationships with this variable would be futile because there would not be any subject variance to explain.

Second, do subjects change their action choices over time? As we know from studies assessing moral judgment development, subjects change their concepts of justice over time. But if we find that action choices remain stable over this same period, then any claim for causal links between these variables would be pointless—both variables have to vary over time in order to look for correlations, if there are any causal links to explain.

The results indicate that subjects do differ in action choices. Some dilemmas tend to be more controversial than others. The most controversial is the Heinz story. There, 40, 18, 42 percent of the subjects selected the pro, can't decide, and con action choices, respectively, whereas in the least controversial dilemma (the Webster story), these same numbers were 86, 9, and 5 percent.

Using a second cross-sectional sample, we assessed the pattern of action choices supplied by subjects from the four major age/educational groupings (e.g., junior high school, high school, college, and graduate school). Across the six dilemmas, as one moves from youngest to the oldest/most educated groups, the controversy in selecting action choices declines. The average agreement in junior high school is 59 percent, whereas the average agreement for Ph.D. students was 78 percent.

2. Pursuing these results further, we questioned whether action choices followed a developmental pattern over time. As individuals increase in DIT scores, do their patterns of action choices become increasingly like the pattern of the philosophy students? To address this question, a summary index of action choices was developed, following the procedure suggested by Cooper (1972) mentioned earlier. The index is simply a count of the number of times a subject's action choice agrees with the action choice pattern of the graduate philosophy students (these choices were "steal," "not take over," "not turn in,"

"mercy kill," "hire," and "stop"—see Appendix for the set of dilemmas and action choices). Scores range from 0 (no matches) to 6 (an action choice pattern identical to the philosophy students' pattern). The correlation of this index with the DIT was .31, a modest correlation and one comparable to Cooper's value of .34. The relationship between the action choice index and age was a similarly modest correlation of .29.

The final set of descriptive data on action choice selections addressed the question of whether subjects change their action choices over time or stick with the same action choice and only change their reasons for it. A sample of 221 subjects tested two years apart supplied the data. Of interest was the number of stories on which subjects changed their action choices from those selections made at the earlier time. An index of action choice change was created. Possible values for this index ranged from 0 (no changes, the subject has supplied identical action choice selections at times one and two) to 6 (six changes, the subjects' action choice selections on the second testing was different on all six stories from the first set of action choices). When subject's action choice changes are indexed in this fashion, the average change is slightly more than a third of the stories (2.31 story changes). Thus subjects do seem to change their action choices over time. In addition, no one story elicits significantly more change than the others.

From these analyses, we concluded that there is both within-subject and between-subject variability on action choices that is sufficient to pursue the study of relationships between these choices and moral judgments.

3. Following the descriptive analyses, we questioned whether the failure to find a more substantial correlation (greater than .3) between moral judgments and action choice maturity was due to aggregating across stories without special regard to specific reasons in the stories and the specific action choice decisions. Note that in the studies mentioned so far, indices of moral judgment and action choice were constructed from subject responses to all six stories, perhaps obscuring relationships between specific moral judgments and specific action choices within particular stories. Therefore, analyses were performed that assessed the relationship between story indices of moral judgment (e.g., moral judgment scores based on the Heinz dilemma only, on the student dilemma only, etc.), and the action choice of the corresponding story (scored 1, 2, and 3 for the pro, can't decide, or con action choices, respectively). The results of these analyses did not suggest

that a focus on the individual stories improved the obtained relationship between moral judgment and action choices beyond a correlation of .31 obtained by aggregating subject responses across stories. However, we noticed something else. The direction of the relationship between moral judgment and action choices changed from story to story. In some stories the lower-stage DIT items related to the pro action choice, whereas in other stories the same type of items favored the con choice; thus there is not a simple linear relationship between action choice and moral judgment. This finding indicates that to understand the relationship between action choice and moral judgments one must take into account the particulars of the situation, the degree to which stage-typed items suggest a story-specific choice, as well as the stage properties of the items deemed important by an individual.

4. Following this line of reasoning, we assessed the degree to which individual DIT items are aligned with a particular action choice. That is, can one reliably catalog DIT items as logically implying a pro or con action decision? As an example, consider the first item in the Heinz story, whether a community's laws are going to be upheld. It seems plausible that subjects who select this item as the most important consideration are so concerned about breaking the law that they would conclude that Heinz should not steal the drug. Conversely, the second item in the Heinz story is: "Isn't it only natural that a loving husband would care so much for his wife that he'd steal?" We would think that subjects finding this item most important would favor the pro or "steal" action choice if they understand the logical implications of that item. Accordingly, we asked whether all DIT items could be reliably rated as favoring one or another action choice.

Ten graduate students familiar with moral judgment research agreed to rate the 72 DIT items. Their task was to consider each DIT item and rate on a five-point scale the most likely action choice match for a hypothetical individual rating the item most important. If the graduate student felt confident that an item rated most important would clearly imply the pro action choice, the appropriate rate was 1. If the graduate raters were less convinced but still considered an item as favoring the pro action choice, a 2 was entered. If the graduate rater had no idea which action choice an item implied, then the appropriate rating was a 3. Similarly, a 4 or 5 rating was reserved for items leaning con, or strongly con, respectively. (Hereafter, we will refer to these ratings as "the logical implication ratings.")

Results were clear that the graduate raters found it fairly easy to assign action choice implications to DIT items. For only 19 of the 72 items was there any ambiguity in identifying action choice implications. Also, there was high agreement among raters. If we take variability of the graduate student item ratings as an index of agreement, only 19 (or 26 percent) of the item rates had standard deviations of 1 or more. This finding suggests a majority of the variability in action choice implications is due to differences in the confidence that a given item favored the same action choice, and not confusion over which action choice seemed to be implied by the item.

5. The possibility remains, however, that the ratings of graduate students of items in terms of their logical implications for action might have little to do with the way more typical subjects taking the DIT under normal conditions view these items. Sensitive to this argument, we conducted an analysis to clarify the meaning of the graduate student ratings. This second study addressed the question of whether there was any indication that subjects taking the DIT under normal circumstances are aware of which action choice an item seems to imply, and if so, do the subjects' sense of the action choice implications coincide with the sense of the graduate students?

To address this question we used a sample of 969 subjects completing the DIT under normal circumstances. For each DIT story three groups were formed by dividing subjects on their action choice selections. For example, on the Heinz story, the first group consisted of those subjects who said Heinz should steal the drug, the second group consisted of those who said they can't decide, and the third group consisted of those who said Heinz should not steal the drug. For each of these groups an average rating was computed on all 12 Heinz story issues. This same procedure was repeated on the other five stories (for a total of 72 items). From these three groups, the average rate for each DIT item was computed. The major question here was, do subjects who favor a pro action choice rate the items the same way as subjects who favor a con action choice?

When the group mean item rates were statistically compared, it was found that subjects in one group rate an item differently from subjects in the other groups. For instance, those subjects in the "steal" group rated an item higher if the item favored stealing, whereas those subjects in the "not steal" group rated an item higher than the other groups if the item favored not stealing. In 79 percent (58 items) of DIT items, the rates significantly differed as a function of the action choice groupings. In other words, the ratings of DIT items contain a degree of bias reflecting the subject's own preference for action and the item's implication for action.

6. Now the question arises: How does this bias in rating DIT items correspond to the graduate student's ratings of the logical implications of the items? For instance, if the graduate students thought an item had strong pro action choice implications, then do typical subjects taking the DIT under usual conditions tend to "overrate" that item if they also advocate a pro action choice, and underrate the item if they advocate a con action choice? We followed this procedure: for each DIT item subtract the average rate of the con group from the pro group's rate. For example, suppose on the first Heinz item, the pro steal group rate was 2.6, and the con steal group's rate was 2.1. This pattern of ratings suggests that the con group found Item 1 more important than the pro group (since the DIT rates range from 1, most important, to 5, least important). Following the subtraction procedure we find a positive .5. If on the second item in the Heinz story, these same groups rated the item 1.5 (pro), and 3.0 (con), then the difference would be a negative (- 1.5), suggesting that the pro group found Item 2 much more important than those subjects choosing the con action choice. These two examples indicate that differences between item rates can vary in direction (e.g., whether the difference is positive or negative), and in the magnitude of the difference (e.g., |.5| versus |1.5| in the example above). Both of these influences on group rating differences can be compared to the graduate student logical implications ratings, and we should expect both sources of information to covary if the underlying cause for differences on these values is the same. Specifically, the direction of the difference found by the subtraction procedure should correspond to the graduate student's selection of an item's appropriate action choice match. The magnitude of the difference between average group rates should correspond to the degree of certainty in the logical implications item rates. That is, if our expectations are correct, then we should expect to find the largest group differences on those DIT items identified by the graduate students as the items having the most extreme logical implications for an action choice.

By correlating the difference (from the ratings of 969 subjects) values with the logical implications data, we can simultaneously assess the correspondence between both groups' action choice implications for items. Following this procedure, we found a highly significant correlation ($r = .73, p < .001$). This finding supports the claim that typical subject responses to DIT items do favor specific action choices, and the pattern of correspondence between item and action choice is similar to the pattern predicted by the graduate student ratings.

7. We then wanted to test the notion that action choices could be predicted by knowing the joint influence of situational features and concepts of justice. In our view, concepts of justice guide attention to certain features of a situation and thus provide a specific definition of the situation from which actions logically follow. For instance, consider a Stage 4 reasoner faced with the story of Heinz and the drug. His/her *P* score offers little information in predicting the action choice. This person could define the situation in terms of duty toward the family and thus select the steal option, or could define the dilemma in terms of duty to the laws of the community, and select the not steal choice. If, however, we know the *particular* items selected as important by this person, then by the logical implications of that item (i.e., using the ratings of the graduate students) we can determine which action choice is more appropriate. As an example, if the subject chose the item: "whether a community's laws are going to be upheld," then we know not only that he/she is defining the dilemma in Stage 4 terms, but also that the action choice is most likely "not steal."

To operationalize this procedure, a set of rules was necessary to combine item information and arrive at the predicted action choice. The difficulty one encounters in devising an appropriate methodology is that subjects often mix pro and con items (that is, a subject does not pick all "steal" items or all "not steal" items). A typical pattern on the Heinz story might be the following: the most important item is pro steal, the second and third most important items are not steal, and the fourth most important item is ambiguous (can't decide). Should we expect this subject's action choice to be "steal" because a pro item was selected as most important, or should we predict the "not steal" choice because the majority of selections were not steal items? Or perhaps we should choose the can't decide category because there seems to be some indecision in the item selections. Thus it was necessary to create an algorithm by which item information could be systematically weighted and combined to produce action choice predictions.

We experimented with a dozen algorithms. The algorithm eventually selected in this research involved a complex integration of two major sources of information: the four items ranked as most important by the subject, and the logical implications of items supplied by the ten graduate student raters. The important features of this algorithm are (a) it allows for differences in the degree an item logically implies a specific action choice (e.g., an item may strongly imply an action choice or may only lean toward an action choice), (b) the algorithm weights item information by the subject's importance rankings (e.g., the action choice implications represented by the item rated most important by the subject are weighted more than the second most important item, which in turn is weighted more than the third most important item, and so on), and (c) the algorithm incorporates the consistency of graduate student logical implication rates (e.g., items for which the graduate students had difficulty rating, as evidenced by greater rater variability, were given less weight in the eventual prediction than items of relatively clear logical implications).

Using this algorithm, we found support for the notion that a procedure that focuses on both the individual DIT story and the logical action choice implications of items, can better predict actual action choice decisions than the prior global approaches (i.e., an approach that uses a six-story *P* score). Across stories the average hit rate was 73 percent for predicting the pro choices, and 50 percent for predicting the con action choices. However, the algorithm was ineffective at predicting the action choices of those subjects selecting the can't decide categories, regardless of the story (hit rates ranged from 6 to 22 percent). Thus for some stories and action choice decisions, the algorithm performed very well by predicting a majority of subject's actual choices from information on DIT item endorsement.

8. A surprising finding was that there was little correspondence between DIT items and action choices for some subjects. For instance, some subjects would choose the "not steal" action choice but select items all of which imply the opposite (pro steal). Generally, subjects fell between these two extremes. Table 5.7 presents the distribution of subjects with different numbers of matches between item selections and action choice decisions. A 6 signifies that on each DIT story a correct prediction was made from a subject's DIT item ratings and his/her action choice. Conversely, a 0 number of matches indicates that for these subjects, there was no correspondence between the logical

Table 5.7 Distribution of "hits"

Number of matches:	0	1	2	3	4	5	6
n of subjects	8	46	149	286	257	142	44
% of sample	.01	.05	.16	.31	.28	.15	.05

Source: Compiled by the authors.

implications of items and the subject's action choices. Table 5.7 indicates that the ability to accurately predict action choices from the algorithm is normally distributed, suggesting that algorithm scores can predict action choices for most of the people some of the time.

We interpret Table 5.7 as indicating that there is a normally distributed dimension representing the degree to which concepts of justice influence decision-making in specific situations. This interpretation suggests that some subjects use considerations to decide an action choice different from those embodied in the DIT. For many subjects, the justice concepts exemplified in DIT items capture the key elements in their decision-making about what one ought to do in the situation; nevertheless, some other subjects do not use these justice concepts in making a decision. At this point, we do not know exactly what the other concepts are, but they are not DIT-type ideas. What we do have in our algorithm, however, is a method for identifying those subjects who are using concepts of justice in decision-making versus those subjects who are not using concepts of justice. We refer to this as the "utilizer" dimension (denoting those who use concepts of justice versus those who do not).

Recall the Lawrence study mentioned in the previous chapter. She found that fundamentalist seminarians were capable of mature justice reasoning, but neglected to use those ideas in taking the DIT. When asked to describe how they made moral decisions, these subjects said they relied on religious directives to resolve the dilemmas contained in the DIT stories. Here we see that religious norms were the criteria used in place of justice reasoning. Accordingly, we would expect to find these seminarians at the nonutilizer pole. Consequently, knowing how these subjects rank DIT items would give us little information on how these subjects were really choosing the action choices. And so, for these subjects, there would be little predictability from knowing their DIT scores to their decision-making or behavior. If we regard the utilizer dimension as a mediating variable, low utilizer scores would indicate that for these subjects, DIT-type conceptions have little to do with behavior.

As described earlier, it is our view that the most profitable direction for research on the moral judgment and behavior relationship is to focus on the links and mediators. The Rest and Thoma study (1984) suggests the existence of one such mediator—the utilizer dimension.

9. This hypothesis was tested in a dissertation by Thoma (1985). Thoma reanalyzed five previous studies that had correlated DIT scores

with a measure of behavior. He reanalyzed those studies, including the utilizer dimension, using algorithms he devised to represent the scope of the logically possible ones. Thoma predicted that the degree of utilization moderates the effect of moral judgments on behavior. That is, the predictability from DIT scores to behavior will be enhanced when information about the utilizer dimension is added in. He selected the five studies to represent a range of behavior and attitudes—the behavior measures include delinquency, cooperative behavior, clinical performance of medical doctors, law and order attitudes, and attitudes in the 1976 presidential election. In this way the generalizability of the utilizer effect could be ascertained. If a majority of studies showed a significant improvement in predictability to behavior when the utilizer dimension was included, then we would have confidence that the utilizer variable was an important mediator between concepts of justice and decision-making. On the other hand, if only one or two studies showed improvement, we would not attribute general importance to the utilizer dimension. Table 5.8 presents a brief description of each dependent variable and its respective descriptive statistics.

The overall strategy for the secondary analysis of these studies followed from the hypothesis that the relation between moral reasoning and behavior/attitudes is in part attenuated by differences in the degree of utilization. Thus an appropriate analysis strategy would be one that was sensitive to the influence of the utilizer effect over and above that due to DIT scores alone. The strategy ultimately selected by Thoma was a general linear model approach similar to that used in attitude-treatment interaction studies (cf. Cronbach and Snow 1977), also described as the "classic moderator model" (Tellegen, Kamp, and Watson 1982; Cohen and Cohen 1975). In general, this method is a hierarchical multiple-regression model in which the behavioral or attitudinal criterion is first regressed onto the moral reasoning measure, thus duplicating the original analysis (Step 1), then onto the algorithm score (Step 2), and finally onto a cross-product term derived from the moral judgment and algorithm score vectors (Step 3). It is the last term that is of particular interest to Thoma's hypothesis, because it represents the joint effect of moral judgment and degree of utilization on the criterion measure. If the cross-product term significantly increases predictability to the dependent measures, then we have found support for the claim that the relationship between moral judgment and behavior/attitudes differs as a function of utilization. Furthermore, these results are consistent with the view that utilization represents a link in the moral reasoning and behavior system.

Table 5.8   Behavioral and attitudinal measures

Sample	Behavior/attitude variable	n	$\overline{X}$	SD
McColgan A	Group 1: Matched comparison group (P scores)	26	23.46	12.16
	Group 2: Pre-delinquent group (P scores)	26	17.45	7.97
Jacobs B	Test: Number of cooperative moves (20 possible)	56	10.25	3.77
Law and order C	Law and order test scores	70	3.70	2.23
Political attitudes D	Ford/Dole-Carter/Mondale difference scores	71	-2.39	42.30
Clinical performance E	Rating scores (1 = top rating)	133	2.14	.93

Source: Compiled by the authors.

Thoma's results are presented in Table 5.9. In the first row, which corresponds to Step 1 in the regression analysis, we can view the original relationship between the behavior/attitude measures and DIT *P* scores. As expected, moral judgment is negatively related to group membership in Sample A (see Table 5.8), to law and order scores in Sample C, to intern performance in Sample E, and positively related to cooperative behavior in the total condition of Sample B. While the *P* scores were unrelated to the attitude scores in Sample D, in the original study, the D score was significantly related. For comparability, however, the *P* score is used in Sample D. In addition, the correlation between *P* and the testing condition scores in Sample B (not reported in the original paper by Jacobs) did not reach significance.

The second step in the regression analysis is presented in the second row of Table 5.9. These coefficients represent partial correlations between the criterion measures and utilizer scores, controlling for the original relationship between moral judgment and behavior/attitudes. Thus these correlations assess the contribution of utilization as a variable in its own right. As can be seen, there is little support in these correlations for the claim that utilization separately accounts for a consistent portion of the behavior/attitude variance. This finding does not damage Thoma's hypothesis, since the utilizer effect is expected

Table 5.9 Increases in predictability of behavior/attitudes

Steps in multiple progression	Sample				
	A	B	C	D	E
Step 1 P scores	-.29[a]	.15	.57[a]	-.20	-.22[a]
Step 2 Utilizer scores	-.04	-.04	.18	-.24[a]	-.01
Step 3 P X U scores	.30[a]	.26[b]	-.24[a]	.27[a]	-.18[a]
Multiple R at Step 3	.41[a]	.30[a]	.62[a]	.33[a]	.27[a]

[a]$p < .05$.
[b]$p < .10$.
Source: Compiled by the authors.

to influence criterion variance in *interaction* with moral judgment scores. Thus the appropriate test for the hypothesized effect is carried by the cross-product term presented in Step 3.

In the third row, Step 3 of the regression analysis is presented. As described above, this step directly addresses the hypothesis that utilization operates as a moderator of the moral judgment and behavior/attitude relationship. In support of this hypothesis, a majority of the second-order partial correlations are significant and roughly of the same magnitude. We see, therefore, that utilization in interaction with moral judgments does improve on the original relationship to behavior and attitudes. The specific amount of improvement can be judged by observing the final row in Table 5.9. These coefficients represent the multiple *R* values at the last step of the regression model. By comparing these values to the Step 1 correlations, we can observe that the relationships approximately double. The reader is referred to Thoma's dissertation for much more detail about these analyses, for discussions of the trends and counter-trends, and about the nature of the utilizer dimension.

Having done all these studies and all this computation, what have we gained? In practical terms, Thoma has almost doubled the predictability in the behavioral measures by incorporating a new factor into the analysis, the utilizer variable. This gain in predictability comes at no further testing of subjects, but by performing some additional computations on their DIT questionnaires—something easily done by computer while scoring the questionnaire for the P index. We would encourage other researchers to use this index in their studies. The formulas for calculating a score for "utilization" are given in Thoma's dissertation, and the computer programs for calculating it are given in the new DIT manual (see Appendix for details about its availability).

In theoretical terms, the success of this series of studies culminating in Thoma's dissertation shows the promise of approaching the relationship between concepts of justice and behavior by investigating a series of linkages and mediators. The "utilizer" dimension is only one of many linkages and mediators, but it constitutes a beginning. Hopefully, some of the research strategies we devised in pursuing the utilizer dimension will suggest other strategies to other investigators in pursuing other linkages and mediators. As we think more about the utilizer dimension, a flood of additional questions comes to mind. For example, if nonutilizers are not using concepts of justice to determine what is morally right, what criteria are they using? Of interest here is whether the knowledge of a utilizer dimension can help us understand and identify the class of interpretive systems that compete with moral judgment structures in the process of determining an action within specific moral situations. Second, how does moral sensitivity relate to utilization? Are utilizers more likely to be morally sensitive, or are these components relatively independent? Third, is utilization a phase in the development of moral reasoning? For example, are utilizers those who have consolidated their schemes of fairness and can therefore clearly recognize the implications and utility of this information in decision-making? This suggestion would imply that we should observe quite different utilization levels for individuals at different times in their development. Fourth, we have wondered whether moral education programs might influence utilization. Is it the case that while short-term educational interventions are relatively ineffective in promoting structural change, can they influence utilization?

These are but some of the questions that arise from the work on the utilizer dimension. There seem to be innumerable questions in connection with studies of other linkages and mediators, other components and their interactions. Obviously there is much to do for many researchers. We hope our ventures may encourage others to contribute their efforts to this enterprise.

6
Summary

James Rest

After 500 studies have been completed using the DIT, what can we say is the yield of all of this work? Estimating (conservatively) that an average study represents about half a year's work, we have several centuries of person-years to draw from. What are the advances?

This chapter presents three lists of rather compact, terse statements. The first list is of the major empirical findings that are now reasonably well established. I think researchers can count on replications of these phenomena, and can build and design studies that anticipate these trends. The second list is of conceptual advances that have come from immersion in the phenomena of moral development and further reflection on this experience. In other words, the second list presents some new theoretical perspectives and some proposals for research strategy. The third list consists of new directions for research that emerge from this book (and the hope that someone will figure out how to solve some of these problems).

WELL-ESTABLISHED FINDINGS

1. Moral judgment changes with time and formal education, and it changes in the direction predicted by the theory as a developmental progression. Two meta-analyses of about 10,000 subjects indicate that age/education accounts for 30 to 50 percent of the variance in DIT scores. A dozen longitudinal studies also indicate development in moral judgment (see Chapter 1). Between the variables (chronological

age and years in schooling) the latter (formal education) is the stronger correlate with moral judgment development.

2. Although several articles in the morality literature claim that there is no evidence for the higher stages of the Kohlbergian six-stage typology, this overlooks evidence for the higher stages that comes from the DIT. The major index of the DIT is the "*P* score," which is the sum of Stages 5 and 6. Although the DIT is based on somewhat different stage definitions than the recent Kohlberg scoring system, nevertheless the similarities are more striking than the dissimilarities. And so the 500 DIT studies constitute evidence for the usefulness of the higher stages in the six-stage typology.

3. In several studies on life experiences associated with moral judgment development, it appears that for most people it is not specific moral experiences that foster development (e.g., moral education programs, moral leaders, moral crises, living through moral dilemmas), but rather becoming more aware of the social world in general and one's place in it. The people who develop in moral judgment are those who love to learn, who seek new challenges, who enjoy intellectually stimulating environments, who are reflective, who make plans and set goals, who take risks, who see themselves in the larger social contexts of history and institutions and broad cultural trends, who take responsibility for themselves and their environs. The people who develop are advantaged by receiving encouragement to continue their education and their development, who are in stimulating and challenging environments, and who operate in social milieus that support their work, endeavor to interest them, and reward their accomplishments. As young adults, the people who develop in moral judgment are more fulfilled in their career aspirations, have set a life direction of continued intellectual stimulation and challenge, are more involved in their communities, and take more interest in the larger societal issues (see Chapter 2).

4. Moral education programs designed to stimulate moral judgment development do produce modest but significant gains. This is particularly so for programs emphasizing peer discussion of controversial moral dilemmas. Education programs designed to foster general personality development are also effective. But discipline-oriented, information-laden courses on traditional academic topics seem not to be so effective. In contrast to the popular opinion that morality is fixed in childhood, adults show more change than younger participants in moral education programs. Educational interventions shorter in duration than three weeks do not seem effective, but programs over 12

weeks do not increase gains proportional to the time spent (Chapter 3).

5. An examination of some 20 cross-cultural studies using translations of the DIT indicates that similarities across cultures are more striking than dissimilarities. Cross-cultural studies of age-trends, correlates, and internal structure produce similar findings to studies performed on U.S. samples using the DIT. However, there are difficulties in using translations of the DIT in other cultures, and there are problems in exporting either the DIT or the Kohlberg scoring scheme to other cultures (because such a procedure is biased against finding other concepts or processes for making moral judgments). Nevertheless, it was interesting that other cultures are higher in DIT scores than samples from the United States—in other words, the theory and instrumentation developed in the United States does not exalt our own people above other cultures.

6. Sex differences on the DIT are trivial. Less than one-half of 1 percent of the variance in DIT scores is attributable to male/female differences (compare this to the effect of education, which is 250 times more powerful). Gilligan's view that women appear less sophisticated in justice concepts than males is not at all supported. In fact, where differences exist, it is females who score higher on the DIT than males. For predicting moral judgment scores, ask for a person's level of education, not sex (see Chapter 4).

7. Religion, when represented in terms of conservative versus liberal ideology, is moderately but significantly related to DIT scores. In a number of studies, liberal religious ideology is associated with higher DIT scores, perhaps because these ideologies tend to foster an orientation toward moral decision-making that emphasizes the individual's own responsibility in determining a just balance of claims in a moral dilemma, whereas the more conservative ideologies emphasize obedience to external authority and doctrines (see Chapter 4).

8. A review of over 50 studies shows that the DIT is significantly correlated to a wide variety of behavioral and attitude measures. The measures include behaviors such as cooperative behavior, distribution of rewards, cheating, conscientious objection, voting for different presidential candidates, clinical performance ratings of medical interns, delinquency, and school problem behavior. The attitudes include political liberalism/conservatism, "law and order" attitudes, attitudes toward authority, death, pupil control, school discipline, and capital punishment. Fairly consistent but modest correlations were obtained for this

wide spectrum of behaviors and attitudes. Experimental evidence indicates that moral judgment, however, is not reducible to political liberalism-conservatism. Nevertheless, since there is much variance in these behavioral and attitude measures that is not explained by the DIT, other factors must be taken into account (see Chapter 5).

9. One such additional variable seems to be the "utilizer" dimension (that is, the degree to which people use justice concepts to make decisions). In a reanalysis of five studies relating moral judgment to behavior, the inclusion of the utilizer dimension as a mediator variable almost doubled the amount of variance accounted for in the behavioral measures. Future behavioral researchers would be well advised to include the utilizer variable in their analyses (see Chapter 5).

10. Although the major interest of the 500 studies was not to test the validity of the DIT, nevertheless, the fact that so many studies produced meaningful results indicates that the DIT is a useful measure in moral judgment research.

THEORETICAL ADVANCES

1. The major theoretical advance is the Four-Component Model. This set of ideas does several things for us. It provides a theoretical perspective for integrating and placing different research traditions into a unified picture. Different research traditions largely have addressed different facets of the ensemble of processes involved in the psychology of morality. The Four-Component Model gives a way of viewing the distinctive contributions (and distinctive limitations) of each approach. It provides a way of conceptualizing the relations of thought, affect, and behavior. It provides guides for organizing research. It gives direction for setting educational goals (Chapter 1).

2. In applying the Four-Component Model to DIT research, we reinterpret the cognitive developmental approach (the six-stage typology) as addressing Component 2, namely, how people arrive at judgments of which course of action in a social situation is morally right or wrong. The six stages of moral judgment are interpreted as primarily reflecting people's conceptions of how social cooperation can be organized (i.e., conceptualizing social cooperation in terms of simple exchange of favor for favor, or enduring close relationships, or society-wide networks of cooperation based on law and roles within secondary organizations, or ideal principles for constructing societies, etc.). Each conception of social cooperation entails a distinctive notion of what is fair and just. By and large, as people face social situations involving

moral dilemmas, they invoke their basic conceptions of social cooperation and the attendant notions of fairness, and use those notions as heuristics for deciding what considerations are important and relevant, for deciding how to prioritize the conflicting claims in a situation—in short, for judging what is morally right (see Chapter 1). However, it is not always the case that people arrive at moral judgments in this way—other concepts and processes are sometimes used to make this judgment (e.g., religious or political ideologies). People seem to differ in the extent to which concepts of justice determine their moral judgments (see Chapters 4 and 5).

3. A basic tenet of cognitive developmental theory is that people operate on their experiences in order to make sense of them, and that experiences change the basic conceptual structures by which people construct meanings. A long-standing question has been, *which* experiences are the ones responsible for the transformation of moral judgment structures? The theoretical issue is how to characterize experience (i.e., how to describe experience, what kind of a taxonomy of experiences to employ, what kinds of information about a person's experiences do we have to have in portraying that person's life experiences?). Piaget's notion of "cognitive disequilibrium" and Kohlberg's notion of "role-taking opportunities" have been too vague to lead to operational definitions. At first we tried very concrete characterizations of life experiences. These experiences could be easily operationalized, but they did not produce very powerful data trends in accounting for moral judgment development. As we reflect on a dozen studies that have attempted to relate moral judgment development to life experiences, it now seems that we were too concrete. We need to characterize experience in "deeper" or more general terms. Also, it seems that we need to embody in our descriptions of life experiences information about how the subject reacted to the experience—to encode the subjective aspect as well as the objective aspect. That is, we want to know more than whether the person was exposed to some event; we want to know how the subject reacted to the event as well. Some of the characterizations of life experiences that are emerging from the more "clinical" approaches seem to have greater potential for investigation of life experiences.

4. The question of the universality of the six-stage typology of moral judgment has seemed to some psychologists as preposterous and obviously false, as well as ethnocentric and dangerous. I have tried to present an interpretation of the universality claim that makes it feasible, but not necessary to the core of the cognitive developmental ap-

proach. What is crucial to the cognitive developmental view is the distinction between surface features and underlying structure. Whether or not there is only one set of underlying structures with regard to moral judgment development, I argue, remains an empirical question. Furthermore, the universality of the six-stage typology is not the only interesting issue for cross-cultural research. In addition, treating cultural variation as "natural experiments" in the variation of life circumstances provides opportunities to discover how social variation produces variation in moral development.

5. Our basic approach to studying the relation of moral judgment with behavior is to assume that there are many factors that codetermine behavior. Confining one's investigation to analysis and reanalysis of moral judgment interviews is too limited. Our strategy is to identify the factors and their linkages with moral judgment. Our research on the utilizer variable illustrates one approach. We envision that powerful prediction of behavior will only come when we can assess all four component processes in the real-life situation. This proposal is not capable of being tested now because the technology for measuring each component in real-life situations is not available. However, this theoretical perspective suggests what the task is before us, helps to set research agendas, and suggests new research.

NEW DIRECTIONS FOR RESEARCH

1. Develop assessment instruments for moral judgment occurring not in hypothetical situations but in real-life situations. (We are trying to devise ways of assessing how moral decisions are made on the job in the health field. See Chapter 1.)

2. Develop measures of Components 3 and 4, particularly as they are engaged in real-life situations. Presumably the motivational aspects of morality have to be studied simultaneously with other motives and values since there is a competition for alternative behaviors in any given situation.

3. Study the interaction of the four components, especially in real-life situations, and the ability to better predict real-life behavior by having information from all four components. For instance, it may be that being very sensitive to moral issues (Component 1) lessens the ability to follow through and implement previous moral goals (Component 4), and vice versa.

4. Improve the methodology in evaluation studies of educational interventions (see Chapter 3). Of special interest is the study of how

the direct teaching of Kohlberg's stage theory affects posttest scores (i.e., whether as an artifact or as actual enhancer of development).

5. Research how the other components (besides Component 2, moral judgment) are affected by special educational interventions. (Perhaps it is the case that the impact of an educational program would primarily be to sensitize students to moral problems. Perhaps it is the case that the impact of an educational program would be to increase the utilization of concepts of justice in decision-making, even if not to change one's basic concepts of justice.) Research is also needed to determine how much behavioral change is associated with changes in internal processes instituted through education (i.e., do increases in moral judgment brought about by education also lead to relevant changes in actual behavior?).

6. Further research the life experiences that are associated with moral development. The coding guides developed by Deemer/Spickelmier need to be cross-validated on new and different samples. Other dimensions in addition to the "academic" and "intellectual" dimensions need to be investigated by which to characterize life experience. And all these new dimensions need to be related to development not only of moral judgment, but also other components of moral development. For instance, are the life experiences that foster moral judgment development different from the life experiences that foster moral motivation?

7. Investigations of cultural differences are needed that do not simply translate the DIT or Kohlberg's scoring guides into another language, but which start out inductively, in a mode of exploration rather than in the mode of hypothesis testing (Is Kohlberg's theory universal?). Rather, the study would begin as did Kohlberg in the 1950s, by asking open-ended questions about what people think is right or wrong and why, and then deriving the categories and central concepts inductively. This approach would allow different concepts and different developmental pathways to emerge, if there were really alternatives to the six-stage typology.

The reviews in this book do not exhaust all the issues addressed in the 500 DIT studies. Hopefully some new reviews will be forthcoming. Nor does our list of new directions for research nearly exhaust all the possibilities for future research. Yet we hope that this book has stimulated interest for doing further work in this enterprise. Accordingly, the Appendixes describe some of the tools for doing research, some of the details for obtaining further information about specific studies, and some of the services offered by the group at Minnesota.

APPENDIXES

Appendix A

A. OPINIONS ABOUT SOCIAL PROBLEMS

This questionnaire is aimed at understanding how people think about social problems.* Different people often have different opinions about questions of right and wrong. There are no "right" answers in the way that there are right answers to math problems. We would like you to tell us what you think about several problem stories. The papers will be fed to a computer to find the average for the whole group, and no one will see your individual answers.

Please give us the following information:

Name _____   _____ female
Age _____   _____ male
Class and period _____
School _____

    *   *   *   *   *   *   *   *   *   *

In this questionnaire you will be asked to give your opinons about several stories. Here is a story as an example:

Frank Jones has been thinking about buying a car. He is married, has two small children, and earns an average income. The car he buys will be his family's only car. It will be used mostly to get to work and drive around town, but also sometimes for vacation trips. In trying to decide what car to buy, Frank Jones realized that there were a lot of questions to consider. Below there is a list of some of these questions.

If you were Frank Jones, how important would each of these questions be in deciding what car to buy?

Instructions for Part A: (Sample Question)

On the left-hand side, check one of the spaces by each statement of a consideration. (For instance, if you think that Statement no. 1 is not important in making a decision about buying a car, check the space on the right.)

IMPORTANCE:

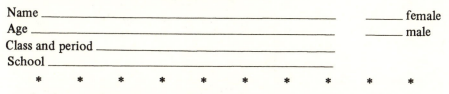

Great Much Some Little No

1. Whether the car dealer was in the same block as where Frank lives. (Note that in this sample, the person taking the questionnaire did not think this was important in making a decision.)

Great Much   Some Little   No

					2. Would a *used* car be more economical in the long run than a *new* car? (Note that a check was put in the far left space to indicate the opinion that this is an important issue in making a decision about buying a car.)
					3. Whether the color was green, Frank's favorite color.
					4. Whether the cubic inch displacement was at least 200. (Note that if you are unsure about what "cubic inch displacement" means, then mark it "no importance.")
					5. Would a large, roomy car be better than a compact car?
					6. Whether the front connibilies were differential. (Note that if a statement sounds like gibberish or nonsense to you, mark it "no importance.")

Instructions for Part B: (Sample Question)

From the list of questions above, select the most important one of the whole group. Put the number of the most important question on the top line below. Do likewise for your second, third, and fourth most important choices. (Note that the top choices in this case will come from the statements that were checked on the far left-hand side—statements no. 2 and no. 5 were thought to be very important. In deciding what is the *most* important, a person would re-read no. 2 and no. 5, pick one of them as the *most* important, and then put the other as "second most important," and so on.)

Most	Second Most Important	Third Most Important	Fourth Most Important
5	2	3	1

Heinz and the Drug

In Europe, a woman was near death from a special kind of cancer. There was one drug that the doctors thought might save her. It was a form of radium that the druggist in the same town had recently discovered. The drug was expensive to make, and the druggist was charging ten times what the drug cost to make. He paid $200 for the radium and charged $2000 for a small dose of the drug. The sick woman's husband, Heinz, went to everyone he knew to borrow the money, but he could get together only about $1000, which is half of what it cost. He told the druggist that his wife was dying, and asked him to sell it cheaper or let him pay later. But the druggist said, "No, I discovered the drug and I'm going to make money from it." So Heinz became desperate and began to think about breaking into the man's store to steal the drug for his wife.

Should Heinz steal the drug? (Check one)

_____ Should steal it   _____ Can't decide   _____ Should not steal it

IMPORTANCE:

Great Much Some Little   No

Great	Much	Some	Little	No	
					1. Whether a community's laws are going to be upheld.
					2. Isn't it only natural for a loving husband to care so much for his wife that he'd steal?
					3. Is Heinz willing to risk getting shot as a burglar or going to jail for the chance that stealing the drug might help?
					4. Whether Heinz is a professional wrestler, or has considerable influence with professional wrestlers.
					5. Whether Heinz is stealing for himself or doing this solely to help someone else.
					6. Whether the druggist's rights to his invention have to be respected.
					7. Whether the essence of living is more encompassing than the termination of dying, socially and individually.
					8. What values are going to be the basis for governing how people act toward each other.
					9. Whether the druggist is going to be allowed to hide behind a worthless law that only protects the rich anyway.

Great   Much   Some   Little   No

					10. Whether the law in this case is getting in the way of the most basic claim of any member of society.
					11. Whether the druggist deserves to be robbed for being so greedy and cruel.
					12. Would stealing in such a case bring about more total good for the whole society or not.

From the list of questions above, select the four most important:

Most important   _____
Second most important   _____
Third most important   _____
Fourth most important   _____

Escaped Prisoner

A man had been sentenced to prison for 10 years. After one year, however, he escaped from prison, moved to a new area of the country, and took the name of Thompson. For eight years he worked hard, and gradually he saved enough money to buy his own business. He was fair to his customers, gave his employees top wages, and gave most of his own profits to charity. Then one day, Mrs. Jones, an old neighbor, recognized him as the man who had escaped from prison eight years before, and whom the police had been looking for.

Should Mrs. Jones report Mr. Thompson to the police and have him sent back to prison? (Check one)

_____ Should report him   _____ Can't decide   _____ Should not report him

IMPORTANCE:

Great   Much   Some   Little   No

					1. Hasn't Mr. Thompson been good enough for such a long time to prove he isn't a bad person?
					2. Every time someone escapes punishment for a crime, doesn't that just encourage more crime?
					3. Wouldn't we be better off without prisons and the oppression of our legal systems?

Great	Much	Some	Little	No	
					4. Has Mr. Thompson really paid his debt to society?
					5. Would society be failing what Mr. Thompson should fairly expect?
					6. What benefits would prisons be apart from society, especially for a charitable man?
					7. How could anyone be so cruel and heartless as to send Mr. Thompson to prison?
					8. Would it be fair to all the prisoners who had to serve out their full sentences if Mr. Thompson was let off?
					9. Was Mrs. Jones a good friend of Mr. Thompson?
					10. Wouldn't it be a citizen's duty to report an escaped criminal, regardless of the circumstances?
					11. How would the will of the people and the public good best be served?
					12. Would going to prison do any good for Mr. Thompson or protect anybody?

From the list of questions above, select the four most important:

Most important _____
Second most important _____
Third most important _____
Fourth most important _____

The Doctor's Dilemma

A woman was dying of cancer, which could not be cured, and she had only about six months to live. She was in terrible pain, but she was so weak that a good dose of pain killer like morphine would make her die sooner. She was delirious and almost crazy with pain, and in her calm periods, she would ask the doctor to give her enough morphine to kill her. She said she couldn't stand the pain and that she was going to die in a few months anyway.

What should the doctor do? (Check one)

_____ He should give the woman an overdose that will make her die

_____ Can't decide   _____ Should not give an overdose

IMPORTANCE:

Great	Much	Some	Little	No	
					1. Whether the woman's family is in favor of giving her the overdose or not.
					2. Is the doctor obligated by the same law as everybody else if giving her an overdose would be the same as killing her?
					3. Whether people would be much better off without society regimenting their lives and even their deaths.
					4. Whether the doctor could make it appear like an accident.
					5. Does the state have the right to force continued existence on those who don't want to live?
					6. What is the value of death prior to society's perspective on personal values?
					7. Whether the doctor has sympathy for the woman's suffering or cares more about what society might think.
					8. Is helping to end another's life ever a responsible act of cooperation?
					9. Whether only God should decide when a person's life should end.
					10. What values the doctor has set for himself in his own personal code of behavior.
					11. Can society afford to let everybody end their lives when they want to?

Great	Much	Some	Little	No	
					12. Can society allow suicides or mercy killing and still protect the lives of individuals who want to live?

From the list of questions above, select the four most important:

Most important	_____
Second most important	_____
Third most important	_____
Fourth most important	_____

Student Takeover

At Harvard University a group of students, called the Students for a Democratic Society (SDS), believe that the university should not have an army ROTC program. SDS students are against the war in Vietnam, and the army training program helps send men to fight there. The SDS students demanded that Harvard end the army ROTC training program as a university course. This would mean that Harvard students could not get army training as part of their regular course work and not get credit for it toward their degrees.

Agreeing with the SDS students, the Harvard professors voted to end the ROTC program as a university course. But the president of the university stated that he wanted to keep the army program on campus as a course. The SDS students felt that the president was not going to pay attention to the faculty vote or to their demands.

So, one day last April, two hundred SDS students walked into the university's administration building and told everyone else to get out. They said they were doing this to force Harvard to get rid of the army training program as a course.

Should the students have taken over the administration building? (Check one)

_____ Yes, they should have taken it over   _____ Can't decide
_____ No, they shouldn't have taken it over

IMPORTANCE:

Great	Much	Some	Little	No	
					1. Are the students doing this to really help other people or are they doing it just for kicks?
					2. Do the students have any right to take over property that doesn't belong to them?
					3. Do the students realize that they might be arrested and fined, and even expelled from school?

Great   Much   Some   Little   No

					4. Would taking over the building in the long run benefit more people to a greater extent?
					5. Whether the president stayed within the limits of his authority in ignoring the faculty vote.
					6. Will the takeover anger the public and give all students a bad name?
					7. Is taking over a building consistent with principles of justice?
					8. Would allowing one student takeover encourage many other student takeovers?
					9. Did the president bring this misunderstanding on himself by being so unreasonable and uncooperative?
					10. Whether running the university ought to be in the hands of a few administrators or in the hands of all the people.
					11. Are the students following principles they believe are above the law?
					12. Whether or not university decisions ought to be respected by students.

From the list of questions above, select the four most important:

Most important   _____
Second most important _____
Third most important   _____
Fourth most important _____

Webster

Mr. Webster was the owner and manager of a gas station. He wanted to hire another mechanic to help him, but good mechanics were hard to find. The only person he found who seemed to be a good mechanic was Mr. Lee, but he was Chinese. While Mr. Webster himself didn't have anything against Orientals, he was afraid to hire Mr. Lee because many of his customers didn't like Orientals. His customers might take their business elsewhere if Mr. Lee was working in the gas station.

When Mr. Lee asked Mr. Webster if he could have the job, Mr. Webster said that he had already hired somebody else. But Mr. Webster really had not hired anybody, because he could not find anybody else who was a good mechanic.

What should Mr. Webster have done? (Check one)

_____ Should have hired Mr. Lee   _____ Can't decide

_____ Should not have hired him

IMPORTANCE:

Great	Much	Some	Little	No	
					1. Does the owner of a business have the right to make his own business decisions or not?
					2. Whether there is a law that forbids racial discrimination in hiring for jobs.
					3. Whether Mr. Webster is prejudiced against Orientals himself or whether he means nothing personal in refusing the job.
					4. Whether hiring a good mechanic or paying attention to his customers' wishes would be best for his business.
					5. What individual differences ought to be relevant in deciding how society's roles are filled?
					6. Whether the greedy and competitive capitalistic system ought to be completely abandoned.
					7. Do a majority of people in Mr. Webster's society feel like his customers or are a majority against prejudice?
					8. Whether hiring capable men like Mr. Lee would use talents that would otherwise be lost to society.
					9. Would refusing the job to Mr. Lee be consistent with Mr. Webster's own moral beliefs?

Great Much Some Little No

					10. Could Mr. Webster be so hard-hearted as to refuse the job, knowing how much it means to Mr. Lee?
					11. Whether the Christian commandment to love your fellow man applies to this case.
					12. If someone's in need, shouldn't he be helped regardless of what you get back from him?

From the list of questions above, select the four most important:

Most important   _____

Second most important   _____

Third most important   _____

Fourth most important   _____

Newspaper

Fred, a senior in high school, wanted to publish a mimeographed newspaper for students so that he could express many of his opinions. He wanted to speak out against the war in Vietnam and against some of the school's rules, like the rule forbidding boys to wear long hair.

When Fred started his newspaper, he asked his principal for permission. The principal said it would be all right if before every publication Fred would turn over all his articles for the principal's approval. Fred agreed and turned in several articles for approval. The principal approved all of them and Fred published two issues of the paper in the next two weeks.

But the principal had not expected that Fred's newspaper would receive so much attention. Students were so excited by the paper that they began to organize protests against the hair regulation and other school rules. Angry parents objected to Fred's opinions. They phoned the principal, telling him that the newspaper was unpatriotic and should not be published. As a result of the rising excitement, the principal ordered Fred to stop publishing. He gave as a reason that Fred's activities were disruptive to the operation of the school.

Should the principal stop the newspaper? (Check one)

_____ Should stop it   _____ Can't decide   _____ Should not stop it

IMPORTANCE:

Great Much Some Little No

					1. Is the principal more responsible to students or to the parents?

Great	Much	Some	Little	No	
					2. Did the principal give his word that the newspaper could be published for a long time, or did he just promise to approve the newspaper one issue at a time?
					3. Would the students start protesting even more if the principal stopped the newspaper?
					4. When the welfare of the school is threatened, does the principal have the right to give orders to students?
					5. Does the principal have the freedom of speech to say "no" in this case?
					6. If the principal stopped the newspaper, would he be preventing full discussion of important problems?
					7. Whether the principal's order would make Fred lose faith in the principal.
					8. Whether Fred was really loyal to his school and patriotic to his country.
					9. What effect would stopping the paper have on the student's education in critical thinking and judgments?
					10. Whether Fred was in any way violating the rights of others in publishing his own opinions.
					11. Whether the principal should be influenced by some angry parents when it is the principal that knows best what is going on in the school.
					12. Whether Fred was using the newspaper to stir up hatred and discontent.

From the list of questions above, select the four most important:

Most important _____   Third most important _____
Second most important _____   Fourth most important _____

Appendix B

B. DESCRIPTION OF THE DEFINING ISSUES TEST

The DIT is based on the premise that people at different points of development interpret moral dilemmas differently, define the critical issues of the dilemmas differently, and have different intuitions about what is right and fair in a situation. Differences in the way that dilemmas are defined therefore are taken as indications of their underlying tendencies to organize social experience. These underlying structures of meaning are not necessarily apparent to a subject as articulative rule systems or verbalizable philosophies—rather, they may work "behind the scenes" and may seem to a subject as just commonsensical and intuitively obvious.

The DIT task is as follows: a subject is presented with a moral dilemma and then presented with a list of "issues" or questions that a person might consider in making a decision about what ought to be done in the situation. The subject's job is to consider each of the issues and then indicate which ones are important in making a decision about what one ought to do. The dilemmas include Kohlberg's classic dilemma about Heinz and the drug and others that he has used, as well as three dilemmas used in a dissertation by Alan Lockwood (1970). Six dilemmas are used, each accompanied by a set of 12 items, for a total of 72 items for the whole test. The items for the DIT were derived from extensive interview material and from the scoring guides developed in connection with each dilemma. Special care was taken to write items with comparable vocabulary and sentence syntax. The items also were written in the form of questions, so that subjects would focus on the form of argument rather than on the action advocated by a statement (e.g., to steal or not steal, in the Heinz dilemma). The items were designed to represent the different considerations that are diagnostic of different schemes of fairness (i.e., moral judgment stages). Note that the items are not designed to represent all pragmatic, ideological, or factual issues that subjects might bring to the dilemmas. The DIT items comprise a set of alternatives that in effect present a forced-choice between different concepts of justice. So if a subject, for instance, consistently selects Stage 4 "law and order" items across the six dilemmas, then we infer that that particular concept of justice is preeminent in the person's thinking. A subject may sometimes select a certain item for idiosyncratic reasons, having nothing to do with his/her underlying concept of justice. But by and large, by aggregating over 72 items in six stories, we expect such idiosyncratic ratings to be randomly distributed and to cancel each other in the aggregated scores.

The most used score from the DIT is the P index, P standing for "principled morality," Stages 5 and 6. The P index is interpreted as the relative importance that subjects attribute to Stage 5 and 6 items. It is calculated by summing the number of times that Stage 5 and 6 items are chosen as the first, second, third, or fourth important consideration, weighting these ranks by 4, 3, 2, and 1, respectively. The score is usually expressed in terms of a percentage, and can range from 0 to 95. The *P* index has shown the most consistent reliability and validity trends of any index based on the DIT.

Other scores are also calculated. Using the procedure for weighted ranks, scores for other stages can also be calculated (for Stages 2, 3, and 4). Davison has derived a summary score, the *D* index, based on latent-trait, unfolding models of scaling theory (in Rest 1979a). In most recent studies (after 1979), however, trends using the *D* index have generally not been as strong as trends using the *P* index. There are also internal validity scores: the M-score, the consistency check, and the A-score (antiestablishment attitude—see discussion in Chapter 5). Chapter 5 also discusses the "utilizer" score and "action choice" indices.

Extensive reliability and validity studies have been carried out (along the lines indicated in the Preface) and are summarized in Rest 1979a, 1983, and in the *Manual for the Defining Issues Test.*

Comparisons with Kohlberg's Research on Moral Judgment

While DIT research is derived from Kohlberg's work, nevertheless there are several important methodological and theoretical differences. The DIT is a multiple-choice test rather than an interview procedure. In the Kohlberg task, subjects generate spontaneous verbalizations, but in the DIT they rate and rank statements set before them. Since subjects usually find recognition tasks (like the DIT) easier than production tasks (like the Kohlberg task), it is not too surprising that the DIT credits subjects with more advanced thinking than does the Kohlberg test. For instance, in Kohlberg's test, any trace of Stage 5 thinking is extremely rare, even among professional, middle-aged adults, whereas in the DIT at least a trace of Stage 5 thinking is present in adolescents (although rarely a predominant amount). The two methods for collecting information have inherent methodological problems, although different ones, and their methods of data collection make each vulnerable to different kinds of errors.

In any recognition task (such as that used by the DIT) there is the inherent problem that subjects can rate items and put check marks down next to items even if they do not really understand them. As an attempt to minimize this problem, the DIT includes an internal reliability check. To check whether a subject is attending to the meaning or more to surface features of an item (such as vocabulary or sentence syntax), a number of meaningless but complex-sounding items are interspersed throughout the DIT. If too many of these items receive top rankings by a subject, we infer that the subject is not attending to meaning, and consequently invalidate that subject's questionnaire. We also have an internal consistency check in the DIT to determine if subjects are randomly responding without attending to any item feature. In general, items were written in a question format and matched on level of vocabulary to encourage selection of items on the basis of meaning rather than verbal sophistication or syntactic complexity (see Rest 1979a, Chapter 4, for further detail).

On the other hand, an inherent problem in any production task (such as that used by Kohlberg) is that a subject is not credited with an idea unless the subject explicitly and articulately verbalizes the idea. When subjects can argue persuasively for an idea, we have great confidence that the subject understands that idea. When a subject is not so articulate, however, can we be sure that the subject does not understand that idea in any sense? The problem here is that some of a subject's thinking may be in advance of the ability to express it sufficiently to meet Kohlberg's stringent criteria in the scoring manual, yet that inarticulated thinking may be influential in the subject's moral decision-making. Some of Kohlberg's own recent research indicates that tacit, more intuitive thinking rather than explicit verbalization is most critical in guiding behavior: "We give credibility to the notion that moral action is responsible choice guided by *intuitions* of moral values not dependent on stage sophistication" (italics added; Kohlberg 1984, 535-36). Therefore, stage scoring according to the Kohlberg system may be underestimating the thought processes of subjects (while the DIT procedure is vulnerable to overestimation).

The different sources of error in the DIT assessment procedure and the Kohlberg procedure probably account for some of the discrepancy between measures. Correlations generally range between .3 and .7, depending on the homogeneity of the samples—evidence that the two procedures are not equivalent. Nevertheless, the two measures show similar kinds of longitudinal trends, correlational patterns, and responsiveness to educational interventions (see Rest 1983). Perhaps the robustness of the underlying phenomena overcomes the particular vulnerabilities of each assessment tool. One special way that the two measures complement each other is in providing empirical support for the full six-stage theory. It is often cited in research reports dealing with the Kohlberg measure that evidence for the first four stages is well established, but the evidence is scanty for Stages 5 and 6. (This may be owing in part to the fact that in order for subjects to be scored above Stage 4 in the Kohlberg system, the subject has to intrude a philosophical lecture on morality in response to dilemmas like Heinz and the drug.) On the other hand, DIT research is weak in providing evidence for the developmental order of Stages 1 to 4 (this is due to the fact that subjects younger than 13-14 years cannot be tested with the DIT). The DIT works because Stages 5 and 6 show orderly patterns in distinction to the lower stages. In fact, if one eliminated Stages 5 and 6 from the DIT, there wouldn't be any scores left worth analyzing.

Another methodological difference between the DIT and Kohlberg's test is in the way that developmental level is indexed. Kohlberg's procedure is to use certain algorithms (attending to the highest stage scored, counting the predominant usage of a stage, etc.), which assign a subject to a stage (i.e., a "Stage 4 subject," "a Stage 2 subject"). In DIT research (Chapters 4, 8 in Rest 1979a) we have not found any algorithm which stage-types subjects that produces strong trends (e.g., longitudinal upward movement, short-term test-retest stability, convergent-divergent patterns of correlations). Instead, we have found two indices that work best with DIT responses: the P index (usually expressed as a percentage, the "$P\%$"), and the D index. Both of these indices represent a subject's developmental level in terms of a continuous variable. The use of these indices rather than stage-typing algorithms was arrived at through systematic experimentation with dozens of indexing alternatives. Developmental theory is not advanced enough to tell us, a priori, which method of indexing will be most useful for a particular data-gathering procedure, and we have therefore arrived at our choice for the DIT through empirical testing. Having a continuous index does not imply that we have given up the structuralist interest in different qualitative patterns of thinking. In fact, the DIT presupposes various structures of thinking in the stage-keying of items. But rather than representing developmental information in terms of assigning a subject to one or another stage, we consider the quantitative usage of each qualitative type, and arrive at a summary score that is expressed in terms of a continuous index. This difference stems in part from our endorsement of a "soft" concept of stage (in which a "stage" is a type of heuristic for determining which of a number of actions is morally right; a person can have and use various "stages" of thinking, depending on many situational factors), rather than Kohlberg's "hard" concept of stage (in which a "stage" is the ruling program of a person's mind, is pervasive and consistent across situations, and follows a strict invariant sequence of development; see Rest 1979a, and Colby et al. 1983 for further discussion).

An important theoretical difference between Kohlberg's test and the DIT is in the way that the six stages are defined. As most readers know, since 1958 Kohlberg has changed his own stage definitions many times. In fact, one study indicated that when the same interviews are coded and recoded, Kohlberg's 1958 scoring system correlates at only about .39 with the latest scoring system (Kohlberg, Colby, and Damon 1978). Of course there are obvious family resemblances between the various Kohlberg stage systems, as there are with the stage definitions presupposed in the DIT. All systems of stage definitions have focused on the concept of justice (in which each stage means something different in what constitutes justice). Kohlberg's latest scoring system, however, emphasizes formalistic terms (i.e., reversibility, universality, prescriptivity), whereas the DIT characterizes the central core of stage definitions as following from different concepts of how social cooperation can be organized. For instance, according to the DIT scheme, a person thinking of social cooperation in terms of face-to-face primary relationships is at a different stage than a person thinking of social cooperation in terms of a society-wide network of role responsibilities within secondary institutions. For Kohlberg, such distinctions are "content" differences, not structural, and these distinctions do not define his stages. He strives to purge such distinctions as considerations, and ends up with very abstract stage criteria. The difference between Kohlberg's system and the DIT, therefore, lies in the degree of abstractness with which stage criteria are defined. He has been most interested in defending a "hard" stage position, and thereby devising a scoring system so as to minimize stage score inconsistency and longitudinal reversals. I have not been so concerned in defending the hard stage position, and it seems to me that the level of definition of stage criteria should be most determined by how well the characterization illuminates how moral decision-making actually takes place. From Kohlberg's view, the DIT confounds structure with content; from my point of view, the Kohlberg system is too abstract to represent optimally how people's intuitions of fairness determine their judgments of morality.

Appendix C

C. SERVICES FROM THE CENTER AT THE UNIVERSITY OF MINNESOTA

At the University of Minnesota, my colleagues and I have organized the Center for the Study of Ethical Development. This is a loose organization of students and faculty who have mutual interests in this area of research. Grant money comes and goes for specific projects, but a group has been meeting together for years and has produced over 100 research reports and studies. We have a large collection of research reports on file sent to us from other universities, a large bank of DIT data (tens of thousands of subjects), and numerous computer routines for scoring and analyzing moral judgment data. We meet to consult about our projects, to generate new ideas, and to commiserate when things don't work out as hoped.

Since the Center is not supported by any external funds, we can only share the services and resources of the Center through cost-sharing. There are a number of papers that can be easily sent to interested people, at cost. And there are a number of services that can be arranged on a cost basis:

1. *The 1986 Manual for the DIT* contains the questionnaire itself (as appears in Appendix A), advice on administering it, instructions for scoring the various indices, printouts of computer programs, guides on interpreting and using the various scores, reliability and validity summaries, and normative data related to various kinds of sample characteristics. Copies can be obtained by writing to the following address:

Center for the Study of Ethical Development
University of Minnesota
206 Burton Hall
178 Pillsbury Drive S.E.
Minneapolis, MN 55455.

2. *A current bibliography of DIT studies*, listing both papers in the public domain (published papers and doctoral dissertations available from University Microfilms, Inc., Ann Arbor, Michigan, or from ERIC) and reports sent to us that are not in the public domain (preprints, unpublished manuscripts, personal communications about DIT studies). Currently there are over 500 listings. Updated at least twice a year. Write to address above.

3. Rest, J.R. 1979a. *Development in judging moral issues.* Formerly from University of Minnesota Press, now out of print, and available in xerox, paper cover from the Center.

4. *Scoring service.* There are a number of ways for getting scores from DIT questionnaires. First, the *Manual* contains directions for scoring the DIT by hand, however these hand calculations do not permit derivation of Davison's "D" score nor Thoma's "U" score. Second, the *Manual* also provides source code for the computer programs that can be adapted to suit the computer you have access to, so you can run the programs at your location. Further arrangements can be made directly with us for purchase of the appropriate computer programs and scoring. Please write for more information.

5. *Copies of articles and papers.* Generally researchers should first try to obtain copies themselves of anything that is in the public domain (published articles, published books, dissertations available from Ann Arbor). Of course, we cannot violate copyright on published materials in books or journals. For materials that are not in the public domain and for which we have received permission from the author for distribution, we will make copies at cost (to cover handling, xeroxing, and mailing). Contact the Center, at above address.

6. *Visits to the Center.* Researchers and students from a number of countries, including the United States, have come to Minnesota, and we welcome these visits. People have come to use the files of research reports, to confer and consult with people here, to see various projects in action, or just to incubate ideas. Usually there are biweekly meetings in the fall quarter, and other occasional meetings throughout the year. We have been able to host some visiting scholars (providing some space and supplies, but no salaries).

7. *Statistical analysis.* Several graduate students who have experience in analyzing data from the DIT in various studies are usually available to provide statistical services on an arranged, per-hour basis.

Bibliography

Adams, R. D. 1982. "The Effects of a Moral Education Seminar upon the Stage of Moral Reasoning of Student Teachers." Doctoral dissertation, University of Tulsa, Oklahoma.

Allen, R. and Kickbush, K. 1976. "Evaluation of the Nicolet High School Confluent Education Project for the Second Year, 1974-75." Unpublished manuscript, Nicolet High School, Glendale, Wisconsin.

Allport, G. W. and Ross, J. M. 1967. "Personal Religious Orientation and Prejudice." *Journal of Personality and Social Psychology 5:* 432-43.

Aronfreed, J. 1968. *Conduct and Conscience.* New York: Academic Press.

Astin, A. W. 1978. *Four Critical Years.* San Francisco, CA: Jossey-Bass.

Avise, M. J. 1980. "A Study to Determine the Growth in Moral Development in Dexfield High School's 1979-80 Fall Peer Helper Program." Unpublished manuscript. Des Moines, IA: Drake University.

Balfour, M. J. 1975. "An Investigation of a School-Community Involvement Program's Effect on the Moral Development of Participants." Master's thesis. Minneapolis, MN: University of Minnesota.

Baltes, P. B. 1968. "Longitudinal and Cross-Sectional Sequences in the Study of Age and Generation Effects." *Human Development 11:* 145-71.

Bandura, A. 1977. *Social Learning Theory.* Englewood Cliffs, NJ: Prentice-Hall.

Bandura, A. and McDonald, F. J. 1963. "The Influence of Social Reinforcement and the Behavior of Models in Shaping Children's Moral Judgments." *Journal of Abnormal and Social Psychology 67:* 274-81.

Bandura, A., Underwood, B., and Fromson, M. E. 1975. "Disinhibition of Aggression through Diffusion of Responsibility and Dehumanization of Victims." *Journal of Research in Personality 9:* 253-69.

Barnett, R. 1982. "Change in Moral Judgment and College Experience." Master's thesis. Minneapolis, MN: University of Minnesota.

Barnett, R. 1985. "Dissimulation in Moral Reasoning." Doctoral dissertation. Minneapolis, MN: University of Minnesota.

Barnett, R. and Volker, J. M. 1985. "Moral Judgment and Life Experience." Unpublished manuscript. Minneapolis, MN: University of Minnesota.

Barrett, D. E. and Yarrow, M. R. 1977. "Prosocial Behavior, Social Inferential Ability, and Assertiveness in Children." *Child Development 48:* 475-81.

Bebeau, M. J., Oberle, M., and Rest, J. R. 1984. "Developing Alternate Cases for the Dental Sensitivity Test (DEST)." Program and Abstracts, abstract no. 228. *Journal of Dental Research 63* (March): 196.

Bebeau, M. J., Reifel, N. M., and Speidel, T. M. 1981. "Measuring the Type and Frequency of Professional Dilemmas in Dentistry." Program and Abstracts, abstract no. 891. *Journal of Dental Research 60* (March).

Bebeau, M. J., Rest, J. R., and Yamoor, C. M. 1985. "Measuring Dental Students' Ethical Sensitivity." *Journal of Dental Education 49,* no. 4: 225-35.

Beck, C. 1985. "Is There Really Development? An Alternative Interpretation." Paper presented at the annual conference of the Association for Moral Education, Toronto, Canada.

Beddoe, I. B. 1981. "Assessing Principled Moral Thinking among Student Teachers in Trinidad and Tobago." Unpublished manuscript.

Benor, D. E., Notzer, N., Sheehan, T. J., and Norman, C. R. 1982. "Moral Reasoning as a Criterion for Admission to Medical School." Paper presented at the AERA Annual Conference, March.

Berkowitz, M. W. 1980. "The Role of Transactive Discussion in Moral Development: The History of a Six-Year Program of Research—Part II." *Moral Education Forum 5:* 15-27.

Berndt, T. J. 1985. "Moral Reasoning: Measurement and Development." In *Research in Moral Development,* M. M. Brabeck (chair). Symposium conducted at the meeting of the American Educational Research Association, Chicago.

Bidwell, S. Y. 1982. "Attitudes of Caregivers toward Grief: A Cognitive-Developmental Investigation." Unpublished master's thesis. Minneapolis, MN: University of Minnesota.

Biggs, D. and Barnett, R. 1981. "Moral Judgment Development of College Students." *Research in Higher Education 14:* 91-102.

Biggs, D., Schomberg, S., and Brown, J. 1977. "Moral Development of Freshmen and Their Pre-College Experience." *Research of Higher Education 7:* 329-39.

Blackner, B. L. 1975. "Moral Development of Young Adults Involved in Weekday Religious Education and Self-Concept Relationships." *Dissertation Abstracts International 35:* 5009A (University Microfilms no. 75-4160).

Blasi, A. 1980. "Bridging Moral Cognition and Moral Action: A Critical Review of the Literature." *Psychological Bulletin 88:* 1-45.

Blasi, A. 1984. "Moral Identity: Its Role in Moral Functioning." In *Morality, Moral Behavior, and Moral Development,* edited by W. M. Kurtines and J. L. Gewirtz, pp. 128-39. New York: Academic Press.

Blatt, M. and Kohlberg, L. 1975. "The Effects of Classroom Moral Discussion upon Children's Level of Moral Judgment." *Journal of Moral Education 4:* 129-61.

Bloom, R. 1978. "Discipline: Another Face of Moral Reasoning." *College Student Journal 12.*

Bloom, R. B. 1977. "Resistance to Faking on the Defining Issues Test of Moral Development." Unpublished manuscript. Williamsburg, VA: College of William and Mary.

Boland, M. L. 1980. "The Effect of Classroom Discussion of Moral Dilemmas on Junior High Student's Level of Principled Moral Judgment." Unpublished manuscript. Louisville, KY: Spalding College.

Bowen, H. R. 1978. *Investment in Learning: The Individual and Social Value of American Higher Education.* San Francisco, CA: Jossey-Bass.

Boyd, C. D. 1980. "Enhancing Ethical Development: An Intervention Program." Paper presented at the Eastern Academy of Management, Buffalo, New York.

Brabeck, M. 1984. "Ethical Characteristics of Whistle Blowers." *Journal of Research in Personality 18:* 41-53.

Brandt, R. R. 1959. *Ethical Theory.* Englewood Cliffs, NJ: Prentice-Hall.

Bredemeier, B. J. and Shields, D. L. 1984. "The Utility of Moral Stage Analysis in the Investigation of Athletic Aggression." *Sociology of Sport Journal 1:* 138-49.

Bridges, C. and Priest, R. 1983. "Development of Values and Moral Judgments of West Point Cadets." Unpublished manuscript, West Point, NY: United States Military Academy.

Bridston, E. D. 1979. "The Development of Principled Moral Reasoning in Baccalaureate Nursing Students." Doctoral dissertation, University of San Francisco.

Broadhurst, B. P. 1980. "Report: The Defining Issues Test." Unpublished manuscript, Colorado State University.

Broverman, I., Vogel, S., Broverman, D., Clarkson, F., and Rosenkrantz, P. 1972. "Sex-Role Stereotypes: A Current Appraisal." *Journal of Social Issues 28:* 59-78.

Brown, D. M. and Annis, L. 1978. "Moral Development and Religious Behavior." *Psychological Reports 43:* 1230.

Bzuneck, J. K. 1978. "Moral Judgment of Delinquent and Non-Delinquent Adolescents in Relation to Father Absence." Doctoral dissertation, Brazil.

Cady, M. 1982. "Assessment of Moral Development among Clergy in Bloomington." Unpublished manuscript. Minneapolis, MN: Augsburg College.

Cain, T. 1982. "The Moral and Ego Development of High School Subcultures." Master's thesis. Minneapolis, MN: University of Minnesota.

Campbell, D. T. and Stanley, J. C. 1963. "Experimental and Quasi-Experimental Research on Teaching." In *Handbook of Research on Teaching,* edited by N. L. Gage, pp. 171-246. Chicago, IL: Rand McNally.

Carella, S. D. 1977. "Disciplinary Judgments of Disruptive Behavior by Individuals and Dyads Differing in Moral Reasoning." Unpublished manuscript.

Charles, R. A. 1978. "The Relationship between Moral Judgment Development and Predictive Ability." Doctoral dissertation. Columbia, SC: University of South Carolina.

Chickering, A. W. 1969. *Education and Identity.* San Francisco, CA: Jossey-Bass.

Clark, G. 1979. "Discussion of Moral Dilemmas in the Development of Moral Reasoning." Unpublished manuscript. Spartanburg, SC: Spartanburg Day School.

Clark, G. 1983. "Leadership and Leader Effectiveness in Small Group Discussion of Moral Dilemmas." Doctoral dissertation. Columbia, SC: University of South Carolina.

Clarke, J. 1978. "Prediction of the Development of Moral Judgment in Primary School Children." Doctoral dissertation. Sidney, Australia: MacQuarie University.

Clouse, B. 1979. "Moral Judgment of Teacher Education Students as Related to Sex, Politics and Religion." Unpublished manuscript. Bloomington, IN: Indiana State University.

Coder, R. 1975. "Moral Judgment in Adults." Doctoral dissertation. Minneapolis, MN: University of Minnesota.

Cognetta, P. 1977. "Deliberate Psychological Education: A Highschool Cross-Age Teaching Model." *Counseling Psychologist 4:* 22-24.

Cohen, J. 1969. *Statistical Power Analysis for the Behavioral Sciences.* New York: Academic Press.

Cohen, J. and Cohen, P. 1975. *Applied Multiple Regression/Correlation Analysis for the Behavioral Sciences.* Hillsdale, NJ: Erlbaum.

Colby, A., Kohlberg, L., Biggs, J., and Lieberman, M. 1983. "A Longitudinal Study of Moral Judgment." *SRCD Monograph* 48 (1-2, serial no. 200).

Collins, W. A., Wellman, H. M., Keniston, A., and Westby, S. D. 1978. "Age-Related Aspects of Comprehension and Inference from a Televised Dramatic Narrative." *Child Development 49:* 389-99.

Cook, C. D. 1976. "Moral Reasoning and Attitude about Treatment of Critically Ill Patients and Performance in Pediatricians." Paper presented at the American Pediatric Society, SUNY, Downstate Medical Center, April.

Cooney, M. D. 1983. "A Comparison of Married and Cohabiting Individuals with Regard to Egoistic Morality and Moral Judgment Development." Doctoral dissertation. Minneapolis, MN: University of Minnesota.

Cooper, D. 1972. "The Analysis of an Objective Measure of Moral Development." Doctoral dissertation. Minneapolis, MN: University of Minnesota.

Copeland, J. and Parish, T. S. 1979. "An Attempt to Enhance Moral Judgment of Offenders." *Psychological Reports 45:* 831-43.

Corcoran, K. J. (n.d.) "Locus of Control and Moral Development and the Impressions of a Confederate in a Trickery Situation." Unpublished manuscript.

Cronbach, L. J. and Snow, R. E. 1977. *Aptitudes and Instructional Methods.* New York: Irvington.

Crowder, J. W. 1978. "The Defining Issues Test and Correlates of Moral Judgment." Master's thesis. College Park, MD: University of Maryland.

Damon, W. 1977. *The Social World of the Child.* San Francisco: Jossey-Bass.

Damon, W. 1984. "Self-Understanding and Moral Development from Childhood to Adolescence." In *Morality, Moral Behavior, and Moral Development,* edited by W. M. Kurtines and J. L. Gewirtz, pp. 109-27. New York: Wiley.

Darley, J. and Batson, C. 1973. "From Jerusalem to Jericho: A Study of Situational and Dispositional Variables in Helping Behavior." *Journal of Personality & Social Psychology 27:* 100-108.

Deal, M. D. 1978. "The Relationship of Philosophy of Human Nature, Level of Cognitive Moral Reasoning and Pupil Control Ideology of Graduate Students in a Department of Curriculum and Instruction." Doctoral dissertation. Stillwater, OK: Oklahoma State University.

Dean, J. 1976. *Blind Ambition.* New York: Simon and Schuster.

Deemer, D. (in press) "Life Experiences and Moral Judgment Development." Doctoral dissertation. Minneapolis, MN: University of Minnesota.

Dewey, J. 1959. *Moral Principle in Education.* New York: Philosophical Library.

DeWolfe, T. E. and Jackson, L. A. 1984. "Birds of a Brighter Feather: Level of Moral Reasoning and Attitude Similarity as Determinants of Interpersonal Attraction." *Psychological Reports 54:* 303-308.

Deyoung, A. M. 1982. "A Study of Relationships between Teacher and Student Levels of Moral Reasoning in a Japanese Setting." Doctoral dissertation. Lansing, MI: Michigan State University.

Dickinson, V. 1979. "The Relation of Principled Moral Thinking to Commonly Measured Sample Characteristics and to Family Correlates in Samples of Australian Highschool Adolescents and Family Triads." Doctoral dissertation. Sidney, Australia: MacQuarie University.

Dickinson, V. and Gabriel, J. 1982. "Principled Moral Thinking (DIT P Percent Score) of Australian Adolescents: Sample Characteristics and F Correlates." *Genetic Psychology Monographs 106:* 25-29.

Dispoto, R. G. 1977. "Moral Valuing and Environmental Variables." *Journal and Research in Science Teaching 14:* 273-80.

Donaldson, D. J. 1981. "Effecting Moral Development in Professional College Students." Doctoral dissertation. St. Louis, MO: University of Missouri.

Durkheim, E. 1961. *Moral Education.* New York: Free Press.

Eberhardy, J. 1982. "An Analysis of Moral Decision Making among Nursing Students Facing Professional Problems." Doctoral dissertation. Minneapolis, MN: University of Minnesota.

Eisenberg, N. (ed). 1982. *The Development of Prosocial Behavior.* New York: Academic Press.

Ellis, A. 1977. "Rational Emotive Therapy: Research Data that Supports the Clinical and Personality Hypothesis of RET and Other Modes of Cognitive-Behavioral Therapy." *Counseling Psychologist 7:* 2-42.

Emler, N., Renwick, S., and Malone, B. 1983. "The Relationship between Moral Reasoning and Political Orientation." *Journal of Personality and Social Psychology 45,* 1073-80.

Enright, R., Lapsley, M., and Levy, M. 1983. "Moral Education Strategies." In *Cognitive Strategy Research: Educational Applications,* edited by M. Pressley and I. Levin, pp. 43-83. Springer-Verlag.

Erickson, B. L., Colby, S., Libbey, P., and Lohmann, G. 1976. "The Young Adolescent: A Curriculum to Promote Psychological Growth." In *Developmental Education,* edited by G. D. Miller. St. Paul, MN: Minnesota Department of Education.

Erikson, E. 1958. *Young Man Luther.* New York: Norton.

Ernsberger, D. J. 1977. "Intrinsic-Extrinsic Religious Identification and Level of Moral Development." *Dissertation Abstracts International 37:* 6302B (University Microfilms no. 77-11, 510).

Ernsberger, D. J. and Manaster, G. J. 1981. "Moral Development, Intrinsic/Extrinsic Religious Orientation and Denominational Teachings." *Genetic Psychology Monographs 104:* 23-41.

Eyler, J. 1980. "Citizenship Education for Conflict: An Empirical Assessment of the Relationship between Principled Thinking and Tolerance for Conflict and Diversity." *Theory and Research in Social Education 8,* no. 2: 11-26.

Eysenck, H. J. 1976. "The Biology of Morality." In *Moral Development and Behavior,* edited by T. Lickona, pp. 108-23. New York: Holt, Rinehart & Winston.

Farrelly, T. 1980. "Peer Group Discussion as a Strategy in Moral Education." Doctoral dissertation. Lakeland, FL: University of South Florida.

Felton, G. M. (n.d.) "Attribution of Responsibility, Ethical/Moral Reasoning and the Ability of Undergraduate and Graduate Nursing Students to Resolve Ethical/Moral Dilemmas." Unpublished manuscript.

Fincham, F. D. and Barling, J. 1979. "Effects of Alcohol on Moral Functioning in Male Social Drinkers." *Journal of Genetic Psychology 134:* 79-88.

Finkler, D. 1980. Personal communication.

Fleetwood, R. S. and Parish, T. S. 1976. "The Relationship between Moral Development Test Scores of Juvenile Delinquents and Their Inclusion in a Moral Dilemmas Discussion Group." *Psychological Reports 39:* 1075-80.

Fleiss, J. L. 1969. "Estimating the Magnitude of Experimental Effects." *Psychology Bulletin 72:* 273-76.

Forsyth, M. 1980. Personal communication.

Fox, P. 1982. "Stages of Moral Development in Greek and English Schools." Unpublished manuscript, England.

Frankena, W. K. 1970. "The Concept of Morality." In *The Definition of Morality,* edited by G. Wallace and A. Walker, pp. 146-73. London: Methuen.

French, M. D. 1977. "A Study of Kohlbergian Moral Development and Selected Behaviors among High School Students in Classes Using Values Clarification and Other Teaching Methods." Doctoral dissertation. Auburn, GA: Auburn University.

Galbraith, R. E. and Jones, T. M. 1976. "Moral Reasoning: A Teaching Handbook for Adapting Kohlberg to the Classroom." Minneapolis, MN: Greenhaven Press.

Gallagher, W. 1978. "Implication of a Kohlbergian Value Development Curriculum in Highschool Literature." Doctoral dissertation. New York: Fordham University.

Geis, G. 1977. "The Relationship between Type of Peer Interaction and Development in Moral Judgment." Unpublished manuscript. Ambassador, CA: Ambassador College.

Gendron, L. 1981. "An Empirical Study of the Defining Issues Test in Taiwan." Unpublished manuscript. Taiwan: Fujen Catholic University.

Getz, I. 1984. "The Relation of Moral Reasoning and Religion: A Review of the Literature." *Counseling and Values 28:* 94-116.

Getz, I. 1985. "The Relation of Moral and Religious Ideology to Human Rights." Doctoral dissertation. Minneapolis, MN: University of Minnesota.

Gibbs, J. C. and Widaman, K. F. 1982. *Social Intelligence: Measuring the Development of Sociomoral Reflection.* Englewood Cliffs, NJ: Prentice-Hall.

Gilligan, C. 1977. "In a Different Voice: Women's Conceptions of the Self and Morality." *Harvard Educational Review 47:* 481-517.

Gilligan, C. 1982. *In a Different Voice.* Cambridge, MA: Harvard University Press.

Glass, G. V. 1977. "Integrating Findings: The Meta-Analysis of Research." *Review of Research in Education 5:* 351-79.

Goddard, R. C. 1983. "Increase in Moral Reasoning as a Function of Didactic Training in Actualization and Assertiveness." Unpublished manuscript. Big Rapids, MI: Ferris State College.

Goldiamond, I. 1968. "Moral Development: A Functional Analysis." *Psychology Today,* September, 31ff.

Greene, J. A. 1980. "A Study to Investigate the Effects of Empathy Instruction on Moral Development." Doctoral dissertation. Nashville, TN: Vanderbilt University, George Peabody College for Teachers.

Gunzburg, D. W., Wegner, D. M., and Anooshian, L. 1977. "Moral Judgment and Distributive Justice." *Human Development 20:* 160-70.

Gutkin, D. and Suls, J. 1979. "The Relation between the Ethics of Personal Conscience-Social Responsibility and Principled Moral Reasoning." *Journal of Youth and Adolescence 8:* 433-41.

Hanford, J. J. 1980. "Advancing Moral Reasoning in Bioethics with Nursing Students: A Report of a Faculty Research Project." Unpublished manuscript. Big Rapids, MI: Ferris State College.

Harris, A. T. 1981. "A Study of the Relationship between Stages of Moral Development and the Religious Factors of Knowledge, Belief and Practice in Catholic Highschool Adolescents." *Dissertation Abstracts International 42:* 638A-639A (University Microfilms no. 8116131).

Hau, K. T. 1983. "A Cross-Cultural Study of a Moral Judgment Test (the D.I.T.)." Master's thesis. Hong Kong: Chinese University.

Hay, J. 1983. "A Study of Principled Moral Reasoning within a Sample of Conscientious Objectors." *Moral Education Forum 7,* no. 3: 1-8.

Hays, L. V. and Olkin, I. 1980. *Statistics for Psychologists.* New York: Holt, Rinehart & Winston.

Hedges, L. V. 1981. "Distribution Theory for Glass's Estimator of Effect Size and Related Estimators." *Journal of Educational Statistics 6:* 107-28.

Heyns, P. M., Niekerk, and Rouk, J. A. 1981. "Moral Judgment and Behavioral Dimensions of Juvenile Delinquency." *International Journal of Advanced Counseling 4:* 139-51.

Hoffman, M. L. 1976. "Empathy, Role-Taking, Guilt and Development of Altruistic Motives. In *Moral Development and Behavior: Theory Research and Social Issues,* edited by T. Lickona, pp. 124-43. Chicago, IL: Holt, Rinehart & Winston.

Hoffman, M. L. 1981. "Is Altruism Part of Human Nature?" *Journal of Personality and Social Psychology 40:* 121-37.

Hogan, R. 1975. "Moral Development and the Structure of Personality." in *Moral Development: Current Theory and Research,* edited by D. J. Depalma and J. M. Foley, pp. 153-63. Hillsdale, NJ: Erlbaum.

Hogan, R. and Emler, N. P. 1978. "The Biases in Contemporary Social Psychology." *Social Research 45,* no. 3: 478-534.

Holley, S. 1978. "Change in the Pattern of Use of Different Levels of Moral Reasoning Associated with Short-Term Individual Counseling." Doctoral dissertation. University of Texas at Austin.

Hurt, B. L. 1974. "Psychological Education for College Students: A Cognitive-Developmental Curriculum." Doctoral dissertation. Minneapolis, MN: University of Minnesota.

Isen, A. M. 1970. "Success, Failure, Attention, and Reaction to Others: The Warm Glow of Success." *Journal of Personality and Social Psychology 15:* 294-301.

Ismail, M. A. 1976. "A Cross-Cultural Study of Moral Judgment: The Relationship between American and Saudi Arabic University Students in the Defining Issues Test." Doctoral dissertation. Oklahoma University.

Jacobs, M. K. 1977. "The DIT Related to Behavior in an Experimental Setting: Promise Keeping in the Prisoner's Dilemma Game." In *Development in Judging Moral Issues: A Summary of Research Using the Defining Issues Test,* edited by J. Rest. Minneapolis, MN: Minnesota Moral Research Projects.

Jacobson, L. T. 1977. "A Study of Relationships among Mother, Student and Teacher Levels of Moral Reasoning in a Department of Defense Middle School." Doctoral dissertation. East Lansing, MI: Michigan State University.

Johnson, J. A. and Hogan, R. 1981. "Moral Judgments and Self Presentations." *Journal of Research in Personality 15:* 57-63.

Johnson, S. F. 1984. "The Relationship between Parent Occupation and Education and Student Moral Development." Master's thesis. Institute, WV: West Virginia College of Graduate Studies.

Johnston, M., Lumbomudrob, C., and Parsons, M. 1982. "The Cognitive Development of Teachers: Report on a Study in Progress." *Moral Education Forum 7,* no. 4: 24-36.

Kagarise, L. E. 1983. "Male Juvenile Delinquency Type of Crime and Level of Moral Maturity." Master's thesis. Millersville, PA: Millersville University.

Kaseman, T. C. 1980. "A Longitudinal Study of Moral Development of the West Point Class of 1981." West Point, NY: United States Military Academy, Department of Behavioral Sciences and Leadership.

Keller, B. B. 1975. "Verbal Communication Characteristics of Couples at Principled, Conventional or Mixed Levels of Moral Development." Master's thesis. Williamsburg, VA: College of William and Mary.

Kenvin, W. A. 1981. "A Study of the Effect of Systematic Value Instruction on Level of Moral Judgment." Doctoral dissertation. New Brunswick, NJ: Rutgers University.

Killeen, O. P. 1977. "The Relationship between Cognitive Levels of Thinking and Levels of Moral Judgment as Compared in Adolescents 12-18 in Catholic and Public Schools." *Dissertation Abstracts International 38:* 6621A (University Microfilms no. 7804596).

Kitchner, K., King, P., Davison, M., Parker, C., and Wood, P. 1984. "A Longitudinal Study of Moral and Ego Development in Young Adults." *Journal of Youth and Adolescence 13:* 197-211.

Kohlberg, L. 1958. "The Development of Modes of Moral Thinking and Choice in the Years 10 to 16." Doctoral dissertation. University of Chicago.

Kohlberg, L. 1969. "Stage and Sequence: The Cognitive-Developmental Approach to Socialization." In *Handbook of Socialization Theory and Research,* edited by D. Goslin, pp. 347-480. Chicago, IL: Rand McNally.

Kohlberg, L. 1971. "From Is to Ought: How to Commit the Naturalistic Fallacy and Get Away with It in the Study of Moral Development." In *Cognitive Development and Epistemology,* edited by T. Mischel, pp. 151-236. New York: Academic Press.

Kohlberg, L. 1984. *Essays on Moral Development. Volume II. The Psychology of Moral Development.* New York: Harper and Row.

Kohlberg, L. 1985. "The Just Community Approach to Moral Education in Theory and Practice." In *Moral Education: Theory and Application,* edited by M. W. Berkowitz and F. Oser, pp. 27-88. Hillsdale, NJ: Erlbaum.

Kohlberg, L. and Candee, D. 1984. "The Relationship of Moral Judgment to Moral Action." In *Essays on Moral Development. Volume II. The Psychology of Moral Development,* edited by L. Kohlberg, pp. 498-581. New York: Harper & Row.

Kohlberg, L., Colby, A., and Damon, W. 1978. "Assessment of Moral Judgment in Childhood and Youth." Grant proposal to the National Institute of Health.

Kraack, T. 1985. "The Relation of Moral Development to Involvement and Leadership Experiences." Doctoral dissertation. Minneapolis, MN: University of Minnesota.

Krebs, D. 1975. "Empathy and Altruism." *Journal of Personality and Social Psychology 32:* 1124-46.

Krebs, R. L. 1967. "Some Relations between Moral Judgment, Attention, and Resistance to Temptation." Doctoral dissertation. University of Chicago.

Kurtines, W. and Grief, E. 1974. "The Development of Moral Thought: Review and Evaluation of Kohlberg's Approach." *Psychological Bulletin 81:* 453-70.

Kurtines, W. and Gewirtz, J. (eds.) 1984. *Morality, Moral Behavior, and Moral Development.* New York: Wiley.

Lab of Comparative Human Cognition. 1983. "Culture and Cognitive Development." In *Handbook of Child Psychology, Vol. 1: History, Theory, and Methods,* 4th ed., edited by W. Kessen, pp. 295-356. New York: Wiley.

Laisure, S. and Dacton, T. C. 1981. "Using Moral Dilemma Discussion for Para-Professional Staff Training in Residence Hall." Unpublished manuscript. Kent, OH: Kent State University.

Lapsley, D. K., Sison, G. G., and Enright, R. D. 1976. "A Note Concerning Moral Judgment, Authority Biases and the Defining Issues Test." Unpublished manuscript. University of New Orleans.

Lawrence, J. A. 1979. "The Component Procedure of Moral Judgment Making." *Dissertation Abstracts International 40:* 896B (University Microfilms no. 7918360).

Lawrence, J. A. 1980. "Moral Judgment Intervention Studies Using the Defining Issues Test." *Journal of Moral Education 9:* 14-29.

Leming, J. S. 1978. "Cheating Behavior, Situational Influence and Moral Development." *Journal of Educational Research 71:* 214-17.

Leming, J. S. 1981. "Curricular Effectiveness in Moral/Values Education: A Review of Research." *Journal of Moral Education 10:* 147-64.

Letchworth, G. A. and McGee, D. 1981. "Influence of Ego-Involvement, Attitude and Moral Development on Situational Moral Reasoning." Unpublished manuscript. University of Oklahoma.

Levine, A. 1980. *When Dreams and Heroes Died: A Portrait of Today's College Student.* San Francisco, CA: Jossey-Bass.

Lockwood, A. 1970. "Relations of Political and Moral Thought." Doctoral dissertation. Cambridge, MA: Harvard University.

Lockwood, A. 1978. "The Effects of Values Clarification and Moral Development Curricula on School-Age Subjects: A Critical Review of Recent Research." *Review of Educational Research 48:* 325-64.

London, P. 1970. "The Rescuers: Motivational Hypotheses about Christians Who Saved Jews from the Nazis." In *Altruism and Helping Behavior,* edited by J. Macaulay and L. Berkowitz. New York: Academic Press.

Lonky, E., Reihman, J., and Serlin, R. 1981. "Political Values and Moral Judgment in Adolescence." *Youth and Society 12:* 423-41.

Lorr, M. and Zea, R. L. 1977. "Moral Judgment and Liberal-Conservative Attitude." *Psychological Reports 40:* 627-29.

Lupfer, M. 1982. "Jucidial Sentencing and Judge's Moral Development." Unpublished manuscript. Memphis, TN: Memphis State University.

Lupfer, M., Cohn, B., and Brown. 1982. "Jury Decisions as a Function of Level of Moral Reasoning." Unpublished manuscript. Memphis, TN: Memphis State University.

Ma, H. K. 1980. "A Study of the Moral Development of Adolescents." Master's thesis. University of London.

Malinowski, C. I. and Smith, C. P. (in press). "Moral Reasoning and Moral Conduct: An Investigation Prompted by Kohlberg's Theory." *Journal of Personality and Social Psychology.*

Malloy, F. J. 1984. "Moral Development and the Study of Medical Ethics." Master's thesis. University of Wisconsin-Madison.

Mamville, K. 1978. "A Test of Cleary's Hypothesis with Respect to Teaching Methodologies." Doctoral dissertation. Boston University.

Maratsos, M. 1983. "Some Current Issues in the Study of the Acquisition of Grammar." In *Handbook of Child Psychology, Vol. III: Cognitive Development,* 4th ed., edited by J. H. Flavell and E. M. Markman, pp. 707-86. New York: Wiley.

Marston, D. 1978. "Social Cognition and Behavior Problems in School: A Three Year Follow-Up Study of 38 Adolescents." Unpublished manuscript. University of Minnesota.

Martin, R. M., Shafto, M., and Van Deinse, W. 1977. "The Reliability, Validity, and Design of the Defining Issues Test." *Developmental Psychology 13:* 460-68.

Masters, J. C. and Santrock, J. W. 1976. "Studies in the Self-Regulation of Behavior: Effects of Contingent Cognitive and Affective Events." *Developmental Psychology 12:* 334-48.

McColgan, E. B., Rest, J. R., and Pruitt, D. B. 1983. "Moral Judgment and Antisocial Behavior in Early Adolescence." *Journal of Applied Developmental Psychology 4:* 189-99.

McGeorge, C. 1975. "The Susceptibility to Faking of the Defining Issues Test of Moral Development." *Developmental Psychology 11:* 108.

McGeorge, C. 1976. "Some Correlates of Principled Moral Thinking in Young Adults." *Journal of Moral Education 5:* 265-73.

McKenzie, J. 1980. "A Curriculum for Stimulating Moral Reasoning in Highschool Students Using Values Clarification and Moral Development Interventions." Doctoral dissertation. Boston College.

Meehan, K. A., Woll, S. B., and Abbott, R. D. 1979. "The Role of Dissimulation and Social Desirability in the Measurement of Moral Reasoning." *Journal of Research in Personality 13:* 25-38.

Mentkowski, M. and Strait, M. 1983. "A Longitudinal Study of Student Change in Cognitive Development and Generic Abilities in an Outcome-Centered Liberal Arts Curriculum." *Final Report to the National Institute of Education,* no. 6. Office of Research and Evaluation, Alverno College, Milwaukee, Wisconsin.

Meyer, P. 1977. "Intellectual Development: Analysis of Religious Content." *Counseling Psychologist 6,* no. 4: 47-50.

Miller, C. 1979. "Relationship between Level of Moral Reasoning and Religiosity." Unpublished manuscript. Wellesley, MA: Wellesley College.

Mills, C. and Hogan, R. 1978. "A Role Theoretical Interpretation of Personality Scale Item Responses." *Journal of Personality 46:* 778-85.

Mischel, W. 1974. "Processes in Delay of Gratification." In *Advances in Social Psychology, Vol. 7,* edited by L. Berkowitz. New York: Academic Press.

Mischel, W. 1976. *Introduction to Personality,* 2d ed. New York: Wiley.

Mischel, W. and Mischel, H. 1976. "A Cognitive Social-Learning Approach to Morality and Self Regulation." In *Moral Development and Behavior,* edited by T. Lickona, pp. 84-107. New York: Holt, Rinehart & Winston.

Moon, Y. L. 1984. "Cross-Cultural Studies on Moral Judgment Development Using the Defining Issues Test." Unpublished manuscript. Minneapolis, MN: University of Minnesota.

Moon, Y. L. 1986. "An Examination of Sex Bias of Test Items in the Defining Issues Test of Moral Judgment." Doctoral dissertation. Minneapolis, MN: University of Minnesota.

Morrison, T., Toews, O., and Rest, J. 1973. "An Evaluation of a Jurisprudential Model for Teaching Social Studies to Junior High School Students." Study in progress. University of Manitoba, Canada.

Mosher, R. I. and Sprinthall, N. 1970. "Psychological Education in Secondary Schools: A Program to Promote Individual and Human Development." *American Psychologist 25:* 911-24.

Nardi, P. and Tsujimoto, R. 1978. "The Relationship of Moral Maturity and Ethical Attitude." *Journal of Personality 7:* 365-77.

Nichols, K., Isham, M., and Austad, C. 1977. "A Junior High School Curriculum to Promote Psychological Growth and Moral Reasoning." In *Developmental Theory and Its Application in Guidance Program,* edited by G. D. Miller. St. Paul, MN: Pupil Personnel Services Section, Minnesota Department of Education.

Nisan, M. and Kohlberg, L. 1982. "Universality and Cross-Cultural Variation in Moral Development: A Longitudinal and Cross-Sectional Study in Turkey." *Child Development 53:* 865-76.

Nitzberg, M. 1980. "The Relationship of Moral Development and Interpersonal Functioning in Juvenile Delinquent Subgroups." Doctoral dissertation. Long Island, NY: Nova University.

Nucci, L. 1981. "Conceptions of Personal Issues: A Domain Distinct from Moral or Social Concepts." *Child Development 52:* 114-21.

Oberlander, K. J. 1980. "An Experimental Determination of the Effects of a Film about Moral Behavior and of Peer Group Discussion Regarding Moral Dilemmas upon the Moral Development of College Students." Doctoral dissertation. Los Angeles, CA: University of Southern California.

O'Gorman, T. P. 1979. "An Investigation of Moral Judgment and Religious Knowledge Scores of Catholic Highschool Boys from Catholic and Public Schools." *Dissertation Abstracts International 40:* 1365A (University Microfilms no. 7920460).

Oja, S. N. 1977. "A Cognitive-Structural Approach to Adult Conceptual Moral and Ego Development through in Service Education." In *Developmental Theory and Its Application in Guidance Program,* edited by G. D. Miller, pp. 291-98. St. Paul, MN: Minnesota Department of Education.

Olson, A. A. 1982. "Effects of Leadership Training and Experience on Student Development." Doctoral dissertation. Seattle, WA: Seattle University.

Panowitsch, H. R. 1975. "Change and Stability in the Defining Issues Test." Doctoral dissertation. Minneapolis, MN: University of Minnesota.

Park, J. Y. and Johnson, R. C. 1983. "Moral Development in Rural and Urban Korea." Unpublished manuscript. Seoul, Korea: Hankkook University of Foreign Studies.

Piaget, J. 1965. *The Moral Judgment of the Child.* M. Gabain, trans. New York: Free Press (originally published 1932).

Piaget, J. 1970. "Piaget's Theory." In *Carmichael's Manual of Child Psychology, Vol. 1,* edited by P. H. Mussen, pp. 703-32. New York: Wiley.

Pittel, S. M. and Mendelsohn, G. A. 1966. "Measurement of Moral Values: A Review and Critique." *Psychological Bulletin 66:* 22-35.

Piwko, J. 1975. "The Effects of a Moral Development Workshop." Unpublished manuscript. Winona, MN: St. Mary's College.

Prahallada, N. N. 1982. "An Investigation of the Moral Judgments of Junior College Students and Their Relationship with the Socio-Economic Status, Intelligence and Personality Adjustment." Doctoral dissertation. University of Mysore, India.

Preston, D. 1979, "A Moral Education Program Conducted in the Health and Physical Education Curriculum." Doctoral dissertation. Athens, GA: University of Georgia.

Radich, V. M. 1982. "Conservatism, Altruism, Religious Orientation and the Defining Issues Test: With Catholic, Brethren and Non-Religious Adolescents." Unpublished manuscript. Murdoch University, Murdoch, Australia.

Radke-Yarrow, M., Zahn-Waxler, C., and Chapman, M. 1983. "Children's Prosocial Dispositions and Behavior." In *Handbook of Childhood Psychology,* (edited by P. Mussen), Vol. 4: *Socialization, Personality, and Social Development* (edited by E. M. Hetherington), 4th ed., pp. 469-547. New York: Wiley.

Rawls, J. 1971. *A Theory of Justice.* Cambridge, MA: Harvard University Press.

Reck, C. 1978. "A Study of the Relationship between Participants in School Services and Moral Development." Doctoral dissertation. St. Louis, MO: St. Louis University.

Redman, G. 1980. "A Study of Stages of Moral and Intellectual Reasoning and Level of Self Esteem of College Students in Teacher Education." Unpublished manuscript. St. Paul, MN: Hamline University.

Rest, G. 1977. "Voting Preference in the 1976 Presidential Election and the Influence of Moral Reasoning." Unpublished manuscript. Ann Arbor, MI: University of Michigan.

Rest, J. 1975. "Longitudinal Study of the Defining Issues Test: A Strategy for Analyzing Developmental Change." *Developmental Psychology 11:* 738-48.

Rest, J. R. 1976. "New Approaches in the Assessment of Moral Judgment." In *Moral Development and Behavior,* edited by T. Lickona, pp. 198-220. New York: Holt, Rinehart & Winston.

Rest, J. R. 1979a. *Development in Judging Moral Issues.* Minneapolis, MN: University of Minnesota Press (Available from MMRP, University of Minnesota).

_____. 1979b. *Revised Manual for the Defining Issues Test.* Unpublished manuscript. MMRP Technical Report. Minneapolis, MN: University of Minnesota.

_____. 1983. "Morality." In *Manual of Child Psychology* (edited by P. Mussen). *Vol. 3: Cognitive Development,* edited by J. Flavell and E. Markham, pp. 556-629. New York: Wiley.

_____. 1984. "The Major Components of Morality." In *Morality, Moral Behavior, and Moral Development,* edited by W. Kurtines and J. Gewirtz, pp. 24-40. New York: Wiley.

Rest, J., Davison, M., and Robbins, S. 1978. "Age Trends in Judging Moral Issues: A Review of Cross-Sectional, Longitudinal, and Sequential Studies of the Defining Issues Test." *Child Development 49:* 263-79.

Rest, J. R., Cooper, D., Coder, R., Masanz, J., and Anderson, D. 1974. "Judging the Important Issues in Moral Dilemmas—an Objective Measure of Development." *Developmental Psychology 10:* 491-501.

Rest, J. R. and Thoma, S. 1984. "The Relation of Moral Judgment Structures to Decision-Making in Specific Situations: The Utilizer and Nonutilizer Dimension." Unpublished manuscript. Minneapolis, MN: University of Minnesota.

Rest, J. R. and Thoma, S. J. 1985. "Relation of Moral Judgment Development to Formal Education." *Developmental Psychology 21:* 709-14.

Riley, D. A. 1981. "Moral Judgment in Adults: The Effects of Age, Group Discussion and Pretest Sensitization." Doctoral dissertation. New York: Fordham University.

Sach, D. A. 1978. "Implementing Moral Education: An Administrative Concern." Doctoral dissertation. Cambridge, MA: Harvard University.

Sauberman, D. 1978. "Irrational Attribution of Responsibility: Who, What, When and Why." Paper presented to the Eastern Psychological Association, Washington, D.C.

Schaie, K. W. 1970. "A Reinterpretation of Age-Related Changes in Cognitive Structure and Functioning." In *Life-Span Developmental Psychology: Research and Theory,* edited by L. R. Goulet and P. B. Baltes. New York: Academic Press.

Schlaefli, A., Rest, J. R., and Thoma, S. J. 1985. "Does Moral Education Improve Moral Judgment? A Meta-Analysis of Intervention Studies Using the Defining Issues Test." *Review of Educational Research 55,* no. 3: 319-52.

Schomberg, S. F. 1978. "Moral Judgment Development and Freshmen Year Experiences." *Dissertation Abstracts International 39:* 3482A (University Microfilms no. 7823960).

Schwartz, S. H. 1977. "Normative Influences on Altruism." In *Advances in Experimental Social Psychology, 10,* edited by L. Berkowitz. New York: Academic Press.

Shafer, J. 1978. "The Effect of Kohlberg Dilemmas on Moral Reasoning, Attitudes, Thinking, Locus of Control, Self-Concept and Perceptions of Elementary Science Methods Students." Doctoral dissertation. Fort Collins, CO: University of Northern Colorado.

Shantz, C. U. 1983. "Social Cognition." In *Manual of Child Psychology* (edited by P. Mussen), *Vol. 3: Cognitive Development* (edited by J. Flavell and E. Markman), 4th ed., pp. 495-555. New York: Wiley.

Sheehan, T. J., Hustad, S. D., and Candee, D. 1981. "The Development of Moral Judgment over Three Years in a Group of Medical Students." Paper presented at AERA Convention, Los Angeles.

Sheehan, T. J., Husted, S. D., Candee, D., Cook, C. D., and Bargen, M. 1980. "Moral Judgment as a Predictor of Clinical Performance." *Evaluation and the Health Professions 3:* 393-404.

Siegal, M. 1974. "An Experiment in Moral Education: AVER in Surrey." Paper presented at Annual Conference, Canadian Society for Study of Education, Toronto, Ontario.

Simpson, E. L. 1974. "Moral Development Research: A Case of Scientific Cultural Bias." *Human Development 17:* 81-106.

Smith, A. 1978. "The Developmental Issues and Themes in the Discipline Setting: Suggestions for Educational Practice." Unpublished manuscript. Wittenberg University, West Germany.

Snarey, J. R. 1985. "Cross-Cultural Universality of Social-Moral Development: A Critical Review of Kohlbergian Research." *Psychological Bulletin 97:* 202-32.

Snarey, J. R., Reimer, J., and Kohlberg, L. 1985. "The Development of Social-Moral Reasoning among Kibbutz Adolescents: A Longitudinal Cross-Cultural Study." *Developmental Psychology 20* (1): 3-17.

Spickelmier, J. L. 1983. "College Experience and Moral Judgment Development." Doctoral dissertation. Minneapolis, MN: University of Minnesota.

Sprechel, P. 1976. "Moral Judgment in Pre-Adolescents: Peer Morality Versus Authority Morality." Master's thesis. Madison, WI: University of Wisconsin.

Sprinthall, N. A. and Bernier, J. E. 1977. "Moral and Cognitive Development for Teachers: A Neglected Area." Chapter for Fordham University Symposium: *Programs and rational in value-moral education.* New York: Fordham University Press.

St. Denis, H. 1980. "Effects of Moral Education Strategies on Nursing Students' Moral Reasoning and Level of Self-Actualization." Doctoral dissertation. Catholic University of America.

Staub, E. 1978, 1979. *Positive Social Behavior and Morality, 1-2.* New York: Academic Press.

Steibe, S. 1980. "Level of Fairness Reasoning and Human Values as Predictions of Social Justice Related Behavior." Doctoral dissertation. University of Ottawa.

Stevenson, B. 1981. "Curriculum Intervention." Doctoral dissertation. Minneapolis, MN: University of Minnesota.

Stoop, D. A. 1979. "The Relation between Religious Education and the Process of Maturity through the Developmental Stages of Moral Judgment" (doctoral dissertation, University of Southern California, 1979). *Dissertation Abstracts International 40:* 3912A.

Tellegen, A., Kamp, J., and Watson, D. 1982. "Recognizing Individual Differences in Predictive Structure." *Psychological Review 89,* no. 1: 95-105.

Thoma, S. J. 1983. Defining Issues Test scores. Unpublished raw data.

————. 1984. "Estimating Gender Differences in the Comprehension and Preference of Moral Issues." Unpublished manuscript. Minneapolis, MN: University of Minnesota.

————. 1985. "On Improving the Relationship between Moral Reasoning and External Criteria: The Utilizer/Nonutilizer Dimension." Doctoral dissertation. Minneapolis, MN: University of Minnesota.

Thornlindsson, T. 1978. "Social Organization, Role-Taking, Elaborated Language and Moral Judgment in an Icelandic Setting." Doctoral dissertation. Iowa City, IO: University of Iowa.

Tsaing, W. C. 1980. "Moral Judgment Development and Familial Factors." Master's thesis. National Taiwan Normal University.

Tsuchiya, T., Bebeau, M. J., Waithe, M. E., and Rest, J. R. 1985. "Testing the Construct Validity of the Dental Ethical Sensitivity Test (DEST)." Program and Abstracts, Abstract no. 102. *Journal of Dental Research 64:* 186.

Tucker, A. B. 1977. "Psychological Growth in Liberal Art Course: A Cross-Cultural Experience." In *Developmental Theory and Its Application in Guidance Programs: Systematic Efforts to Promote Growth*, edited by G. D. Miller, pp. 225-49. St. Paul, MN: Pupil Personnel Section, Minnesota Department of Education.

Turiel, E. 1966. "An Experimental Test of the Sequentiality of Developmental Stages in the Child's Moral Judgments." *Journal of Personality and Social Psychology 3,* no. 6: 611-18.

————. 1978. "Social Regulations and Domains of Social Concepts." In *New Directions for Child Development,* edited by W. Damon, pp. 45-74. San Francisco, CA: Jossey-Bass.

Villanueva, E. S. 1982. "Validation of a Moral Judgment Instrument for Filipino Students." Doctoral dissertation. Quexon City, Philippines: University of the Philippines System.

Volker, J. M. 1979. "Moral Reasoning and College Experience." Unpublished manuscript. Minneapolis, MN: University of Minnesota.

————. 1984. "Counseling Experience, Moral Judgment, Awareness of Consequences, and Moral Sensitivity in Counseling Practice." Doctoral dissertation. Minneapolis, MN: University of Minnesota.

Wahrman, I. S. 1981. "The Relationship of Dogmatism, Religious Affiliation and Moral Judgment Development." *Journal of Psychology 108:* 151-54.

Walgren, M. B. 1985. "Relationship between Moral Reasoning and Career Values." Master's thesis. Minneapolis, MN: University of Minnesota.

Walker, L. J. 1974. "The Effect of Narrative Model on Stages of Moral Development." Unpublished manuscript. University of New Brunswick, Canada.

————. 1980. "Cognitive and Perspective-Taking Prerequisites for Moral Development." *Child Development 51:* 131-39.

————. 1985. "Sex Difference in the Development of Moral Reasoning: A Critical Review." *Child Development 55:* 677-91.

Walker, L. J., de Vries, B., and Bichard, S. L. 1984. "The Hierarchical Nature of Stages of Moral Development." *Developmental Psychology 20:* 960-66.

Walster, E. and Walster, G. W. 1975. "Equity and Social Justice." *Journal of Social Issues 31:* 21-43.

Walters, T. P. 1981. "A Study of the Relationship between Religious Orientation and Cognitive Moral Maturity in Volunteer Religion Teachers from Selected Suburban Chicago Parishes in the Archdiocese of Detroit." *Dissertation Abstracts International 41:* 1517A-1518A (University Microfilms no. 8022800).

Watson, W. 1983. "A Study of Factors Affecting the Development of Moral Judgment." Unpublished manuscript. Monash Chirering, Clayton, Victoria, Australia.

Whiteley, J. 1982. *Character Development in College Students.* Schenectady, NY: Character Education Press.

Willging, T. E. and Dunn, T. G. 1982. "The Moral Development of Law Students." *Journal of Legal Education 31:* 306-58.

Wilson, E. O. 1975. *Sociobiology: The New Synthesis.* Cambridge, MA: Belkap Press of Harvard University Press.

Wilson, T. 1978. "Work and You (W.A.Y.): A Human Development Oriented Guidance and Work Experience Program." Unpublished manuscript. Newport Harbor High School, Newport Beach, CA.

Wolf, R. J. 1980. "A Study of the Relationship between Religious Education, Religious Experience, Maturity, and Moral Development." *Dissertation Abstracts International 40:* 6219A-6220A (University Microfilms no. 8010312).

Wong, J. M. B. 1977. "Psychological Growth for Women: An In-Service Curriculum Intervention for Teachers." In *Developmental Theory and Its Application in Guidance Programs: Systematic Efforts to Promote Growth,* edited by G. D. Miller, pp. 265-85. St. Paul, MN: Pupil Personnel Section, Minnesota Department of Education.

Zajonc, R. B. 1980. "Feeling and Thinking: Preferences Need No Inferences." *American Psychologist 35:* 151-75.

Index

About the Authors

Robert Barnett received the Ph.D. degree at the University of Minnesota in 1985 in counseling and is presently with the MDA Consulting Group, Inc., a Minneapolis-based industrial/organizational psychology consulting firm.

Muriel Bebeau is an Associate Professor at the University of Minnesota School of Dentistry and directs a project for research and curriculum development in dental ethics. Formerly she directed the National Dental Quality Assurance Curriculum Project. Her ethics and quality assurance curriculum materials are used by dental schools nationwide, and earned her the 1984 Lever Brothers' Award for Outstanding Educational Innovation. She is Education Director of the Center for the Study of Ethical Development.

Deborah Deemer is currently teaching at Macalester College, St. Paul, Minnesota, and is completing her doctoral dissertation in Educational Psychology at the University of Minnesota.

Irene Getz recently completed her Ph.D. degree in counseling at the University of Minnesota. Her review of the relation of moral judgment and religion was cited by *Counseling and Values* as Outstanding Article of the Year. She is currently a member of the executive staff of the national office of the American Lutheran Church based in Minneapolis.

Yong Lin Moon is Senior Researcher of moral education and research at the Korean Educational Development Institute. Until 1981 he was an Assistant Professor of Psychology at King Sejong University, Seoul, Korea. He recently completed the Ph.D. at the University of Minnesota.

James R. Rest is Professor in Educational Psychology, Coordinator of the program in Counseling and Student Personnel Psychology, and Research Director of the Center for Ethical Development at the University of Minnesota.

James Spickelmier is Director of Field Education and Placement, and Director of the Doctor of Ministry Program at Bethel Theology Seminary, St. Paul, Minnesota. He received the Ph.D. from the University of Minnesota in Higher Education.

Stephen J. Thoma has recently completed the Ph.D. in Educational Psychology at the University of Minnesota with a double major in developmental psychology and in measurement-statistics. He teaches at the University in personality-social development and in measurement-statistics.

Joseph Volker is a psychologist at the Cleveland State University Counseling Center and adjunct Assistant Professor of Psychology at Cleveland State University, Cleveland, Ohio.